WOMEN IN GLOBAL SCIENCE

WOMEN IN
GLOBAL SCIENCE

Advancing Academic Careers through International Collaboration

Kathrin Zippel

Stanford University Press
Stanford, California

Stanford University Press
Stanford, California

Printed in the United States of America on acid-free, archival-quality paper

Library of Congress Cataloging-in-Publication Data

Names: Zippel, Kathrin, author.
Title: Women in global science : advancing academic careers through international
    collaboration / Kathrin Zippel.
Description: Stanford, California : Stanford University Press, 2017. | Includes
    bibliographical references and index.
Identifiers: LCCN 2016029021 (print) | LCCN 2016030430 (ebook) |
    ISBN 9781503600393 (cloth : alk. paper) | ISBN 9781503601499 (pbk : alk. paper) |
    ISBN 9781503601505 (ebook)
Subjects: LCSH: Women scientists—United States. | Career development—United
    States. | Women in science—United States. | Science—International cooperation.
Classification: LCC Q130 .Z56 2017 (print) | LCC Q130 (ebook) | DDC 507.1/073—dc23
LC record available at https://lccn.loc.gov/2016029021

Typeset by Thompson Type in 10/14 Minion

For Dirk

Contents

Preface and Acknowledgments

W E NEED AN INCLUSIVE GLOBAL ACADEMIA TO CREATE the knowledge necessary to tackle the problems of our world. When countries pursue isolationist (science) policies, shut down their borders through travel bans for academics, and fail to provide adequate support for research across borders, the political dimensions of international research collaborations become visible. Cooperation among academics across national borders holds both academic and political significance.

This book grew out of the question what happens to gender inequalities when academics engage in international collaborations? Or in short does globalization of science and academia open doors to women or create more hurdles? Faculty at U.S. universities increasingly participate in research collaborations with colleagues abroad; compared to academics in many countries, they do enjoy many privileges. But they also experience obstacles and often lack support for international collaborations; this is especially true for women scholars.

I offer my sincere gratitude to all my research participants for their openness and willingness to devote time for my research and to the many colleagues who have informally shared with me their stories of navigating the frontiers of global academia. Because about one-third of the faculty in STEM fields in research universities in the United States are foreign born and educated, U.S. universities have benefited from "brain drain" from other countries and/or brain circulation. Although for many academics this mobility is voluntary, other international scholars find themselves unable to return to their own countries for multiple reasons, including personal, family, academic, economic, or political ones. Their struggles became even clearer to me as I interviewed the academics for this book, and they have convinced me even more deeply of the urgency and importance of international collaboration among academics. And without the contributions of these participants, this book would not have been possible.

Growing up in Germany I had the privilege of having a high school education and first university degrees in publicly funded German educational institutions, before my graduate education and most academic positions took me to the United States. I am citizen of both countries now, and, when I travel around the world, I also benefit from my academic nationality, the status of being affiliated with and educated at U.S. institutions of higher education—what I call the .edu bonus. My research has benefited from an international academic life in many ways; thus I bring to this project a positive inclination toward valuing cosmopolitanism in academia.

This material is based on work supported by the National Science Foundation under Grant No. OISE-0936970 and HRD-0811170. I want to thank John Tsapogas and Jessie DeAro, who were wonderful to work with. I have carried this project across the Atlantic several times, including with a generous research fellowship from the Alexander von Humboldt Foundation. I have had wonderfully stimulating research stays and working conditions at the Women and Public Policy Program, Harvard Kennedy School; Ludwig-Maximilian University of Munich; the Max Planck Institute for the Study of Societies in Cologne; the Social Science Research Center Berlin; and the Minda de Gunzburg Center for European Studies at Harvard. For their hospitality and support I want to thank the staff and directors, including Iris Bonet, Hannah Riley Bowles, Victoria Budson, Paula Irene Villa, Jens Beckert, Jutta Allmendinger, Patricia Craig, and Grzegorz Ekiert. I want to thank Northeastern University for institutional support and the Northeastern University ADVANCE Team, Sara Wadia-Fascetti (PI) and the other Co-PIs, Jacqueline Isaacs, Luis Falcon, and Graham Jones, as well as Mary Loeffelholz for supporting this project in its early stages.

My involvement in the U.S. ADVANCE community sparked my initial interest in gender and the internationalization of academia leading to this book on international research collaborations. So I am grateful to the broader ADVANCE community, who, like me, have been wrestling with gendered inequalities in academia and beyond, trying to bring about enduring transformations in institutions to create more gender equality. I cannot list them all individually, but the writing workshop in gender, science, and organizations and the participants of the NSF-sponsored workshop on gender and international collaborations stand out. Some portions of this book previously appeared as reports of this workshop. Other portions also appeared as part of chapters, journal articles, and reports.

I have benefited also from the stimulating discussions, critical questions, and constructive advice I received from my collaborators on various pieces of this project, including Laura Kramer, Alice Hogan, Lisa M. Frehill, and Amy Lubitow. My former students and now collaborators Katrina Uhly and Laura Visser helped me push some ideas forward by testing them with very different survey data. I also want to thank Sorina Vlaicu and Debra Guckenheimer, who conducted some of the interviews and focus groups and started some of the analysis. I owe much gratitude to my research assistants, especially Katrina Uhly but also Ethel Mickey and Emily Smykla, who helped with coding as well as with commenting on various versions of the chapters. Saleha Chaudry, Laura Trachte and Morgan Whitney also provided invaluable research assistance.

I am especially indebted to Myra Marx Ferree. Her interest and trust in my research have inspired me. She has commented on several parts of the book. I owe her the name of the concept "glass fences," and much more. I have also been fortunate to receive thoughtful feedback from colleagues and friends, especially Sarah Bracke, Catherine Espaillat, Laura Frader, Tim Kimmel, Lynnette Madsen, Laurie McIntosh, Eileen McDonagh, Kimberly Morgan, Liza Mügge, Lisa Prügl, Nina Sylvanus, Berna Turam, and Claudia Zilla. In addition, I have greatly benefited from discussions with and support of my colleagues, Anna (Enobong) Branch, Susanne Baer, Frank Dobbin, Jeff Hearns, Patricia Hill Collins, Liisa Husu, Mary Frank Fox, Julian Hamann, Heike Kahlert, Dagmar Simon, Gerhard Sonnert, Gaye Tuchman, Marieke van den Brinck, Angelika von Wahl, Maya Widmer, and Alison Woodward.

For critical questions and helpful comments and suggestions from colleagues at invited talks, I am grateful to my own department as well as to colleagues at the Ludwig-Maximilian-University, Technical University Munich, University of Konstanz, University of Hamburg, Social Science Research Center Berlin, Ruhr-University of Bochum, Vrije Universiteit Brussels, Harvard University, University of Miami, and University of Wisconsin-Madison.

I want to thank the critical audiences at workshops organized by the Swiss Science Foundation, the Qatar National Research Foundation, the National Science Foundation, the Society for Women in Marine Science, Woods Hole Oceanographic Institution, the Project Directors' Conference "International Cooperation in the Field of Higher Education and Training" organized by the U.S. Department of Education and the European Commission 's Directorate General for Education and Culture, and the DAAD-Alumni Meeting of the German Academic Exchange Service in São Paulo, Brazil.

I am also thankful to colleagues at conferences where I presented ideas for this project, including the American Association for the Advancement of Science; the American Sociological Association; Sociologists for Women in Society; the Eastern Sociological Association; the Council for European Studies; the Seventh European Conference on Gender Equality in Higher Education in Bergen, Norway; the European Conference on Politics and Gender; the International Sociological Association; and the German Studies Association.

My editor Kate Wahl at Stanford University Press deserves special recognition. I also want to thank Alison Anderson and Margaret Pinette, who copyedited the entire manuscript with great care, as well as Rebecca Steinitz, Amber Ault, and Sheri Englund, who all helped me to transform my ideas into a readable book manuscript! I also want to thank Stanford's anonymous reviewers for their encouraging feedback and suggestions. I take all responsibility for any remaining shortcomings.

Finally, I want to thank my mother Bärbel Zippel, my sister Sonja Seidenspinner and her husband Hans-Jörg Seidenspinner, and my other family for supporting me in getting this book out of the door. My partner Dirk has survived yet another book with his enduring humor and encouragement. He has been the best "portable" supportive partner I could wish for, and we spent many hours on video-conference calls while living on two different continents. I am grateful that we get to share our lives and ways of seeing the world. I dedicate this book to him.

WOMEN IN GLOBAL SCIENCE

1 A World of Opportunity

Science, Gender, and Collaboration

THELMA, A PROMINENT PROFESSOR OF BIOTECHNOLOGY AND a member of the National Academy of Sciences, has enjoyed a successful academic career.[1] The collaborative research she has pursued for decades with colleagues in Spain and China has been crucial to that success. Leading these collaborations has been stimulating and fruitful even though language and cultural differences, funding and bureaucratic issues, and international travel have added a layer of challenge further complicated by her responsibilities in her family and laboratory life. In identifying potential collaborators, she has sought out experts in the United States and abroad whose work complements that of her research team. Her collaborators include former graduate students and postdocs who have returned to their home countries, as well as colleagues she has met over the years at international conferences or during her stays at international institutes. Although Thelma has found it increasingly difficult to obtain U.S. funding for these projects, she is part of a large European Union (EU) funded research collaboration that gives her access to resources her U.S. university cannot provide.

Thelma feels respected by her colleagues abroad and enjoys her interactions with them. Reflecting on her career path, she believes that extending her circles to include international collaborations has been crucial for her career. She describes how she has often felt more valued in her international collaborations than at home. Her international colleagues have provided opportunities to break out of an academic environment that was characterized by exclusionary networks and given her meaningful academic exchange as well as the recognition and encouragement that she needed to advance her career.[2] Thelma sends her students abroad to exchange knowledge and gain experience in international scientific settings, which she believes are critical for preparing them to be global scientists.

In this book, I use science, technology, engineering, and mathematics (STEM) fields as a case to explore what such international research collaborations mean for U.S. faculty, how they are gendered, and how they are shaped by the global position of U.S. science.[3] Experts concerned about challenges to U.S. scientific dominance consider Thelma a model and envision more U.S. academics following in her footsteps. Policy makers expect that elite academics will be engaged both at home and abroad to foster scientific progress and maintain U.S. economic and scientific leadership worldwide. Globalization of scientific and engineering knowledge has been rapidly evolving over the past decades in the broader political context of competition among national knowledge economies, and international collaboration is a key aspect of this process.[4] Nation-states compete in higher education and research around the production of scientific knowledge. The United States increasingly finds both competitors and partners in other parts of the world, primarily Asia and Europe, leading some to ask whether U.S. science is in decline.[5] Thus international collaborations have not only scientific and economic, but also political, importance, as the National Science Foundation (NSF) considers them crucial for the future of the United States.[6]

As U.S. universities compete to create a globally savvy, culturally literate workforce, much public attention and research on globalization and internationalization of higher education—as well as the efforts of many colleges and universities—focus on students. University internationalization strategies are directed at study-abroad programs, satellite campuses in other countries, and teaching collaborations across universities and countries, such as Massive Open Online Courses (MOOCs). International research cooperation and faculty mobility have received less attention, despite the fact that faculty play a crucial role in internationalization of universities.[7] This oversight is startling to those engaged with the European Union ideology that explicitly equates international mobility with excellence in research. And it is surprising to those familiar with elite programs in Asia, Latin America, and Africa that seek to increase international connections by encouraging mobility among postdoctoral fellows and faculty as well as students.

Although scientists in the United States have been slower than their colleagues abroad to engage in international mobility and collaboration,[8] international coauthorships among U.S. scientists have also been rising dramatically over the past decades. Academics increasingly need and are expected to engage in international scientific networks and collaborations. These new expectations create an ideal of the global scientist who is a cosmopolitan academic entrepreneur, an internationally mobile and hyperflexible jet-setter reflecting a neoliberal understanding of unattached individuals.[9] The American Association for the Advancement of Science (AAAS) has also recognized the importance of "global scientific engagement," dedicating its 2016 conference to this theme.[10] Although this conference focused on collaborative activities across national borders, mobility refers to both research stays and jobs.

As internationalization has become a major concern in academia, so has gender equality.[11] Women are seen as an important human resource in the worldwide battle for talent in STEM fields, academic areas that are highly valued in today's knowledge economies.[12] In 2013, President Barack Obama declared the increase of women and girls in STEM to be of national and international interest:

> Increasing the representation of women and girls in scientific and technical fields is not only a national imperative, it's a global one. As STEM skills become ever more important in an increasingly interconnected global economy, the potential for progress is enormous. However, the Administration can't be satisfied when more than half the world's population is not participating in this progress.[13]

This imperative suggests that when highly qualified women academics do not fulfill their potential, their failure is not personal but signals a missed opportunity for everyone. I argue that, if we seek to promote women effectively in academia, we need to understand international dimensions of academia more broadly as the new frontier for women. We must look at globalization of scientific knowledge, internationalization of academia, and promotion of gender equality together.

By "the globalization of academia," I mean the dynamic process of acceleration of flows and exchange of knowledge and people across national borders over the past decades and the emergence of global norms and values in academic practices. More concretely, Richard Freeman's definition is useful when he points out five key components in the globalization of scientific and engineering knowledge: the growth of higher education worldwide, the increasing numbers of international students, the flow of scientists and engineers (immigration), "non-immigration trips: academic visitors, conferences," and rising international coauthorship and copatenting.[14] I focus in this book on one core element of globalization of academia: international research collaborations. I refer to "internationalization" as an ongoing process in which institutions respond to globalization of scientific knowledge through adopting new or modifying existing policies and practices.[15] These institutions include funding agencies, universities, and professional associations that act as gatekeepers because they can provide resources, policies, and practices to support international mobility and collaboration.

The United States serves as a fascinating case study for these intersections because of its position as a world leader in science and academia in general.[16] I focus on STEM fields, including social science,[17] because—as we will see—they have some of the highest rates of international collaborations[18] but also some of the lowest representations of women. Women's experiences with international collaborations in STEM fields provide broad insights into globalization of academia because these fields are increasingly used as models to restructure universities,[19] with important implications for gender dynamics and inequalities in academic career paths in general.[20]

In the rapidly changing world of academia so far, we know little about what international collaborations mean for faculty members and their career paths and even less about the gendered implications of the challenges and opportunities in these paths. We do not even know whether there is a gender gap in international research activities among faculty in the United States (studies to date have been inconclusive).[21] In this book, I ask: How does gender matter in international research collaborations? What are the obstacles and opportunities for faculty—especially women? More broadly, what does the globalization of academia mean for women in STEM fields, in which they have long been underrepresented? Is globalization helping or hindering the integration and advancement of women in these fields?

Good News, Bad News

The good news is that international engagement can provide opportunities for women (and men from underrepresented groups) to leverage their experiences, pursue their career goals, and gain footing toward more gender equality in U.S. academia. We might expect that the condition of being a woman *and* a foreigner would accumulate disadvantages; however, I find that being a woman scientist from the United States can create a crucial advantage because "academic nationality" is often more salient than gender. For U.S. academics, I call this the *.edu bonus*, on the basis of the .edu domain name, available only to institutionally accredited U.S. postsecondary institutions and visible to the world in academic email and website addresses. I propose that, although white heterosexual male academics benefit from the .edu bonus, those with lower status or who are marginalized at home benefit even more.[22] The inequalities in international science create a positive situation for women of all racial/ ethnic groups and men from underrepresented groups who are excluded from the U.S. scientific elite.

The less good—but also less surprising—news is that the globalization of scientific knowledge entails disadvantages for women and perpetuates gendered inequalities. Whereas international dimensions of academic work are challenging for many academics, women academics face gendered challenges as well when they attempt to cross national borders. I call these gendered challenges *glass fences*. Like glass ceilings for women managers, academics, and politicians who climb the hierarchal upward ladder in organizations, glass fences are invisible barriers embedded in the gendered organization and culture of academia, though they are horizontal and demarcate national borders. For example, individual women may believe that it is their individual problem that they have difficulty being successfully engaged in research abroad; however, I find a broader pattern—many women interviewees bump into similar barriers when attempting to conduct such research. These fences can amplify the gendered obstacles in U.S. academia or can be unique challenges. Still, unlike their issues with the seemingly robust glass ceilings and borders faced by women managers,[23] women academics are overcoming the fences, although this takes them more effort than it does for their male colleagues. Ironically, many of the obstacles and fences are built precisely by the institutions— universities, funding agencies, professional associations—that support U.S. involvement in global science and academia more broadly and stand most to benefit from it. But this also means that these fences can be dismantled.

Aside from the good news that these fences are not built of stone, the overall hopeful message is that when U.S.-based women cross national boundaries, the .edu bonus awaits them. The .edu bonus opens doors and enables women to engage in productive exchanges with colleagues abroad. It thus creates an incentive and makes it worthwhile to get through, around, or over the fences. With the .edu bonus, U.S.-based women can draw their professional circles wider, extending them abroad. International collaborations allow women—like Thelma—to circumvent potentially exclusionary networks at home and experience enriching collaborations abroad. Senior women faculty experience that their reputation and status among colleagues is at times higher outside than inside their institutions and especially closer to home in their own departments.

Therefore, moving horizontally across borders can help women faculty rise vertically through glass ceilings, given how important collaborations are for academic careers in many STEM fields. And even though U.S. faculty at times find that their international engagement is discounted, publications with international coauthors receive more attention and are published in higher-quality journals than those with national coauthors. Thus, moving horizontally across borders can enable faculty to move vertically.[24]

Mapping a New Domain: International Gender, Science, and Organizations

Global academia is therefore not gender neutral because it is organized in gendered ways. On the one hand, the globalization process has important implications for gender relations in academia. On the other hand, gendered inequalities shape the process. This book focuses on faculty in STEM fields at research universities to explore the (gendered) meanings of international collaborations for faculty and their universities to shed light on the role of gender in an internationalized academia in the context of the changing global position of U.S. science. Internationalization takes place at interrelated organizational levels—national policy, funding agencies, and universities, as well as individual faculty careers—and decisions and actions at each level directly influence the others. I explore the effects of these dynamics on faculty and universities. Administration, evaluation, and resource policies and practices can create obstacles for international research. I investigate how STEM faculty members perceive and negotiate these barriers and how academic institutions continue to prop them up in the face of their own good intentions and ostensible priorities.[25]

This book is thus the first to systematically consider the challenges and opportunities globalization of scientific work brings to the career paths of U.S.

academics, especially women faculty. It maps a new scholarly domain: analysis of globalization of science and gender, in which two processes intersect, as the globalization of science reconfigures gender arrangements and internationalizes U.S. universities.

Globalization processes intensify and amplify some of the gendered inequalities in academia. I argue that the internationalization of U.S. academia is a gendered process with deeply intertwined status inscriptions based on national affiliations. In particular, gender shapes international collaborations and mobility, and I show that international research collaborations carry gendered meanings, as both globalization and internationalization (re)create the stratified and hierarchical organizations of academic work while at the same time shifting some of these hierarchies.[26] This study thus seeks to synthesize two bodies of scholarship by bringing gender into discussions of the globalization of science and academia and by internationalizing debates about gender and career paths in academia and science in particular.

With regard to globalization of academia, I investigate what increased national competition means for participation in and access to academic work, asking how academic work can become more democratic and merit based and less elitist.[27] I examine the ethnocentrism inherent in U.S. conceptions of the globalization of science, in particular international research and collaboration. Despite claims about the universality of science,[28] research and other academic work remains organized and governed by institutional norms and practices at the local and national level, and national borders still matter and become visible in the globalization of science. And, as we will see, faculty notice these national boundaries when they engage with international colleagues.

With regard to gender, I bring an international lens to the ongoing debates about the steady attrition of girls and women in STEM fields from secondary and higher education up to academic leadership. Some continue to argue that the underrepresentation of women in STEM fields is due to biological differences or gendered educational and career preferences.[29] A large social science literature,[30] however, identifies the institutional and organizational factors that produce gendered inequalities in science, primarily at the national level.[31] I examine a less explored but increasingly important terrain: how these gendered structures in academia at the local and national level might be replicated or reproduced at the international and global levels. So we could understand how globalization of scientific work—in particular, international collaboration—might contribute to the underrepresentation of women in STEM fields and gender inequalities in academia, even as internationalization of research networks might provide opportunities for individual women to pursue STEM careers.

Women faculty are relatively invisible in global academia. This invisibility of women professors is even more striking because undergraduate and graduate women students participate at higher rates in international study abroad programs and earn more degrees abroad than do men.[32] However, this gender pattern seems to reverse at the postdoctoral level, and men are more internationally mobile than are women.[33] And furthermore we find that women faculty are underrepresented in international leadership positions and have fewer international awards, such as Nobel Prizes, Fulbright research fellowships, and German Alexander von Humboldt professorships and prizes.[34] For example, the international Fields Medal, the highest honor for a mathematician, was first awarded to a woman, Maryam Mirzakhani, in 2014.[35] This invisibility, I argue, is due to various fences.

We might also expect a gender gap in international collaborations if women academics simply collaborate less than men. Interestingly, however, research on this question is inconclusive.[36] Some recent U.S. studies find no significant gender differences in collaboration for academics,[37] but a large body of research has shown that women are more isolated and less integrated into international research networks in particular. Women tend to have fewer collaborators and less cosmopolitan networks[38] and coauthor more within their own lab teams[39] and are more nationally oriented in their coauthorships.[40] Extensive research in European countries and Canada finds that women tend to be less included particularly in international collaborative research and coauthorship networks.[41] Explanations for such a gender gap include women's family responsibilities and persistent gendered inequalities in academia across the world.[42] Research in European countries is also inconclusive as to whether there is a gender gap in international mobility.[43]

Collaborations are crucial for academic career advancement as they further the exchange of ideas, skills, and expertise.[44] Not surprisingly, faculty more engaged in collaborations are more productive in terms of publications,[45] and an analysis of published articles worldwide demonstrates that collaborations drive research output and scientific impact.[46] International collaborations in particular can have high rewards, as they bring more citations and publications in higher-impact journals than papers with only domestic authors.[47] International collaborations of U.S. faculty are also associated with higher publication rates and attainment of senior rank.[48] Therefore, we need to understand gender matters in international collaborations and how collaborations in general are evaluated.[49]

This book provides a theoretically grounded analysis of interview and focus group data on U.S. academics and explores why we would expect gender to matter and how. I show that if women academics can overcome fences, they can benefit from international collaborations because of the .edu bonus. Drawing on theoretical work on gender and organizations,[50] and on research that looks at gender, science, and academia,[51] I examine how gender inequality is reconfigured in an internationalized academic world. My particular study of elite U.S. STEM faculty illuminates both what happens to gender inequalities when work internationalizes and how international academic work is organized in gendered ways.[52]

This research has important implications for policy makers, university administrators, and others concerned about promoting (gender) equality in academia. As international collaborations become more important for U.S. academics' research agendas and career paths, we need to understand how to include and support all faculty, including women and those from diverse backgrounds. For those interested in promoting international collaborations, my analysis offers important insights into how access to international academia can be structured in more participatory ways. I provide a tool kit of practical advice for integrating diversity concerns into internationalization strategies, and I map how gender equality initiatives can benefit from attention to the internationalization of scientific work.

What It Means to Collaborate Internationally

An article in *Science* on the genomic changes and social evolution of bees has fifty-two coauthors from eleven countries.[53] When U.S. faculty are on a crew on a research vessel in the Antarctic, work in a research lab in the Andes, conduct field work in the Amazon River basin or in the African Sahara desert, work in the research labs in European or Asian cities, attend international scientific conferences, or coauthor with colleagues abroad, the various forms of collaborations they engage in are part of a broader dynamic of globalization of scientific and technological knowledge. STEM fields have become increasingly reliant on collaborations, international collaborations in particular, and although the form of collaborations varies by field, more scientific papers are produced by teams, and these teams are getting larger.[54]

The dramatic increase in international collaborations is fueled by several factors. The information technology revolution and lower travel costs facilitate more international exchange of knowledge, resources, and scientific communication. The nature of the scientific project calls for collaborations to study global phenomena like climate change and epidemics because oceans and viruses simply do not respect national borders. Faculty networks can expand beyond borders, allowing researchers to connect with specific experts and tap into new knowledge bases,[55] research infrastructure, facilities, laboratories, and equipment. A research team with diverse disciplinary, technical, and national backgrounds can be better equipped to address questions that transcend intellectual and technological boundaries.[56]

Though (national) elite universities still drive both national and international collaborations, global networks have been undergoing important changes.[57] Patterns of global networks have been reconfigured toward becoming somewhat more inclusive; countries that used to be excluded from networks among scientific superpowers are now emerging powerhouses.[58] Of course, persistent inequalities in resources and research capacities continue to influence who gets to collaborate with whom. Despite notions of academia as inherently without boundaries, and with universal scientific values, academia positions faculty on the basis of their national and organizational contexts.[59] Although joint research is ideally based on free, cosmopolitan exchange of knowledge, it is also based on instrumental and economic logics, for example, allowing academics to circumvent inconvenient national research regulations or conduct research less expensively abroad than at home.[60] For example, after the fall of the Berlin Wall, U.S. academics "outsourced" research by hiring postdocs in Russia for a fraction of the salaries they would have paid in U.S. institutions.

These contexts, along with disciplinary and research fields, shape faculty motivations for, attitudes toward, and decisions about international collaboration. Particle physicists at CERN, the European particle physics laboratory in Geneva, Switzerland, will see international collaborations as more important for their careers than faculty in fields where the United States is considered a leader, such as motor neuroscience or other fields in computer science, biotech, and the Earth sciences. And worldwide astronomers and geoscientists have the highest rates of international coauthorship, whereas engineers and social scientists have the lowest.[61] In particle physics and other lab-based fields, the particular institute or lab counts more than which country it is located in.

Engagement in international collaborations among U.S. scientists also depends on who their employers are: PhDs who work in businesses have higher rates of collaboration than those in government and academia.[62] Workplace organizations provide the context in which individuals make decisions and choices; opportunities and potential barriers in their organizations shape scientists' behavior. Because academic institutions are the locus of basic research and the training grounds for future generations of scientists, I focus in my book on these.

But in academia itself, national contexts can vary greatly. Asian, Latin American, and European countries consider strategies to create world-class, internationally linked, high-quality research universities. They invest in the international mobility of their academic elites, young scholars, and scientists in the hope they will engage in global knowledge production. The notion of "excellence" in hiring, merit, and promotion at universities shapes incentives for faculty to engage in international collaborations, and international educational or research experience becomes an expectation in the PhD and postdoc phases of academic career paths.[63]

By contrast, career paths in the United States are constructed around mobility primarily between U.S. institutions and labs. Although many non-U.S. universities see faculty collaborations with U.S. colleagues as a sign of excellence, the value attributed to such collaborations in U.S. universities is more ambiguous (see Chapter 2). I find that despite the benefits of international collaborations for U.S. faculty, some administrators and colleagues place more weight on national presence and devalue international research engagement because they presume it to be of lower quality. I argue that this devaluation of international engagement creates obstacles for U.S. faculty. Ironically, then, without broad-based institutional supports international collaborations risk being elite activities, undertaken primarily by those who can afford risks on the basis of their rank and resources. This attitude has implications for all women and for men from underrepresented groups, who tend to be in more marginal academic positions with less job security and fewer resources.[64]

For the United States, international exchange and collaborations are not primarily organized by U.S. faculty going abroad but have been fueled by mobile international academics who visit the United States for both short and extended periods of time and may migrate long term. Although U.S. faculty have low rates of engaging in international collaborations compared to their counterparts in other academically strong countries,[65] the United States has been a magnet for academics worldwide—the dominant destination country.[66] The United States relies heavily on international recruitment of graduate students, postdocs, and faculty, especially in the STEM fields.[67] Although faculty from the United States show little international mobility and fewer collaborations, international academics bring the world to the United States and create a dynamic context for creating meanings around international collaboration. For example, the idea that the "best academics" are in the United States emerges from this notion of the United States as a magnet for top talent with a comparably good research infrastructure. These returning students and postdocs then help fuel collaborative networks for U.S. faculty in the future without the U.S. faculty leaving their country.[68]

An Unequal Process: International Gender, Science, and Organizations

The globalization of science is a gendered process that intertwines with national affiliation as international research collaborations and mobility are organized in gendered ways. What I call *international gender, science, and organizations* is a new field of study that brings together theoretical frameworks from sociology and gender studies to explore the globalization of science from a gender perspective. A gender lens reveals how social and cultural aspects of academia profoundly structure who participates in international exchange and collaborations: in particular, women's more limited access to international research and collaborations itself might be gendered. Universities provide the institutional contexts, including opportunities and potential barriers, within which individuals make decisions and choices.[69] Glass fences reveal how these organizational structures are both nationally oriented and gendered. My approach seeks to map a framework for studying these processes by focusing on the organizational and institutional contexts in which faculty develop international collaborations.

The .edu Bonus and Glass Fences
To understand how gender matters for U.S. academics' engagement in the globalization of scientific and engineering knowledge, I develop two key con-

cepts: the *.edu bonus* (see Chapter 3) that reveals the particular opportunities that the global position of U.S. science brings, and *glass fences*, gendered obstacles or barriers (see Chapters 4 and 5) that shape women's participation in international research and collaborations. These fences are embedded in the institutions—universities, funding agencies, professional associations' journals—that structure international academic work (see Chapters 2 and 6).

The .edu bonus benefits academics affiliated with U.S. institutions when the global position of U.S. science trumps gender, race/ethnicity, or immigration status; that is, when being an American scientist (or a scientist associated with an American university) is more salient than being a woman, a nonwhite man, or a member of any culturally marginalized status group in U.S. academia. Drawing on Benedict Anderson's[70] notion of nationality as imagined communities, I introduce "academic nationality" to mean belonging to a particular national academic community through training or job affiliation.

The .edu bonus, based on U.S. academic nationality, helps identify how the global positioning of U.S. science provides opportunities and privileges for individual faculty members. Because the internet has become such an important medium also for academics, status is also signaled through email and web addresses. Because academia is organized hierarchically,[71] it is important to consider how faculty stratification, status, and access to resources work at the international level with its own dimension of hierarchy. Despite claims of universalism and meritocracy, status in scientific organizations and professional networks is crucial for accessing resources, such as funding, graduate students, and postdocs (who can be potential future collaborators).[72] Research suggests that the status of faculty members, related to their human, social, and academic capital, correlates with their desirability as collaborators, both at home and internationally.[73]

I build on Cecilia Ridgeway's work on status[74] to explain how these status categories intersect and become more or less salient in particular academic and social contexts. When gender becomes less salient for women scientists abroad because their status as U.S. scientists is more salient, beliefs about U.S. scientific competence counteract with worldwide held beliefs about gender and science that depict women as less competent.[75] The .edu bonus creates a crucial opportunity to experience being valued and seen as desirable collaboration partners even though they might feel or be excluded in the United States. Going abroad can therefore be liberating for women temporarily escaping confining gendered beliefs at home.[76]

Historically, U.S. women academics benefited from educational opportunities abroad and circumvented closed doors at home. In the nineteenth century, before women were admitted to colleges in the United States, they went to Germany and other European countries for their education, and on their return they founded women's colleges.[77] Although German professors did not allow German women to study, U.S. women were seen as less of a threat because they were expected to return to teach in the United States.[78]

The experience of empowerment abroad has some similarities to that of African American writers, artists, and musicians who lived and worked in Paris at the beginning of the twentieth century. Josephine Baker, James Baldwin, and others experienced a kind of freedom away from home. As James Miller explains, they were foremost seen as Americans: "The European treats the American—white and black—as an American, whether the American likes it or not."[79] Their national affiliation was in certain situations more salient than their race or ethnicity. They could not entirely escape gendered and racial stereotyping in France, and their race/ethnicity and gender were still at times salient, as was class,[80] but moving across the Atlantic opened new doors and allowed them to live very different lives from what the racial politics and inequalities in the United States would have permitted. The .edu bonus allows U.S.-based women scientists such an experience.

Many obstacles for academics to engage in international collaborations appear invisible, for they are rarely direct prohibitions but are woven into the policies, practices, and values of universities, funding agencies, and government bureaucracies. Clearly visible prohibitions include, for example, U.S. federal laws that restrict technological exchange in sensitive areas of national security (arms, nuclear energy, and so on). Many obstacles can be surmounted, but with difficulty. The Fly America Act, for instance, requires researchers with public funding to fly on U.S. airlines even if their prices are higher, which protects domestic airlines at the (literal) cost of U.S. researchers (and taxpayers). By draining already scarce funding for international collaborations, this act creates a material obstacle.

Finally, faculty, for example, notice that their international work frequently requires doing things "outside the box" because they do not fit into university and funding policies and practices. It is possible for universities and funding agencies to eliminate these obstacles or support individual faculty, for example by providing extra funding to cover the extra costs.

The obstacles are constructed in the context of a stratified international academia. Research and development resources and expenditures vary widely in different countries, as do research capacities, training infrastructures, supplies of skilled labor, and cultural and political contexts. And these complex global inequalities raise questions about how to set up international collaborations in ethical ways; for example, how to create partnerships that avoid exploitative relations between U.S. researchers and those abroad. These are important challenges; however, they go beyond the scope of this book.

Although research content and disciplines seem to be increasingly globally linked, university workplaces and funding agencies are still largely organized nationally (though universities have always been at once local, national, international, and global).[81] These obstacles, whether institutional, structural, cultural, symbolic, or political, reveal how academia is still organized in national ways. Internationalization strategies often seek to identify and tackle these obstacles because they can have unintended consequences that keep faculty from engaging in international collaborations.

The term *glass fences*, then, describes the gendered obstacles academics face in international collaborations and research, obstacles that have potentially different implications for women and men. The term *glass ceilings* has been useful for describing the barriers women face on the path to leadership positions in business and academia. The term *glass borders* has been used in business literature to discuss the barriers that prevent women managers from participating in a globalizing business world.[82] I find the border imagery, with its implications of permanence, too sturdy for academia. The notion of fences, which can be of different heights, suggests that faculty can find ways to jump them or even climb over them with the help of ladders. In my analysis of fences, I build on conceptualizations by Joan Acker and others[83] of how organizations are gendered, not only through formal and informal rules but also through practices such as division of labor and at the symbolic level of images. Fences show how international academic work amplifies and intensifies some gendered inequalities in academic careers. In short, rather than explaining gendered patterns of faculty involvement in international collaborations with human capital theories, fences embedded in the structures of academia reveal how academia is organized in gendered ways. Fences also point to how institutional support could help faculty to circumvent or climb over them.

Although not all international collaborations require mobility, faculty who have previously lived abroad seem to be able to jump over obstacles more easily and are more likely to be involved in international research collaborations than faculty who have not left their own country.[84] Faculty from family backgrounds and communities where travel abroad is common, and who embrace cosmopolitan values, are also more likely to find (additional) personal funds if necessary as well as supports to go abroad. Thus, not only gender but also class and race/ethnicity shape some of the so-called soft factors, including the ease and comfort level for operating in a different cultural environment abroad.[85] U.S. students of color are underrepresented in study-abroad programs.[86] U.S. faculty of color or from economically disadvantaged family backgrounds might have less cultural capital to engage in international collaborations, though Hispanics and others who speak additional languages might have the advantage of being able to connect to people in different countries in their native language.

Although most studies consider globalization of scientific and engineering knowledge to be a gender-neutral process, I explore its implications for gender arrangements.[87] A gender lens with a social constructionist perspective allows us to explore how the globalization of science is enmeshed with gender through the .edu bonus and fences. The globalization of academia creates forms of inclusion and exclusion that are constructed and in flux; these processes can reproduce gendered inequality, through fences that amplify existing or add more obstacles for women but can also reconfigure or challenge existing inequalities, for example by empowering women through the .edu bonus that offers opportunities in international networks that are exclusionary at home.[88] Feminists studying the impacts of globalization in the Global South have emphasized its negative implications for women;[89] my approach considers the multifaceted effects of globalization of science on gender relations in the North, including its potential benefits for U.S. STEM women professors. As high-status persons in (global) science, they can take advantage of the inequalities in (global) science.

The United States in the World of (Global) Science

As this is an exploratory study, designed to investigate a growing issue and demarcate a new field, I focus on the United States as a case, arguing that its particular positioning and institutional settings shape how its academics gain access to international research collaborations, which in turn has implications for obstacles and fences. To avoid the pitfalls of comparing incommensurable institutional contexts, I focus more specifically on STEM faculty at public and private research universities.[90] And although I make no claims about the generalizability of my specific findings, the framework I offer can provide a template for studying other institutions and countries, even as some of the aspects are particular to U.S. academia. In addition, because U.S. academics are sought after as cooperation partners around the world, understanding the economic, political, social, and cultural context in which they make decisions about collaborations is of broader interest.

The United States is an especially interesting case because of its hegemonic status at the center of science worldwide in terms of research networks and research productivity, including "funding, total scientific output, highly influential scientific papers, Nobel Prize winners."[91] However, policy makers and academics have been debating whether the United States will maintain its dominance in STEM in the twenty-first century and what the implications for the U.S. economy will be, if any.[92] Some argue that the U.S. position is threatened by international competition, especially from Asia, as most prominently expressed in two widely debated reports by the National Academy of Sciences, National Academy of Engineering, and Institute of Medicine, *Rising above the Gathering Storm* (2007, 2010). These reports argue for more public investment in U.S. higher education, particularly in STEM, to strengthen the scientific labor force and stop the decline of U.S. STEM. On the other hand, several economists challenge these alarming depictions of the shortage of scientific talent, pointing out that education, immigration, and workplace policies influence each other in complex ways and that the problem is not a current shortage of U.S. educated workforce but the relatively low wages that make STEM for U.S. talent unattractive.[93]

Historians of science have pointed out that U.S. dominance in science is a relatively recent development. The world center of science has moved several times over centuries, from England, France, and Germany.[94] The growth of U.S. science and engineering was fueled during the Cold War by the "space race." Competition with the Soviet Union led to U.S. investments in military and space developments in particular, and concerns about espionage limited cross-national collaborations because exchanges of knowledge were seen as potential threats to national security.[95] Today, competition among countries has shifted to the global "race for talent." The rationale is that a country's economic performance is fueled by knowledge production and innovation in science and technology.[96] Thus, STEM fields stand not only for economic progress but also for national power and security.

As we will see (Chapter 2), this global position creates a contradictory context for international engagement of U.S. faculty. Given its leadership position, U.S. universities, funding agencies, and publishing practices have developed a self-referential national orientation.[97] And although some argue that the United States needs to get more involved in international research collaborations, others view them as secondary, insisting that the United States is the world leader. The conception of the United States as an isolated island and gold standard for scientific progress, however, carries, among other issues, the risk of invisible power relations between countries and particular privileges of U.S. academics, such as English as the lingua franca.

Furthermore, over the past few decades, changes in academia and scientific developments worldwide have challenged the U.S. position. Overall data, however, support the notion that, as Yu Xie[98] puts it: "The nation's position relative to other countries is changing, but this need not be reason for alarm." For example, rising global competitors, especially from China and to some extent the EU, have been investing in research and development and growing their knowledge economies (see Figure 1.1.).[99]

Although the United States remains the leader in research and development (R&D) expenditures, the business sector finances much of these, often largely for development. The United States has also been the main spender in basic research ($74 billion), followed by Japan ($18 billion) and France ($13 billion), though it should be noted that the United States has a larger population.[100] However, as other regions have increased funding for research and universities, changes in U.S. funding for research and higher education have been starving both public and private universities.[101]

These changes were triggered through the financial crisis in the 2000s and include shrinking endowments, falling charitable contributions, and cutbacks in government support. For example, federal funding for research has remained flat since 2004 and, in 2011, after a temporary boost from the Recovery Act, dipped for the first time in decades.[102] Universities rely on such funding, particularly for basic research; 55 percent of overall college and university R&D funding comes from federal agencies, so these developments are a major concern.[103] In addition, state revenues for higher education between 2000 and 2012 decreased by 37 percent, and federal sources did not pick these

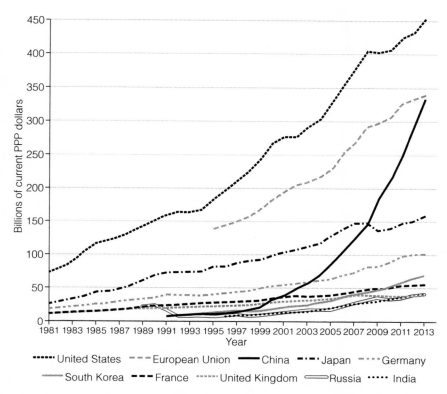

FIGURE 1.1. National trends and international comparisons of GDP on R&D funding, 1981–2013.

SOURCE: NSB Science and Engineering Indicators 2016.

up entirely.[104] Public colleges and universities that educate more than two-thirds of the students are especially hard hit by these changes, as federal and state revenues constitute 37 percent of their total budget.[105]

Along with funding challenges, U.S. universities are experiencing tremendous institutional changes, as ongoing struggles over rationalization, bureaucratization, and modernization characterize a general trend toward a more corporate model of academia.[106] The neoliberal components of what critics call "academic capitalism" impinge on academic institutions in various ways.[107] Institutions experience increased pressure and competition over funding sources and national and international rankings, which lead to heightened pressure on faculty to seek external funding, intensified monitoring of faculty

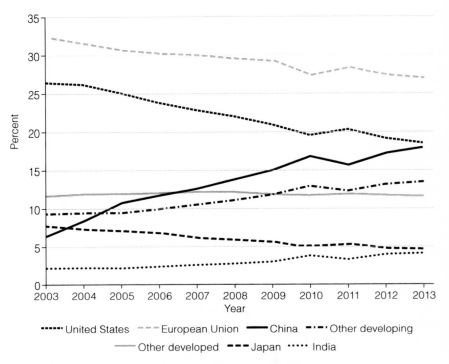

FIGURE 1.2. Science and engineering articles worldwide, 2003–2013.
SOURCE: NSB Science and Engineering Indicators 2016.

"productivity," and greater emphasis on measurable notions of scholarly excellence and knowledge production.[108]

Globalization of scientific and engineering knowledge has reframed competition in academia as not only national but also international.[109] To date, the
United States has been the world leader in research outputs as measured by
publications, with the highest number of articles in science and engineering
for a single country. However, Asian countries are showing dramatic growth
rates and increasingly challenging this lead. China's share alone rose from
3 to 18.2 percent between 1997 and 2013. In 2013, the U.S. share of the world's
total science and engineering articles was 18.8 percent, down from 30 percent
in 2001, while the EU share also dropped from 35 percent in 2001 to 27.5 percent in 2013 (see Figure 1.2).[110]

In this changing context of international scientific knowledge production,
policy makers and academics view international collaborations as increas-

ingly important, in particular as a (seemingly paradoxical) strategy to maintain U.S. leadership and be part of cutting-edge scientific developments. One concern is that collaborations among other countries, especially EU member states and China, could undermine U.S. leadership. As U.S. funding for research and higher education in general stagnates or even decreases, while funding increasingly becomes available elsewhere, international cooperation can be a welcome source of faculty research support. Overall, these developments, including changes in resource allocation and research output, challenge the notion of the United States as *the* undisputed world leader in science and engineering, generating complex and contested attitudes toward international collaboration (see Chapter 2).

STEM Fields, Gender, and Internationalization

The STEM disciplines are the ideal place to consider gender and internationalization, for they currently have the highest status and levels of internationalization in U.S. academia, along with some of the lowest participations by women. STEM fields have been valued highly, not only in the economic competition among countries but also in the competition between U.S. universities. This prioritizing of STEM fields is in part due to their promise of (large) federal government research grants that include facilities and administrative costs. These so-called indirect costs provide much desperately needed revenues for both public and private universities in the aftermath of the financial crises and otherwise dwindling public funding for higher education. Universities have been generalizing expectations for scientific work and increasingly imposing them on other fields, for instance, introducing rankings of publications and impact factors, reorienting expectations from monographs toward article publications, and expecting faculty to pay for their own research and support graduate students and postdocs with external funds.[111] Thus developments in these fields are highly relevant for understanding changes in academia as a whole.

In general, gender inequalities continue to characterize U.S. higher education and academic careers despite important changes over the past decades: Although women now constitute the majority of U.S. college students, they remain underrepresented across all academic ranks in many STEM fields.[112] Women compose less than 20 percent of U.S. STEM faculty in research universities, though integration varies across fields (women's presence in social and life sciences has grown more quickly than in physical sciences and engineering). The United States ranks around the EU average for women's representation in academia.[113]

STEM fields are also a central locus for globalization of scientific and technical knowledge, fueled by mobility of students, postdoctoral researchers, and faculty and collaborative activities, including large international research collaborations and laboratories. The international exchanges are fueled by the international funding resources, publication outlets, workshops, and conferences that promote the internationalization of science.

Academics in these fields increasingly engage internationally, as demonstrated by dramatically rising numbers of research collaborations and co-authored publications from different institutions. In 1988, just over half the articles in STEM fields had authors from multiple institutions; by 2012, that proportion was two-thirds. Scholars around the world are particularly publishing more internationally coauthored articles: In 1990, only 12 percent of overall articles had international coauthors; in 2010, that number was 32 percent. Between 1990 and 2010, the share of coauthored articles rose; articles with only domestic coauthors remained at 43 percent of all articles, while the percentage of internationally coauthored articles almost tripled (see Figure 1.3).[114]

In general, multi-institutional coauthorships have been rising, and international coauthorships have had a remarkable rise, reaching 33 percent in 2013.[115] Researchers from China, the UK, and Germany are the three most frequent coauthors of U.S. scientists.[116] The United States is also tightly intermeshed into the network of leading European nations according to patterns of citations—that is, who cites whom.[117] However, the growth of the global network has, interestingly, not led to an increased clustering.[118]

U.S. STEM faculty rank low in international mobility compared to their counterparts in other academically strong countries. In thirteen of sixteen countries, the majority of scientists have international experience; only 19.2 percent of U.S. scientists have worked abroad, and only 5 percent were abroad in 2011.[119] Because mobility is linked to international collaborations, it is not surprising that U.S. STEM faculty also collaborate less than faculty in other comparable countries.[120] Approximately one-third of STEM PhDs in the NSF Survey of Earned Doctorates stated that they have international collaborators; this is similar to the percentage of coauthored science publications.[121] The rising mobility, coauthorship, and collaboration in the United States

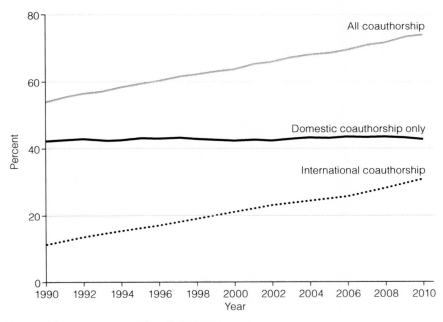

FIGURE 1.3. U.S. scientific collaboration, 1990–2010.
SOURCE: NSB Science and Engineering Indicators 2012.

demonstrate that international collaborations are increasingly important for U.S. scientists, but they also raise the question of why the United States is an outlier. I argue that the particular global positioning of the United States creates obstacles and fences that keep U.S. faculty from engaging in international collaborations and being mobile themselves. Of course, the size and relatively high level of resources of U.S. academia make it easier for faculty to find collaborators within national borders.[122] Furthermore, because the United States has been an international magnet for students, researchers, and faculty, U.S. faculty have opportunities to interact with non-U.S. scholars without leaving home.

In the postwar decades, the United States has been the ne plus ultra for scientific training and scientific labor the dominant destination country.[123] It relies heavily on international recruitment of graduate students, postdocs, and faculty, especially in the STEM fields.[124] International academics "bring the world" to the United States and create a dynamic context for creating meanings around international collaboration. For example, the idea that the "best academics" are in the United States emerges from the notion of the United States as a magnet for top talent with a comparably good research infrastructure. Although many students and postdocs prefer to stay in the United States, those who return to their home countries help create collaborative networks for U.S. faculty (outside the United States) without those faculty leaving their country,[125] creating "brain circulation" that furthers international exchange. Foreign-born academics[126] who stay in the United States may contribute to "brain drain" in other countries; for some, however, family and cultural ties also create motivation to engage in international collaborations. I subsume the foreign-born scientists under "U.S. scientists" because in the international academic community they are considered "American scientists" due to their *academic nationality*, their affiliation with U.S. research institutions, regardless of their citizenship status. And I define international collaborations of U.S. faculty as collaborations they engage in with academics in other countries, independent of the national or immigration backgrounds of those involved.[127]

Faculty in Research Universities

Finally, I focus on faculty in public and private research universities[128] because the high stratification in U.S. higher education means that these academics have comparatively more resources of time (for research and building collaborations) and support (in the form of internal funding, infrastructure, and personnel, including graduate students and postdocs) that enable them to participate in international research and collaborations.[129] They have the status and the resources to apply for the larger grants they need to fund international collaborations. Most universities, whether public or private, will not provide such large research funds. Because faculty encounter not only economic but also noneconomic, symbolic, cultural, and institutional barriers, it is not surprising that I found no systematic differences between public and private universities' overall support of faculty's international engagements.

Stratification occurs within research universities as well. I focus on tenure track and tenured faculty, who are more able to engage in collaborations for the same reasons as having access to these necessary resources.[130] Instructors, contract staff, and others with precarious employment situations are less able to take "risks" to build international collaborations due to lack of funding, short-term planning horizons, and other such barriers.

By selecting the most privileged U.S. STEM faculty, I can investigate the range of freedom of academics to create international collaborative research practices and how gender matters in these. Because these faculty generally have more access to the necessary resources, they allow me to identify what other barriers and fences U.S. academics encounter in international research and collaborations. And despite some variation among fields, the overall percentage of women in STEM faculty positions in research universities remains the lowest compared to other fields and universities. Thus, faculty in research universities in STEM disciplines in the United States can provide important insights into how the globalization of scientific and engineering knowledge shapes and reconfigures gender (in)equalities.

Data and Methods

I have drawn the data for this book from several related projects on international collaboration and mobility, including two U.S. NSF-funded research projects. Data on the international experiences of STEM faculty include a survey of 100 principal investigators of NSF-funded international STEM projects (2009); phone and in-person interviews with more than 100 university STEM faculty (2007–2015); and eight focus groups with eighteen STEM faculty (2009–2010). Participants represent thirty-eight research universities across the United States; 57 percent of these are public and 43 percent are private. The interviews lasted between twenty minutes and two hours and were recorded and transcribed. Because this study is exploratory in nature, the sampling strategies sought faculty from a range of disciplines, regions, ages, ranks, genders, and minority statuses, with or without children living in the household.[131] Although most faculty who participated in the study had some international research, collaboration, or mobility experiences, some did not.

Although faculty are the ones who actually collaborate, funding agencies and universities shape opportunities for engaging in international research and collaboration. To study these institutional contexts, I conducted interviews about opportunities and barriers for international collaboration and mobility with thirty department chairs and university administrators, seventeen funding agency personnel, sixteen policy makers, and thirteen academic experts in the United States and Europe (2007–2015). The interviews were coded for common themes and analyzed to reflect both recurring themes and variation of views, using NVIVO to organize the data analysis. A content analysis of policy documents and materials from funding agencies and policy makers complements the interview data. Finally, I draw on the results of an international expert workshop on international research collaboration I organized with Lisa Frehill at the NSF in Washington, D.C., in 2010.[132]

The Plan of the Book

In the following chapters, I show how the globalization of scientific and engineering knowledge creates a new frontier for the inclusion of women in STEM fields, with concomitant challenges and opportunities. Chapter 2 examines the institutional context for faculty decisions about engagement in international collaboration and research. I investigate the contrast between faculty perceptions of international research and collaborations as extremely positive—a highlight of their careers—and their experiences of lack of institutional recognition and support. Part of this dynamic is the construction of international collaboration as an activity for elite faculty. I also explore the meanings of international research for U.S. funding institutions and universities. By analyzing U.S. faculty constructions of (global) science, I identify how U.S. institutions position themselves globally. Although claims to U.S. scientific supremacy persist, there is also a call for international collaborations as in the "national interest" in maintaining its global position, which suggests a sense of threat to that supremacy. Not surprisingly, given these competing imperatives, faculty members use contradictory rationales to explain why international academic work is meaningful to them in the context of constructions of U.S. superiority, competition, the universality of scientific work, and international research as a "risky" activity.

In Chapter 3, I explain the benefits offered to women in international academic work. I argue that cultural schemas for U.S. scientists reveal an .edu bonus that depicts U.S. scholars as competent and overshadows stereotypes of women as less so. Academics marginalized at the national level by gender, minority background, or field can benefit particularly from the .edu bonus, drawing on the positive aspects of being a U.S. scholar in an international environment. For many women researchers, being a woman and a foreigner is thus a positive combination rather than an accumulation of disadvantages. Persistent stereotypes and myths hold that U.S. women scientists are not effective in cultural environments where no native women hold equal positions of power. But women scientists report that they are seen foremost as foreigners and treated as such, making their gender status less salient. This .edu bonus can serve to expand networks internationally and demonstrates the importance of analyzing the intersection of gender and foreigner status of U.S. scientists.

In Chapter 4, I focus on the glass fences, the various gendered challenges in international research collaborations. Because academia is still organized in gendered ways, these fences tend to have a more powerful impact on women's careers. Gender is embedded in the international collaboration policies and practices of nation-states, funding agencies, universities, and researchers. I illustrate how these fences emerge in specific international work settings and research practices, examining in particular the implications for women's access to and opportunities to participate in, organize, and operate international conferences, research sites, and fieldwork. I suggest that fences emerge when institutions and individuals construct safety abroad as a gendered issue. I argue that (global) academia is gendered through the organization of academic work around norms, values, and expectations that fit the ideal of an elite male global scientist with the personal, social, and academic resources to climb fences. The very structure of international collaboration thus privileges men over women and re-creates gendered inequalities in academia, globally and in the United States.

In Chapter 5, I challenge the conventional wisdom that family barriers make it impossible for faculty to engage in international collaborations and mobility. Despite discourse that suggests that children amplify family burdens for international research for mothers in particular, I debunk the notion that families (meaning those with young children) construct an insurmountable fence for women and hinder international work only for mothers. Diverse family commitments in various constellations can potentially be constraining, but they can also motivate and even support research abroad. Faculty with international family ties might have extra incentive to spend time in other countries and forge transnational academic careers, whereas "portable" or "supportive" partners (or lack thereof) can be another important factor in individual mobility.

The final chapter considers what these findings mean for research institutions. Drawing on the implications of the .edu bonus and glass fences for gender equality policies at funding agencies and universities, I argue that these institutions need to design internationalization strategies that recognize the diversity of both international research collaborations and their participants and take gender inequalities at the international and national level into account. I suggest ways to support international research collaborations that are inclusive of women, individuals from marginalized groups, and those with limited mobility due to caregiving. By promoting international collaboration and mobility, being transparent about support allocation, eliminating obstacles and fences through bureaucratic procedures and policies, and "broadening participation" along demographic lines, U.S. funding agencies and universities have the opportunity to help create a more inclusive (global) academia. I conclude with a cautionary note. When international collaboration and mobility become normative expectations for academic career paths, they might contribute to reproducing gender inequalities in academia because women might fit less the ideal of this kind of global scientist. Instead, the United States can do even more to engage other countries at the policy level to promote gender equality in academia at various levels, toward building an inclusive and innovative world of (global) academia.

2 Traveling Abroad, Coming Home

Ambivalent Discourses on the U.S. Role in (Global) Science

WHEN ACADEMICS WHO HAVE COLLABORATED INTERNA-
tionally are asked whether they would do it again, they respond
enthusiastically. Jordan, an associate professor of Earth and atmospheric
science, described her research abroad as a highlight of her career: "I love
working overseas with people. I think the cultural experience, the scientific
experience, everything is great. So I'm always working and looking for opportunities." Indeed, her main obstacle to further collaboration is lack of institutional support: "If the funding was easier, I'm sure I would have a lot more!"
Richard, an associate professor of pharmaceutical sciences, found collaboration with international colleagues valuable not only for his research but also
for his teaching and graduate student mentoring:

> It adds breadth to the research and visibility in such a way that you're able to use
> it to bring additional people to work with you, grad students. It will certainly
> impact the way that you teach your classes because it gives you broader expo-
> sure to a context in a different country and the way that they look at this type of
> question in other disciplines and in other cultures for that matter.

Richard also noted that he gained visibility, which would in turn translate
into visibility for his university: "It enhances the reputation of the institution, which I think is very important." Many faculty members identified international research and collaboration experiences as pinnacles of their careers. They described these experiences as important, exciting, intense, and

fulfilling. Professionally, they found that international collaboration was intellectually stimulating and had positive impacts on their research projects. Personally, they enjoyed intercultural exchanges and cultivation of friendships abroad and appreciated the good treatment, respect, and appreciation they received from international colleagues. Some faculty members, however, found it challenging to secure the resources they needed for collaboration, especially funding and time. Though they found collaboration valuable, and official rhetoric concurred, they were disappointed by the obstacles and sometimes barriers put up by colleagues, universities, and funding agencies, which give little recognition and support to international research.

This chapter explores how these contradictory experiences emerge in the particular institutional contexts of U.S. universities, which discursively frame international collaboration in conflicting ways, while creating obstacles to international work. Thus faculty who wish to collaborate abroad face a set of burdens and challenges whose effect is powerful, albeit differently felt at different levels. The official construction of the globalization of scientific and engineering knowledge in the United States depicts it as an inherently positive development for scientific progress, which also bolsters the U.S. economy, national and global security, and universities themselves, not to mention intellectual and scientific leadership. Yet at their home institutions, faculty members who conduct research abroad report that some colleagues deploy a range of strategies that diminish the value of their international experiences and collaborations and that their institutions do not recognize their research endeavors.[1] Although they regard these efforts as crucial to their research agendas and career progress, they come up against beliefs that STEM fields in the United States are superior and that international research and collaboration are intellectually unnecessary, trivially touristic, and an expensive hobby of elite academics, beliefs that lead to undervaluation of their work in tenure, promotion, and merit reviews, as well as resource decisions.

The broader institutional contexts explain to some extent the tension between the worth assigned to international collaborations by U.S. faculty who participate in them and the ambivalent responses of their colleagues and institutions. Exploring the construction of international scientific engagement by different U.S. stakeholders, I argue that these contradictory experiences are a consequence of the stratification of (global) science and the efforts of U.S. institutions of higher education to maintain or expand their position within it. Some countries enjoy far more scientific status than others (see also Chapter 3), in a hierarchy that reflects economic power as well as differing scientific research capacities, infrastructures, and (human) resources, which result in a changing yet still unequal division of labor worldwide.

By positioning itself as the leader of the global scientific world, the United States constructs other countries as its scientific inferiors, which shapes U.S. perceptions of the benefits of international research collaborations and the discursive strategies used to diminish the value of faculty engagement in research outside the United States.[2] There is evidence that this sense of U.S. primacy is shifting, providing motivation for some academics to work abroad. But overall the sense of superiority remains a powerful discursive and material engine for U.S. science overall, creating ambivalent meanings toward international collaboration.

In the following pages, I discuss several key rationales offered by national funding agencies and universities for the U.S. stake in the globalization of scientific and engineering knowledge, whereby international collaboration is seen as benefiting the United States, science itself, institutions of higher education, and individuals (faculty and students).[3] I then explore the negative take on international collaboration that creates obstacles faced by faculty and show how these obstacles are tightly woven into these discursive and material constructs.

Science is Global:
Universalism, Diversity, and Cooperation

One key academic rationale for international collaboration is the idea that science is a global enterprise that takes place in a worldwide community and has a cosmopolitan ethos visible in the commitment of scientists to the value of universality.[4] This notion philosophically positions science as universal, that is, beyond containment within national borders. If good research and scholarship are seen as naturally global, then it does not matter with whom you work or from where they come. Greg, a full professor of engineering, explained, "What I find is that the world is global anyway. With email and all this communication, it kind of blurs the boundaries in terms of dialogue and sharing information. So for me, the fact that somebody is in a different country isn't so intrinsic as, what is their knowledge, what is their expertise?" Because only the best work counts, and the best scientists in the world can be anywhere, this ethos holds that science should be an enterprise without national constriction.

Mitchell, an associate professor in the social sciences, pointed out that this rationale applies not only to individual researchers but also to institutions and entire fields:

> The U.S. isn't an island. Knowledge and the dissemination of knowledge, teaching, all benefit immensely from those kinds of international collaborations and comparative contexts. I have a hard time imagining that any academic institution that aspires to any level of standing could be so isolated that it never considers international dimensions of whatever field one's looking at. Presumably even things like engineering, we think of as more narrowly defined, I'm sure they also would benefit from international context.

As Mitchell's final comment implies, albeit in a slightly different context, the extent to which scholars endorse the notion of scientific universality varies by discipline. Mathematicians and physicists, for example, sometimes insist that their work can be done anywhere and is the same everywhere, regardless of the location or sociocultural background of any researcher or research team, but few social scientists would agree that this conception of universality applies to their disciplines—or to science in general. They argue that culture indeed matters for the kind of knowledge they produce, rendering universality a myth.[5] Most famously, Sharon Traweek critiques the idea of science as a "culture of no culture" among physicists, the notion of an "extreme culture of objectivity . . . which longs passionately for a world without loose ends, without temperament, gender, nationalism, or other sources of disorder—for a world outside human space and time."[6] Sociologists insist that science as a workplace is stratified by access to resources, training, and expertise and that these inequalities in the international division of scientific labor create unequal patterns of collaboration around the world (see Chapter 1).

Another academic rationale for international collaboration embraces the idea that approaches to scientific work have local and cultural variations and argues that intellectual cross-pollination enhances scientific progress. In this prodiversity argument for international science, different scientific perspectives contribute to innovative thought and creativity, and differences in research approaches improve scholarship and generate scientific innovation. International collaboration thus becomes intrinsically valuable as an important way of bringing diversity to the table, based on the assumption that different ways of doing science across cultures enhance scientific progress, especially when capitalized on in cross-national collaboration. Michael, a full professor of health sciences, pointed out that such collaboration "gives opportunities to our faculty as well as to our students to participate in research outside the country. And I think you get different perspectives in different countries and different ways of approaching problems that expand your understanding of specific problems."

This diversity discourse values cosmopolitanism and exposure to different views, along with the ability of academics to work across borders. Not surprisingly, social scientists were most likely to endorse this perspective in interviews, pointing to U.S.-centrism in the social sciences in a (self-) critical and reflective way. Nonetheless, scholars in other disciplines often agreed that the quality of one's scholarship depends on knowledge of the rest of the world. Andrea, a full professor of physical sciences, said, "We need to think internationally; we need to collaborate internationally. That's the only way we can keep science alive in the United States." In this context, international collaboration allows scholars from the United States to position themselves and their approaches through comparison with others and to engage in dialogues that improve creativity and innovation as they learn from and with others. Attending conferences abroad provides one such opportunity for meeting colleagues and encountering scholarship that is less visible in U.S. circuits of knowledge.

Although the universality and diversity arguments were the key academic rationales offered for international collaboration, others exist. Some interviewees pointed to the justification that global problems, such as climate change and human and animal health epidemics, need global science solutions. Another instrumental, rational logic is that some research endeavors, like particle physics generators such as CERN, are too large and expensive to be conducted and financed by one country alone. Others noted that international collaborations strengthen research quality by making it possible to find strong partners and keep up with cutting edge research. In small fields in particular, scholars emphasized that finding the best people often meant looking overseas. Also, the selectivity argument economists use states that when faculty can choose the best place to do their work and the best collaborators without being constrained by national borders, we would expect them to be able to produce high-quality research.[7]

Creating a transnational space for academic work itself might also have a positive impact on innovation. As German-American MIT professor Wolfgang Ketterle explained, "Being a foreigner allows one to develop one's own style. When I did things in a certain way, my colleagues in the United States would say, 'Ah, he's doing it the German way,' and my German colleagues commented: 'Ah, he must be doing it the American way.'" Because he was seen as an outsider, neither American nor entirely German, he did not have to fit cultural expectations of how things are done in the lab, he was granted more freedom to experiment with new ways of doing science, and he used these opportunities for innovation that resulted in a Nobel Prize in physics.[8] Overall, U.S. faculty seem to draw important research and career benefits from these collaborations, as internationally coauthored publications are more likely to appear in higher-impact journals and receive higher citation counts.[9] In short, from the perspective of science itself, there are numerous powerful rationales for international collaboration.

The Home Advantage: Economic and Political Rationales

Although research collaborations have scientific value, they also have significant political importance, in large part because of their presumed economic ramifications. Science policy makers and funding agencies articulate implicit and explicit economic, political, and market rationales for international collaboration that can generate political support for resources; for faculty, these discourses can legitimate their endeavors and translate into tangible incentives and opportunities for funding. Although every country has its particular interests in processes of globalization of scientific and engineering knowledge, the United States occupies a singular role as a long-standing global scientific leader, whose leadership position is debated to be under challenge (see controversies discussed in Chapter 1). The rationale then is that if scientific work is happening everywhere, U.S. science must stay involved with international developments, to assert its continued claim to dominance as well as to control knowledge production, at least as much as possible.

The National Science Foundation (NSF) strategic goals for 2011–2016 include "Keep the United States globally competitive at the frontiers of knowledge by increasing international partnerships and collaborations."[10] The United States aims to remain at the forefront of global knowledge production, as other countries seek to compete as knowledge economies creating information societies. U.S. policy makers and funding agencies view the university sector as crucial to the economy precisely because of the global competition around knowledge production,[11] a view also endorsed by the OECD, UNESCO, and World Bank.[12] Their economic rationales use market imagery, in which competition for world leadership is a key element, to describe the dynamics of globalization of scientific and engineering knowledge, knowledge economies, and knowledge societies. The positioning of the United States in the worldwide competition for knowledge production and knowledge economies is thus key to framing what globalization of scientific and engineering knowledge means for U.S. academics and how international research collaborations are framed in the United States.

U.S. funding agencies and universities also use the discourse of cultivating a scientific workforce with intercultural competences that will enable them to take on leadership tasks abroad; in this, they are responding not only to scientific needs but also to the demands of global business for a culturally savvy workforce. In one example of this commitment, the NSF includes career advancement considerations in research funding opportunities—such as the NSF PIRE program (Partnerships for International Research and Education), which encourages international research experience for both undergraduate and graduate students through institutional partnerships and exchanges— because its mission is linked to developing the U.S. scientific and engineering workforce. The value of cross-cultural competences is currently more visible in the global business world than in academia. Business schools have been responding to the corporate call to provide students with global competences so that U.S. businesses will have a workforce that is able to work with international teams. Similar discourse now characterizes U.S. science, as evident in the PIRE 2015 request for proposal: "In the global context, U.S. researchers and educators must be able to operate effectively in teams with partners from different national environments and cultural backgrounds."[13]

Entirely absent from this discourse, however, is discussion of direct economic benefits to individuals and institutions in the United States. This absence reveals that international collaboration is not as simple as market metaphors would imply. Of course, conducting research abroad can have economic benefits. U.S. scholars, for instance, can benefit from the (unequal) division of labor in scientific work when research costs are lower abroad (see Chapter 3), as when U.S. scientists conduct experimental research in laboratories in China for a fraction of the cost at their U.S. institution.[14] As research budgets grow in other countries (see Chapter 1), U.S. researchers may benefit in the long run. However, at the moment, given that faculty and administrators see U.S. national funding agencies as notoriously underfunding international projects, neither individuals nor institutions can expect high funding levels for international work in the short term.

Indeed, funding structures for international collaborations are one of the key obstacles U.S. scholars face. Faculty cannot expect to generate significant funding for their home institutions from agencies abroad because, in general, national funding agencies will fund researchers only in their own countries. They are also reluctant to pay the high overhead U.S. institutions expect, so even if U.S. faculty can cover research and travel costs from funding outside the United States, their home universities see little financial benefit in terms of much-needed indirect cost rates. In the aftermath of the financial crises and declining public spending on research and higher education in particular, these facilities and administrative cost rates, negotiated by each institution with the Office of Management and Budget, have become substantial funding sources for both private and public universities, ranging from 20 to 85 percent with an average rate of 31 percent of the overall award.[15]

From the university budget perspective, encouraging collaborations supported by U.S. funding sources that promise substantial indirect costs is thus more economically rational than incentivizing faculty to conduct research abroad with international funding sources. Surprisingly, however, neither faculty nor administrators pointed to this misfit of international funding mechanisms, which creates conflicting interests for universities if they pursue an internationalization strategy that encourages faculty to collaborate internationally.

National Funding Agencies and National Interests

Beyond the university level, national funding agencies in particular are called on to further the national interest. Given this imperative, these agencies may adopt a skeptical posture toward research conducted outside the United States or by researchers from other countries. Such research raises concerns about dedicating U.S. resources to efforts that will not directly benefit U.S. taxpayers. Policy makers and national funding agencies tend to counter this skepticism by framing international collaboration as congruent with U.S. national interests. They argue, for instance, that maintaining U.S. leadership in science and the prestige and quality of U.S. research requires cooperation across countries. Ironically, this rhetoric posits that to compete successfully in the world market of knowledge production, the United States must cooperate with strong partners, who are often its strongest competitors. In other words, cooperation is entangled with competitiveness. One way policy makers and national funding agencies mitigate this paradox is by emphasizing the need for U.S. scholars to assume leadership in such international projects to maintain the presence and status of U.S. science around the world.

A second discourse on development also provides a way of linking investments abroad to U.S. national interests. The NSF, for example, claims that international collaborations are useful for academic and human resource reasons, as well as to promote U.S. interests: The goal is to "advance *research* excellence and innovation; develop *human and infrastructure* capacity critical to the U.S. science and engineering enterprise; and promote *global engagement* of scientists and engineers at all career stages" (emphases added).[16] In this context, the challenge of negotiating competition and collaboration is less crucial than the U.S. impetus to "help" others by investing in the research capacities of developing countries to help them address local and global issues—of course, tying the development of research capacities to U.S. national interests. The 2013 Partnerships for Enhanced Engagement in Research (PEER), a joint NSF and United States Agency for International Development (USAID) program, also looks for "collaborative global research in critical areas of development."[17]

A third way that international collaboration is framed in relation to national interests is in the context of promoting global security through collaboration around sensitive research, such as nuclear energy and chemical weapons, that is considered a potential threat to national security, especially in the United States. Harold, a full professor of engineering, remarked:

> In the field of homeland security, there's two sides of the equation: One is that the United States needs to have a sense of its own security; they need to safeguard as best we can. You know our nation has threats from within, but that being said, there are also recognitions of the fact that other countries have the same problem and that we need to be in this together. And so, we have to balance the two, so international dialogue and collaboration are very important in terms of effective measures against international terrorism and things like that.

After September 11, 2001, policy makers had a crucial awakening. Today, the official mantra is that collaboration is in the U.S. national interest because global terrorism requires collaborative efforts with other countries, such as the network research tools that helped track the movements of Al-Qaeda and

Osama bin Laden. However, this understanding balances on a crucial ambivalence between recognition that research can help protect the country and fear that sharing too much information and knowledge can pose security risks, as in the case of research on nuclear energy, which can be used for civilian or military purposes. Overall, however, policy makers and funding agencies seek to express clearly the link between international research and collaboration and U.S. national interests, in order to reproduce a nationally focused discourse that is politically tied to taxpayers' purported interests. National security laws then also get translated into regulations, including restrictions in technology transfer and so on.

Global Rationales for Universities

Rationales about national interests and the global economy shape the framing of international collaboration not only for government bodies but also for U.S. universities, whose logics also prominently feature economic metaphors of competition. In the case of academia, global competition, in image and actuality, centers on research quality and cutting-edge research development, which generate institutional prestige and facilitate recruitment of top international students and faculty because global talent is portrayed as a key human resource in knowledge economies. These elements include a self-fulfilling prophecy: Economic advantages can be derived from institutional research excellence, which depends on attracting top human talent, which itself depends on an institution's research reputation on the international market.

International collaboration is tied to global recruitment because it makes U.S. institutions visible and attractive, enhancing their reputations and positioning them in the "brain race," the global competition for talent. The media have been covering debates about highly mobile, highly skilled workers with great concern, following the 2001 McKinsey study by Michaels, Handfield-Jones, and Axelrod entitled *The War for Talent*, which argues that businesses need to embrace finding talent as a strategic business challenge because of the increased worldwide competition for brainpower.[18] For example, in 2009 the *Economist* published several blogs and articles on the "battle for the brains."[19] This group of internationally mobile, highly educated workers is also becoming a market for a particular branch in the service industry. For example, a Dutch private service called "Battle for Brains" provides services to deal with formalities of immigration and other questions on relocation.

Recent state-funded international recruitment and academic repatriation programs are helping the EU and countries such as China to compete with the United States for U.S.-trained postdoctoral researchers and faculty.[20] The discourse uses "brain race" in analogy to metaphors of the arms race, following the Cold War space race; for example, Ben Wildavsky, a scholar at the Ewing Marion Kauffman Foundation, entitled his book *The Great Brain Race: How Global Universities Are Reshaping the World*.[21] Overall, the United States has been successful in the battle for scholarly talent, effectively framing itself as the standard for scientific work, a magnet for international collaboration partners, and the leader in the competition between growing knowledge economies.

International recruitment is also considered crucial for the United States because universities depend on attracting top global graduate students, postdoctoral researchers, and faculty, especially in the STEM fields (see Chapter 1).[22] Some argue that the United States faces an increasing lack of qualified U.S. applicants for graduate programs and positions due to lack of return on investments in high school STEM education. Others argue that scientific jobs have become less attractive in comparison to finance, business, and law, which involve equally long hours but better working conditions and pay.[23] In the 2013–2014 academic year, international students constituted 42.3 percent of the total U.S. graduate student population.[24] Temporary residents were half or more of doctoral recipients in engineering, computer sciences, and economics.[25] Attracting top international students and researchers funded by PhD and postdoctoral fellowships from their home countries can also be a perk for U.S. universities.

As international faculty collaborations create a reinforcing cycle for recruiting international talent and fostering international cooperation, the differential access to international talent can be a potential source of inequity among faculty and institutions. International collaborations also emerge from ties established when students, postdoctoral researchers, and faculty from other countries visit the United States, as brain circulation encourages longer-term collaboration.[26] Faculty with strong international networks are also likely to be viewed as attractive advisors. Sydney, an assistant professor of natural sciences, noted that, because she "partake[s] in all kinds of international things," she receives "loads of emails from international students who are thinking about coming to my university." Faculty at U.S. institutions that are part of the international circuit may thus be involved in international collaborations that do not even require them to leave home because they can count on talented international students, postdocs, and other researchers seeking them out, and they can send their own students and postdocs to foreign labs or field stations. However, faculty and universities with smaller international networks and less international visibility and reputation have fewer opportunities to recruit internationally, which creates fewer opportunities for future international collaboration, in a mutually reinforcing negative cycle.[27] Because of their resources, such as research infrastructure and equipment, research universities and Ivy League schools are generally more attractive to international visitors seeking to collaborate with U.S. faculty.

By maintaining international networks with individuals and institutions, faculty believe that they contribute to the modern image and name recognition of their universities. Faculty involvement in international projects is seen as enhancing the university's image as a global and thus modern institution. Oscar, a social scientist and full professor, believed that "[it] would be the mark of a strong university to have strong international research." He talked at length about how engaging in new and exciting research opportunities, such as international collaborations, can enhance the prestige of a school and make it stand out. He noted:

> [My university is] extremely sensitive to the prestige image. . . . Being able to go and start new programs and do new things, I think, really helps the university because it sort of jump-starts things. It allows you to walk around the fact that you're not as old as some of these other schools or whatever. And I also think that [my university's] classic strengths have been in technology, and I think these things also are simply globalizing and the cross discipline areas in certain basic ways are very hard to duplicate in other settings. And I think that gives us an advantage.

In the discourse of the globalization of science, top universities must have an international image. For U.S. universities, international engagement stands for newness, openness, cosmopolitanism, innovation, and excellence. STEM itself stands for progress; in this discourse of modernization, international represents scientific progress and the future, whereas the past is depicted as national and parochial. By positioning *global* as synonymous with *modern*, this discourse redefines what it means to do modern research: To be a modern university entails not only an international faculty and student body but faculty engaged in international collaboration, as well as student exchanges.

For universities, then, a commitment to globalization—whatever that means in a particular case—signals openness to innovative scholarship and exciting cutting-edge research possibilities such as international collaborations. In countries that perceive their scientific outputs to be less competitive, the relationship between international and excellence is even stronger than in the United States. In Germany, for example, international stands for excellence, and evaluators from the United States, the UK, and other prominent research-strong countries have been invited as peer reviewers for its government-funded excellence initiative.[28] Expanding in a global direction is thus crucial for both domestic and international competition. In line with neoliberal discourses around market competition, "branding" an institution as global is a crucial element of this move.

Rationales for international collaborations construct them as contributing to the U.S. leadership position in science by advancing research and knowledge and helping to recruit talent from around the world to U.S. universities. Global competition shapes the discourses around international collaboration, and recruitment is one important aspect of understanding this process in the United States, where a temporary workforce of graduate students, postdoctoral researchers, and technicians does much of the STEM research. The United States thus has a particular stake in positioning itself as the home of top-notch research by continuing to attract others for study, training, and collaboration. The assumption is that the United States does not have to go into the world to engage in outstanding scientific work; the world should come to the United States.

Mixed Messages at Home

Despite positive official discourses about international collaboration, unofficial or informal discourses can offer a contradictory take. Faculty who engage in international collaboration encounter myriad negative perspectives from colleagues, administrators, and funding agencies, which create discursive obstacles with material consequences. Universities and funding agencies also use these negative discourses to justify their lack of support for collaboration across national borders. Faculty researchers thus receive mixed messages about the value of international collaboration. Even if their subfields are highly internationalized, their disciplines, departments, or universities may attach very different values to their international engagement.

When You Have the Best

One discursive strategy used to discourage international collaboration reflects the same global positioning of U.S. scientific superiority used to justify it. In this account, there is no need to go abroad because everything worthwhile is happening at home, including the best research, the most prestigious conferences, the highest-status publications, and the world's best talent. When asked about the importance of international research collaboration for his career, Morris, a full professor of natural science, explained:

> I think actually sometimes scientists in my field in the United States are very insular, because they sort of take it for granted that anything interesting that's going on is going on in the United States. . . . I think there's just sort of an assumption, and maybe this is universal; I don't mean to pick on Americans, but I think there's an assumption, a very implicit assumption, that . . . the top work is going on in the United States. And that to really understand the field, you don't really necessarily have to pay attention to work that is going on elsewhere.

Although Morris did not share this view, his description of his colleagues illustrates the common perspective that U.S. scholars can limit their expertise to knowledge produced in the United States. Matilda, a social scientist who decided to take an academic position abroad, worried about the effect of this perspective when she was considering leaving the United States:

> There's a very strong sense in U.S. academia that it's "U.S. academia or bust." That the U.S. universities are the world's best, and why would you leave them? And I must say that influenced me, as well, in my thinking. I wasn't so sure it was such a smart career move to move to [a European country].

Although the strength of this parochialism varies by discipline, it was echoed by faculty members across a wide range of science and engineering fields. Eric, a full professor of engineering, argued that, as one could always find a suitable collaborator in the United States, there was no reason to seek international partners. And although Kenneth, a full professor in the social sciences, gets information from his international colleagues, he has not co-authored publications with them because "very often they're not trained the same way that people are in the United States, so they're not necessarily going to help you with your research." He did, however, hope that the new generation of non-U.S. scholars trained in the United States would potentially be collaborators and coauthors. Interestingly, U.S. and foreign-born faculty shared these sentiments, in which the reasoning goes simply: Training abroad is inferior, so the skills of colleagues abroad are inferior; their research infrastructure is inferior, so the quality of their research is inferior; and thus, there is little motivation for scholars in the United States to engage in international collaboration.

The notion that the United States is a magnet for the top talent of the world further supports this rationale of U.S. superiority. Olivia, an assistant professor of biomedical sciences, explained that the draw U.S. academia has for international faculty even creates a situation in which U.S. faculty perceive themselves as being in the center of science worldwide:

> So people feel that—for each of these annual conferences [of the U.S. national professional organization] you have people from different countries coming— especially from Canada, South America, and Europe, some from Asia and other places—so it's almost, I don't call that cultural chauvinism, but it's kind of feeling, "We are the best." If we are not the best, at least we are more developed, almost like the center. In this field, the international is not as important.

Even beyond conferences, the academic world is depicted as a "human resource market," in which scholars are geographically mobile and all topnotch scholars (independently of national background) are assumed to desire to work in the United States. Therefore, the best and most highly qualified graduate students, postdoctoral researchers, and faculty will, of course, be found in the United States. Interestingly, again there is silence about the lack of qualified graduate students from the United States in STEM fields.

An exception is made for the group of U.S.-trained international collaborators who return to their own countries. Yet, this exception serves again to reaffirm the superiority of U.S. training, a rationale highly reminiscent of (post)colonial cultural imperialism, applied indiscriminately to former colonies in Asia, Africa, and Latin America but also to European countries, with the exception of a few British universities, namely Oxford and Cambridge.[29] Academics are also stereotyped based on their non-U.S. backgrounds. Distinctions among the rest of the world do appear when the tape recorder is turned off and faculty explain the international division of labor in the production of scientific work worldwide. Bill, a full professor of chemical sciences who grew up and was trained in Europe, pointed out that among his U.S. colleagues the saying is that Asians are good at technical tasks but have less leadership potential and cannot write due to their limited language skills;

Europeans have superior theoretical reasoning; and Americans are needed to write up research results and are good at management. This division of labor on the basis of ethnic or racialized stereotypes entitles U.S. and European faculty to leadership on U.S. campuses and in international collaborations.[30] These offensive interpretations and stereotyping are about skills, not about the unequal distribution of resources in science, yet these stereotypes both reflect and reproduce global inequalities in the academic status, as we will see in Chapter 3.

The discourse of ethnic or racially based skills and the resulting "research quality" of "international" scholars implies that professors in the United States justifiably make decisions about international collaboration based on "merit" and scientific expertise while being silent about the ethnic and racial stereotypes underlying these judgments as well as the role of status markers in science. The variations of research infrastructures and capacities among countries is ignored, and the consequences of the economic power and political influence of the United States in the "rest of the world" become invisible. Furthermore, the notion of U.S. academics and academia as superior to the rest of the world does not recognize the range of training and skills among U.S. academics or the stratification of research capacities in U.S. institutions. This silence serves to reify the taken for granted elite status of universities as the centers of science worldwide.

Paris in June and Going Home

Although perceived scientific value is one major strategy for devaluing international collaboration, another is to attribute faculty motivation to personal rather than scholarly interests. Depicting international trips as a travel perk, an expensive hobby for elite faculty, or a way for faculty from other countries to visit home discounts the overall value of international collaboration, not to mention its scientific worth. International collaborations are sometimes represented as the guilty pleasure of scholars who like to go on exotic holidays, perceived by colleagues at home as a waste of time with no real scientific payoff. Paige, an associate professor of chemical sciences, described returning to her department after an exhausting airplane trip home from an intensive academic conference that she had paid for privately because her grant did not cover it, only to be met by colleagues who treated her as if she had returned from vacation, rather than acknowledging the academic value of her internationally recognized work:

If you have money to go someplace, to travel, that's not something they'd value; they'd think, "Oh, that's just the perk you get from your own grant," and "Good for you, you get to travel." That's the impression I get; it's not like, "Hooray, you get a gold star for collaborating through the international community." It's more like, "Oh, well, aren't you lucky." . . . Actually I heard that—I went to Vienna for a conference, which I didn't even have enough grant money to pay for, so I had to pay for out of my own pocket, most of it. And the comments I heard were, "Oh, so you're going to Vienna, hmmm." It was not like, "Oh, congratulations on presenting your work."

The discourses that serve to devalue the academic contributions of international collaboration as simply a travel perk contribute to the depiction of those collaborations as an elite activity. Outside academia, internationality carries high cultural status. Historically, as Anne-Catherine Wagner points out, bourgeois cultural exchange and travel have served as signs of cosmopolitanism in Europe, and the idea of the voyage has served an important function in the formation of elites.[31] Connections with the world and cosmopolitanism function as a shield against parochialism and provide individuals with cultural capital.[32] This cultural capital carries value for faculty, who benefit from an enhanced status when they return from their travels with tales of Europe, Asia, and the like. International collaboration thus bears some resemblance to the impetus for undergraduate students to study abroad in Rome, Florence, Paris, or London. However, although it is important to think critically about the meanings of international travel and reflect on how they serve to reproduce class privilege, reducing international collaborations to tourist jaunts belittles them and diminishes their academic worth.

The argument that international collaboration is an elite activity for scholars who can afford it, almost like an expensive hobby, is in fact contradicted by data about seniority. Research on academic collaboration suggests that social, academic, and human capital predict collaboration rates, but in complicated ways.[33] Generally speaking, elite academics with more status and resources are more involved in collaborations because they are seen as attractive partners to collaborate with. As institutional affiliations help shape networks among academics, faculty at resource-rich universities are more likely to be able to find resources and partners for research collaborations.[34] We might predict that those with the greatest academic capital in terms of seniority, who are also generally the wealthiest, both personally and in terms of research budgets, would be most likely to collaborate internationally. However, a review of the literature found that in the United States tenure status is not associated with likelihood to be involved in international research collaborations.[35] This perhaps counterintuitive finding invites us to question the claim that international collaborations are based principally on seniority.

Faculty with international backgrounds, approximately one-third of the STEM faculty in the United States, face slightly different responses to their international collaborations, but the result is the same.[36] Rather than treating research collaborations abroad as a marker of distinguished, excellent scholarship requiring specific language and intercultural competencies, U.S. colleagues see them as what one would obviously expect a scholar from another country to do. This process of naturalization masks the effort these collaborations require, as well as the quality of the research itself, personalizing international relationships rather than considering their academic value. As Lindsey, a social science associate professor, put it, "I feel like they think that, 'Oh, she only cares because she's [from that country],' and it's not because it is an interesting problem." As in comments about vacations, colleagues of faculty members with roots in other countries remark on research projects that involve desirable locations and provide opportunities to reconnect with their cultures. Jeffrey, an associate professor of engineering felt compelled to minimize the impression that he was just going home by insisting that his motivation was not the place but the research opportunities:

> But of course the fact that [my collaborator] is in [European city] and [that European country] is in fact my country it was always a plus for me, so sometimes if you like a place—and say it's a nice place that I would like to go to and also this guy who's a good guy in my field that does things that I am interested in is also there—that's fun. And so when I say to everybody, for instance, that I was going to spend six months on sabbatical in [European country], everybody told me, "poor guy." Who knows why? Well it's my country, it's a beautiful place, but at the same time, you know, I have a proven and strong record of research with this person.

Of course, some faculty members do perceive international travel to interesting places as a perquisite of academic life. All-expenses-paid conferences and workshops with added days of sightseeing have a definite appeal, and exchanges with colleagues and friendships across national and cultural borders are rich sources of enjoyment as well as intellectual stimulation. Returning home to work with colleagues in one's own language and culture is undoubtedly a boon for U.S. faculty from other countries. But to mistake these pleasures as the sole value of international collaboration is to powerfully underestimate their scholarly benefits.

Contestations of Superiority:
The Changing Story of Global Science

The broader discourse of U.S. scientific superiority is under challenge, and the theme of change appeared in many interviews and focus group discussions across disciplines, reflecting current challenges to the status of U.S. scientific scholarship in the global landscape. One counterdiscourse to the view that excellent scholarship can be contained within the United States compares the U.S.-centric past of costly travel, cumbersome knowledge exchange, and lack of suitable collaboration partners to today's modern world of technology-enhanced (global) science with its communication and research capacities. Faster and cheaper data transmission, collaborative online workspaces, inexpensive phone communication, and video conferencing make science a borderless space where information and knowledge are accessible across the world. Improvements in travel allow scholars to move more easily and cheaply when they do need to meet in person or do research in remote sites, creating an academic world without borders. Larry, a full professor of life sciences, described the changes he has witnessed:

> I'm sure everybody can attest to this. In the last ten or fifteen years, we really thought at one time everything being done that was any good was being done in this country, and that has just changed. There is just wonderful science being done everywhere. In my field of magnetic resonance imaging, even emerging markets now are building scanning facilities and the rest. So there's just good science being done everywhere, and you don't want to act ignorant anymore. You want to embrace it. With international meetings now, there's more and more of this; it's just right there. What were journals you wouldn't read before, now you're looking for them. There is still some regionality to what's being published in certain kinds of journals, but there is just open access to other science. There is access to a lot of information. So the climate has changed. It's more global. And I think it's reaching out to everyone, if you care about your science.

As the research quality in other countries catches up, U.S. scholars are increasingly required to go outside the box for the state of the art in their fields. In some fields, laboratory and research institutions outside the United States now have stronger reputations and status than their U.S. counterparts and attract postdoctoral researchers from the United States. Shannon, an assistant professor of Earth and atmospheric sciences, explained that although doing a postdoc in Europe would have been the end of a career in the United States twenty years ago, today it is considered a positive career move. Looking abroad is productive for U.S. faculty, as Brooke, an assistant professor of chemistry, points out; her goal is "to collaborate with the best people . . . , the people who have the expertise who will help what I do. And if those people are overseas or in Canada or are international, then you know that is where I go." She finds that in her field attitudes around international boundaries are diminishing, and she wonders, "I honestly don't know if there is a distinction made in the United States or international."

These changes reflect the ever, if slowly, changing history of scientific prestige and scholarship: In the nineteenth and early twentieth centuries, U.S. scholars went to European countries, including Germany, for high-status academic training.[37] Although some faculty explained that current changes mean the United States is no longer the scientific leader, others acknowledged that in their fields it never was. Ultimately, however, the view that other countries have been catching up with the United States and the view that the United States was never ahead arrive at the same destination: the understanding that academic excellence can be found elsewhere.

The discourse of modernizing science implies an easy transition from U.S.-centric to international science, but in fact globalization of scientific and engineering knowledge is a challenging process for universities, funding agencies, professional associations, and individual faculty. Clearly, a change in faculty attitudes will be necessary for fruitful international collaboration in this new world. Crystal, an assistant professor of physical science, views the old U.S. attitudes toward international collaborators, held by some of her colleagues, as problematic. "You can't go there, wherever you're going, with this prejudice that, 'I'm better than you. We're Americans. We do things the best,'" she said, suggesting instead that they be "open minded." Calling for broader respect for and acceptance of diversity in cultures and approaches, Roy, an engineering associate professor with an international background, echoed Crystal's call for open-mindedness and flexibility in the advice he would offer colleagues: "Don't think of the United States as a gold standard; just accept the way the other countries are, operate." These comments point directly to continuing contradictions in U.S. attitudes toward and status attributions to colleagues and institutions outside the United States.

Institutionalized Discourses of International Collaborations

Although international collaboration provides faculty with career highlights, meaningful intellectual and personal relationships, and scholarly rewards, faculty do not trust that their institutions will reward their efforts. Indeed, the highly ambivalent and ambiguous discourses around these collaborations create obstacles for U.S. faculty who seek to collaborate internationally, not just at the level of discourse but also in concrete rules and practices. U.S. funding agencies and universities are one locus for these obstacles. Their resource distribution practices, administrative procedures, and evaluation processes can privilege U.S. research. These practices and regulations are fueled by but also reproduce the ambivalent discourses discussed earlier.

Funding agencies and universities may explicitly limit some funding mechanisms to national research and collaboration. More circuitously, rules for international travel reflect ambivalence about its necessity. Proposals to funding agencies have separate budget lines for domestic and international travel and require justification for each. University rules often treat international travel differently from domestic travel (in part due to government regulations),[38] requiring faculty members to ask for permission to travel abroad, among other hoops they must jump through. And as we saw in Chapter 1, the Fly America Act even adds material obstacles in the form of high travel costs.

Viewing international collaboration as a nonessential perk means that when institutions need to cut expenses, these extra costs are first in line, even when cutting them makes no financial difference. Brian, a full professor of engineering, was astonished that his dean prohibited all international travel, even though he had outside funding for his trip. By creating obstacles that faculty must overcome, these kinds of institutional regulations further the sense that international travel is superfluous and needs to be contained.

Nationally oriented evaluation rules and practices can also create hindrances for faculty who seek to engage in international collaboration. Given the discursive strategies that diminish the academic value of such collaboration for individual faculty members and institutions overall, it is not surprising that many faculty believe their institutions do not care about their international collaborations and do not support their efforts.[39] Arthur, an associate professor of natural sciences, summed up his advice to colleagues:

> If they have their interests in international sphere, they should pursue it. They shouldn't expect a lot of support, probably no rewards and institutional support. You have to essentially decide that that's what you want and you're going to pursue it. It's going to cost you. You're probably not going to get acknowledged in promotion, tenure, salary—but it's not all about money. If you want to enjoy the world, there are lots of people out there, lots of things to do.

In some circumstances, international collaboration can be perceived as a way for faculty to stand out. Amy, an associate professor of engineering, explained:

> Yeah, I don't think it's necessarily gotten to the point where it's some little check box you have to check off. But I think it's made me more visible at my university. So if you get a main thing like a Fulbright, then they brag about it for a little while. And if you do something for your sabbatical that's a little bit out of the box, then people sort of remember that. And I think that was a good thing.

However, institutions frequently use narrowly defined standards and criteria of "merit" and scholarly excellence for their reward and support structures. These standards are oriented toward U.S.-centric measurements of excellence in scholarship, including publications in recognized, peer-reviewed journals, grant dollars, and grant-funded graduate students. Only 8 percent of doctoral institutions had guidelines how international efforts should be considered in faculty promotion and tenure decisions.[40]

Not surprisingly, faculty do not trust these reward structures to recognize the value of often resource-intensive international collaborations. When internationalization efforts are deemed unimportant, faculty fear that their efforts will not be recognized as valuable scholarly contributions unless they can garner U.S. funding or publication in high-impact English-language journals.[41] The growth of so-called predatory journals that offer open-access publication for hefty publication fees without a robust peer-review process has also fueled distrust in evaluations of international publications and collaborations because assessing the quality of journals and distinguishing legitimate from predatory journals can be cumbersome.[42] Rules and practices for hiring, evaluation, pay increases, tenure, and promotion thus reinforce the idea of the United States as the gold standard in science.[43]

Because international collaborations stand apart from career expectations in U.S. departments, universities, and funding agencies, a different kind of selection process leads faculty to become involved in international collaborations. Professors who have such international standing that they get invited to international collaborations without having to pay their own expenses, faculty members who can afford to take risks because of their positions in university hierarchies—as determined by tenure, access to resources, overhead slush funds, and so on—and faculty with personal resources that enable them to afford these collaborations are the ones who engage in them. As in Fox and Xiao's discussion of faculty decisions about collaborating with industry, untenured faculty, minorities, and white women, who feel less assured of their positions and status, are less likely to take these risks.[44] Those who are less able to take risks, then, are also less able to benefit from international collaborations when they pay off in research and career advantages.

Negative depictions of the value of international collaboration can deter junior faculty from embarking on such endeavors. Untenured faculty are generally advised, with all good intentions, to stay away from high-risk activities, and international collaboration is perceived as one such activity. If colleagues and administration suggest that international collaboration is less valuable than other scholarly work, we should not be surprised that, once tenured, these same faculty will still not want to engage in international collaboration. Under these circumstances, some faculty will continue to participate in internationalization efforts because of the demands of their discipline or field, or because they consider it sufficiently important. However, expanding international collaboration to involve more faculty will require the adjustment of academic reward structures and cultural understandings in the United States.

When faculty members perceive international research collaboration as risky because of high start-up costs, funding, and administrative time, these risks may have gendered outcomes. As we will see in Chapter 4, women tend to be in less privileged positions in scientific organizations including universities. They are more likely than men to be in resource-poor, teaching-oriented institutions, untenured, or in positions without tenure. And even in research-intensive universities, if women academics have smaller grants than their colleagues, they will also have less "overhead money" for "risky" start-up costs or costs not covered by grants. Studies show that women do have less access to resources, for example, lab space and administrative staff, making it harder to house visitors and deal with complicated paper work for their visas.[45] So women might not get the same institutional resources to start larger international collaborative projects; gendered inequalities in domestic scientific organizations then reproduce inequalities of access to the international world of science.

Although notions of U.S. scientific leadership linger on, the claims of U.S. scientific superiority are under challenge, and discourses around international collaboration seem to be changing. Although some of these discourses continue to create obstacles for faculty seeking to engage in science internationally, competing alternative discourses frame international collaboration as in the U.S. national interest, position international scientific engagement as modern, and align with business mantras about the value of diversity for the innovation prized by academics. These forward-looking discourses call for the United States to maintain its position on the cutting edge by engaging in collaborations across the globe. They also point to a new frontier for women's integration into STEM fields, as some of their scientific worlds shift increasingly to the global realm. As we will see in the following chapter, the globally stratified world of science also carries privileges for U.S.-based women academics.

3 The .edu Bonus

Gender, Academic Nationality, and Status

WHEN MARIA, A LATINA ASSOCIATE PROFESSOR OF SOCIAL
science at a public university in the Midwest, went abroad, she
believed that her ethnicity and gender were less salient than in the United
States. Early in her career, Maria sought out collaboration partners in Europe
and Latin America, where she felt she was treated with great professional respect, something that did not always happen in the United States: "I feel way
more dismissed at home—I have never felt dismissed internationally." Un-
ambiguous acceptance as an American scholar came as a novelty and a relief,
bringing her authority, respect, and a sense of collegiality based on the work
at hand, in place of a focus on ethnicity and gender, markers of difference at
home. Not only did Maria return home more confident about her research,
but her international collaborations turned out to be crucial for her career; a
book she coedited with a European colleague was published by a leading U.S.
university press, an accomplishment that helped her achieve tenure.

Many academics find international research experiences personally and
professionally rewarding, offering stimulation, motivation, and encouragement for their work (see Chapter 2). For some, like Maria, these collaborations turn out to be crucial for advancing their research and careers in the
United States. But women of all racial and ethnic groups and men from underrepresented minority groups noted that they felt more validated in their
research abroad than at home. I argue that these positive experiences are in
large part based on the .edu bonus, a term I have coined to describe the ways

U.S. academics benefit from their status as scholars affiliated with the United States, generally considered the leading nation in academia. This chapter explores how the .edu bonus works to render academic nationality more salient than gender in particular but also than race and ethnicity.[1]

I argue that in international academic work settings, the .edu bonus can trump gender for U.S.-based women academics. In this case, being a woman and a foreigner is a positive combination, not an accumulation of disadvantages.[2] Cultural schemas persist about women's competence in academia and leadership in general, and the effectiveness of U.S.-based women in environments where few native women hold positions of power.[3] But when U.S.-based women enter academic settings abroad, they perceive themselves to be treated foremost as foreigners and U.S. academics, rather than as women. In other words, the .edu bonus reflects how cultural schemas of the competence of U.S. academics overshadow schemas that consider women less competent in such settings.

The .edu bonus works for U.S. scholars in general, but the globalization of academic work brings unique opportunities for academics who are marginalized in the United States because of gender, race, ethnicity, or even the kind of work they do. By expanding their networks internationally, the .edu bonus helps faculty circumvent potentially closed academic communities at home. Creating and conducting successful research collaborations abroad not only facilitates intellectual and social inclusion and recognition for these academics but can also translate into research and publications that enhance their careers in the United States. Thus the .edu bonus provides powerful incentives for women to overcome barriers and glass fences.

The case of U.S.-based women academics reflects how privilege works in intersectional ways: Although they may have elite status with regard to education and access to resources (such as money to travel), they remain marginalized as women, particularly in many science, technology, engineering, and mathematics (STEM) fields. Studies show that U.S. women faculty are less satisfied with the department climate and more likely to feel isolated:[4] They are often excluded from important informal networks,[5] talk less frequently to colleagues about their work,[6] have their work questioned by other academics and students, feel their abilities and competencies as academics challenged, and consequently tend to question their own abilities.[7] Their positive experiences abroad can provide them with welcomed relief while providing us with important insights into how the status of women in academia is deeply contextual. Thus, the mobility of elite academics can produce and reproduce privilege because of the global stratification of academia and the resulting inequalities of academic nationality.

Status in Academia

Status matters greatly in academia because of its highly stratified structure with regard to access to resources and its attachment to beliefs about competence.[8] Several markers register high status; some, such as degrees and academic rank, are formally used in evaluation processes, and others, such as country of origin, race, ethnicity, and gender, are more at play in informal interactions.[9] These informally used characteristics are, of course, controversial because they undermine the ideal of scientific universalism postulated by Robert K. Merton, that scholarship should be valued only for its academic merit, not the personal characteristics of the researchers.

Across countries, academia is stratified by different access to education, training, and resources, as well as institutional prestige and reputation. The United States generally occupies high if not the highest prestige in science and academia in general and is considered the overall world leader, as I discuss in Chapters 1 and 2, creating the .edu bonus. Transnationally, academia is characterized by a status system constituted by "shared, culturally recognized standards of difference."[10] These standards include rank, university reputation, number and quality of publications, citations, grants, awards, academic offices, mentor visibility and reputation, and so on. Although these standards are closely developed vis-à-vis a country's performance in STEM fields, the resulting status extends to the reputation of U.S. universities in general. They are diffusing around the world, but their universality as to how they are implemented and applied still varies across countries.[11]

Not only does the social status of professors vary across countries, but in Asian and some European countries, for instance, age and rank intersect to produce stronger status hierarchies than in the United States, and the rank of endowed full professor generates more deference.[12] In the United States, knowledge production is also stratified, with women more likely to be found in resource-poor institutions than in wealthy research universities.[13]

The transnational context modifies the perception of these categories and highlights the ways the status of foreigners is also relative. People frequently assume that foreign academics belong to their country's academic elite. The thinking goes that only the best are selected to go abroad, so visitors must have undergone a rigid selection process and are thus more competent.[14] The rarity of women academics in particular settings may also enhance their status. Cultural beliefs and stereotypes linger that women managers in business are less effective in different cultural environments, especially those with few women in leadership positions.[15] However, U.S. women managers in Asia have been assumed to be top of the line because women managers have been so unusual and because of the belief that U.S. companies would choose their best employees to represent them abroad.[16] Social psychologists point out that negative gender status beliefs become less salient when people evaluate women who are considered stars because they are seen as exceptions.[17] These status beliefs add to the .edu bonus.

Status in academia is supposedly based on competence, and merit alone supposedly explains success.[18] Sociologists of science and academia have highlighted this foundational myth as a social construction, arguing that status is an important predictor of success because colleagues, other peers, and students attribute competence to those with more status.[19] In other words, rather than competence generating status, status itself generates further status. Status is also linked to assumptions about access to funding and other resources, such as the rank, reputation, and prestige of the institution academics work for; technical, administrative, and teaching support; and power based on the social capital attributed to individual academics. Status becomes a self-reinforcing dynamic, as in the Matthew effect of accumulated advantage.[20] Academics with higher status have more time for research, academia's most valued activity, and those considered more competent have more opportunities to participate in workshops, conferences, and collaborative activities, which in turn bring them more status and social capital. Ultimately, the respect afforded high-status individuals makes a difference, whether objectively bestowed or not. Perceptions play a crucial role in determining experiences for academics at home and abroad. When people feel more respected, they also feel more competent, do better work, get better feedback, and enjoy the experience more.

Gender scholars such as Cecilia Ridgeway identify gender as a "primary category" for perception of status in the United States, along with other "shared category systems based on race, gender, age, occupation, and education."[21] In academia as well, gendered cultural beliefs shape status, produce gender hierarchies, and influence academic confidence. Historically, gendered

cultures associate femininity with emotions, the heart and soul, and culture—
all considered "soft"—whereas masculinity stands for hard work, the intellect,
and abstract thinking. These gendered associations continue to create stereotypes about women and their academic capacities, legitimacy, and leadership
competences.[22] Science in particular has strong connotations of masculinity.[23]
Women traditionally have been seen as less competent in mathematical and
logical thought, both the basis of science.[24]

Academia's high sex segregation, both hierarchical and across fields, may
in part reflect the persistent belief that women are not as suited as men for
academia and science in particular.[25] These beliefs and structures vary, however, among STEM fields and across countries.[26] Perhaps not surprisingly,
countries with higher enrollments of women in science education have lower
national gender-science stereotypes.[27] In the United States, biological and
health sciences have been more open to women faculty than physics and engineering and have lower explicit gender-science stereotypes.[28] These variations provide evidence that stereotypes about women's competence in math
and logical reasoning are socially constructed. Such gendered cultural beliefs
work independently of whether individuals themselves endorse them, and
assumptions about other people's beliefs influence how individuals perceive
their own competence and capacity, for example, for mathematical thinking.
In these ways, gendered cultural beliefs about science and academia create
challenges and threats to women's legitimacy as academics.

In the following, I show what happens when gender becomes less salient
than academic nationality. When women travel abroad we see the ways gender and academic nationality interact and produce advantages in status and
access. I use Ridgeway's and Correll's notion of salience here: that when gender is salient, "Cultural beliefs about gender function as part of the rules of
the game, biasing the behaviors, performances, and evaluations of otherwise
similar men and women in systematic ways."[29] When academic nationality is
more salient than gender, U.S.-based women experience the .edu bonus: Cultural beliefs about U.S. academics outweigh gendered cultural beliefs about
science and academia. This idea of how gender works also supports the idea
that gender is not something women academics carry around as a fixed char-
acteristic. Rather, specific context matters in how intersectionality works to
produce status differences.[30] Depending on context, the status beliefs and
other gendered expectations women experience can vary greatly. Gender
never disappears entirely. But the fact that it can recede at times helps explain

why women enjoy international research experiences and why the experiences make them feel successful and empowered.

The .edu Bonus

As Maria found, the .edu bonus bestows high status on U.S. academics who travel abroad. It rests specifically on academic nationality, which I define as belonging to a specific academic national community, regardless of country of origin: Professors at a California university, whether born in New York or Mumbai, are both American academics, while professors born in New York or Rio de Janeiro who work at a university in Brazil are both Brazilian academics, though this also depends on where they were educated. The international academic community attaches status to academic nationality, and the academic status of individual scholars in part reflects the status of the countries in which they are educated and work. For countries with positive academic reputations or leadership in a specific field, academic nationality generates positive beliefs about academic skills and competence that influence status beliefs about individuals. Given that such estimations of competence are crucial in how academics are viewed as collaboration partners, academic nationality can have a profound effect on international collaborations and collaborators.

The .edu bonus for U.S. academics is based on a set of positive status beliefs that frame U.S. academia—and U.S. science in particular—as the gold standard. As we saw in Chapter 2, U.S. scholars observe that the international reputation of U.S. academia is highly positive, and Chapter 1 showed statistics that help explain this reputation. Clarissa, an associate professor of natural science, explained, "In Europe, people tend to think that academia is more prestigious in the United States." The United States also has a strong reputation in certain fields, for example biotech and computer science and experimental sciences in general. It also houses many Nobel Prize winners, particularly in physics, chemistry, medicine, and economics.[31]

The shine of U.S. academia reflects onto individual U.S. scholars, creating the positive reception that characterizes the .edu bonus. Briana, a life scientist, felt that she was a desirable visitor because she represented U.S. scientific standards:

> Everyone [in my field thought that] the United States was the best, both in the United States and abroad. They would bring you there . . . to see how they relate

to the practice in the United States. That was a method that I guess confirmed [for them] that they were doing things correctly. . . . And often times they were doing things correctly and sometimes with novel, different things.

Being perceived as the standard by which others measure themselves can be a positive experience, demonstrating that colleagues have confidence in one's competences. This baseline acceptance of the value of one's capabilities creates a welcome break from academic cultures at home, imbued with persistent gender-science stereotypes that question women's competences in math and logic.[32]

Another form of value was attached to Julia, a social science professor who visited a European university and found that having specific expertise on the United States gave her significant visibility, as an expert *from* the United States *on* the United States:

The other thing I've had an awful lot of, here, is invitations by all of the think tanks in [Europe], and I think [being] American, this is a big component. I have given so many talks lately about [American politics and transnational cooperation]. So there is clearly an interest here in having that American presence. There's interest on the part of the foundations who are supporting work that is tied to the United States. . . . And it seems a plus, really, that you're international. For me, that's made it fun, too, 'cause when you're one of the few big fish in a small pond, you get to take advantage of that!

Julia benefited from both the perception that she had authentic knowledge about the United States and the interest that comes with being a token. Martha, a full professor of geology, experienced the desirability of U.S. scholars abroad to the point that her collaborators did not want to share her with others. Martha believed they purposely kept her from getting to know other local academics because they wanted to work with her exclusively:

In fact it's one of the negative aspects of my collaborations in [African country] that my collaborators have always tried to prevent me getting to know other professors. There's a protectiveness of the goose that lays the golden egg, and they don't want to lose it by developing intellectual relationships with anyone else.

According to U.S. scholars, the .edu bonus also makes them highly attractive collaboration partners. Jack, a full professor of physical science, described this dynamic: "It's really a benefit to [international colleagues] to be able to claim international collaborations with U.S. researchers. So everybody around the world, it seems—or a lot of people around the world—are looking for these kinds of collaborations and opportunities for exchange." Like Jack, other U.S. academics find that the .edu bonus creates academic settings in which they feel treated very well as guests and academics and are sought after as potential collaborators and contributors to academic debates. Of course, being at times treated like a movie star by hosts and colleagues, which they may perceive as unwarranted, leads to discomfort for some academics about the potential inequalities in relationships with their collaborators, when they cannot return the same hospitality.[33] However, being wanted, highly desirable collaboration partners could be likened to being at a ball where everyone wants to be on the dance card. This experience of courtesy and high respect for their expertise and assumed competence is especially positive for faculty and scholars who at home do not feel valued or experience such ease in setting up collaborations.

U.S. academics are seen as attractive cooperation partners abroad for several reasons, including their academic expertise, resources, and access to U.S. journals, along with a generalized admiration of U.S. academic culture that rarely recognizes how stratified U.S. academia is. A variety of mechanisms reinforce these beliefs, including how the United States draws international talent and the visible role of U.S. academics in high-profile top-ranked international journals (see also Chapter 2).

Because of the U.S. reputation for first-class academic and scientific work, especially in experimental science and applied theory, academics in other countries assume U.S. faculty have access to well-equipped labs and talented, well-trained graduate students and postdocs. The influx of international graduate students and scholars over the past decades supports these expectations. Adam, a full professor of computer science, explained why colleagues from Asia sought out his department for collaborating on graduate student training:

> Institutions in China want to have collaboration with the United States. In the beginning of this year there was a program that wanted to have joint doctoral training in [behavioral science] with us. The United States has the reputation of having developed more applied theories. . . . We have some international students. If it is possible to have some joint training, people are interested.

Colleagues abroad also believe that collaborating with U.S. academics offers access to highly ranked, supposedly international publication outlets that are dominated by U.S. standards. Because publications in internationally peer-reviewed journals carry important weight in university rankings and faculty evaluations around the world, they have become increasingly important, and U.S. academics are participating in and leading multinational teams of coauthors, thus strengthening, reinscribing, and affirming the status of the United States as the core country for scientific productivity.[34] Jason, a full professor of natural science, explicitly articulated this dynamic: "So if you have an American coauthor, or the paper comes from a U.S. address, then it may be more likely to be accepted. These are motivators for why international folks collaborate with Americans."

Given that articles in prestigious journals usually undergo peer review, the perception of bias against non-U.S. authors and institutions might be surprising. Editors select the reviewers, and double-blind peer-review processes, although prevalent in the social sciences and humanities, are less common in science and engineering.[35] Reviewers can often figure out the identities of authors due to high degrees of specialization in fields, when scientists and engineers work with shared equipment, or when they are familiar with their work because they have evaluated grant proposals that include names. U.S.-trained academics are generally more familiar with style and format conventions in U.S. journals, as well as with how they set up problems and explain results. They know better which journal to send articles to. And many U.S.-trained academics have the advantage of being English native speakers or have sufficient practice in writing up research in English. This also makes them attractive partners for collaboration.

Another reason international scholars lean toward U.S. collaborators is their general enthusiasm for their own experiences in the United States, which, in turn, rubs off on U.S. academics. Alicia, a full professor of engineering, explained how a German colleague responded to U.S. academia: "He was so enthusiastic. And this was not the first time he had been at this center. And the atmosphere that you find in the American universities was really something that he told us about. And the freedom for scholars there and this and that." One particular element they admire, as mentioned in the following pages, is that U.S. researchers work in more collaborative, less hierarchical academic cultures, interacting in more collegial ways, such as the first-name basis among scholars.

The positive connotations of the .edu bonus also transcend status differentials among U.S. institutions of higher education. Given the general allure of the United States in the academic world, affiliation with *any* U.S. academic institution is perceived as valuable, not just affiliation with the few Ivy League schools (such as Harvard, Yale, Columbia, Princeton) or even fewer public schools (such as U.C. Berkeley) that are well known abroad. Because the ranking systems in U.S. academia are less well known than the international ranking systems, in which U.S. universities generally rank highly, the domestic status gaps that characterize U.S. institutions matter much less overseas.[36] Sophia, an associate professor of social science originally from Europe, who teaches in a third-tier department at a U.S. research university, explained how the .edu bonus applied in her home country, even though people did not know her university: "It does bring a little bit of a status when you are as an American in Europe, although [my university] does not have the kind of reputation that Harvard has, and people don't know what it is. It's been positive overall when you tell them that the institution is in [the United States]."

The data of this study do not show how U.S. academics are actually treated abroad, or whether foreign colleagues really believe the United States is the best place for academic work. Rather, they reveal what our interviewees perceived. But these perceptions matter because they play a profound role in shaping the experiences of U.S. academics abroad. Status expectancy theory explains that "macrocultural" beliefs based on national academic reputation shape how colleagues expect others and themselves to perform.[37] Ridgeway and Smith-Lovin explain that status beliefs can trigger self-fulfilling processes: Positive evaluation of U.S. academics can lead to increased participation, performance, and influence.[38] The .edu bonus thus creates a context for U.S. scholars to have highly positive and beneficial experiences abroad, even when they themselves are critical of stereotypes. Given that such self-fulfilling processes usually work against women in academia and in science in particular, the .edu bonus is especially important for women, providing a valuable counterbalance to the ways their gender too often works as a negative status marker.

Gender and the .edu Bonus

Although doing research abroad can be a very positive experience, it also involves the challenges of navigating language barriers and cultural expectations. As Tara, a social scientist, who at times felt homesick, put it, "If you can get over the loneliness and confusion, it's a good thing!" I argue, however, that these very cultural differences can work in women's favor. When academic nationality becomes more salient than gender, women academics abroad find themselves excused by their hosts and colleagues from many gendered cultural expectations. The .edu bonus works as a cloak that renders gender unimportant and invisible, allowing U.S.-based women academics to perceive themselves foremost as foreigners, as U.S. academics, not as women academics.

U.S. women academics abroad find that, for them at least, gender beliefs seem less salient, especially in countries with language barriers and stark cultural differences. For many, navigating languages and cultural rules is so overwhelming that gender issues tend to fall away. Jamie, a natural scientist, described her research visit to Japan: "I didn't perceive sexism to be a challenge that was greater than basically cross-culture experiences. I'm not saying that sexism doesn't exist, but, by comparison, it's relatively small compared to the communication challenges." This notion that culture is more overwhelming than gender is based on the shared assumption that cultural differences are not gendered. Kyle, an engineering professor, explained that "the language and culture are the national roadblocks or shocks, and I think you need to spend more time to appreciate some of these other aspects [of gender inequalities]. That would be my guess."

Language differences, however, can become a positive when local academics seek to be fluent in English. Destiny, a full professor of engineering, experienced speaking English as a way to connect with men in Europe:

> I was also the only American, so that was also a sort of oddity . . . I had a good time when I was in [small European country]. People would use me to practice their English, and I was very willing to do that . . . I didn't really have any trouble, I felt as though I fit in. And I worked with the men, and we discussed research and things like that. No gender issue that I saw.

Destiny experienced her status as a foreigner, English speaker, and U.S. academic as more salient than her status as a woman, a classic example of the .edu bonus and its particular benefits for women.

As cultural difference creates a kind of screen for gender, and being a foreigner makes gender matter less, working in a different cultural environment can be advantageous to women. If they experience colleagues in a new environment treating them differently, a default explanation is that the treatment is based on status beliefs about foreigners, not women. Although several women reported that in less familiar cultural settings they had difficulty teasing out what people thought about them and expected from them as foreigners, women, or foreign women, they nevertheless had a respite from the persistent gender pressures they often faced at home.

Ultimately, then, the .edu bonus benefits U.S.-based women abroad in two ways. First, as Destiny experienced, it lets them be seen as U.S. scientists rather than as women. Second, cultural and language differences make it harder to detect subtle sexist practices because gender and power work differently in different cultural and organizational settings. This can create a kind of blissful ignorance, where even if men (U.S. and local) are being treated with more respect and appreciation, the women are not aware of it, another self-fulfilling prophecy that enables them to move forward and flourish. Altogether, the .edu bonus means that U.S. woman academics abroad are freer to operate with status beliefs and behavior expectations based on universal professional academic norms, rather than having to negotiate the gender expectations they face at home or being trapped by the expectations local women face.

The Freedom of Not Having to Fit In

For U.S. women abroad, the lack of shared cultural understandings about gender can be liberating. As foreigners, they have less urgency to fit in in general, so while gender does not disappear, gender status beliefs become less applicable. Both women and men academics experienced different sets of expectations for behavior in social interactions from those locals did. Matthew, an associate professor of mathematics, observed that, in Japan, the status of *gaijin* (foreigner) excused him when he broke rules: "Well, simply whenever you go to Japan you are a *gaijin*. . . . And that's an advantage in a way because you can make all kinds of errors in your social life. You commit all sorts of faux pas, and they excuse it. They say, 'Oh, he's a foreigner, he doesn't know any better' [Laughs]."

For women academics, this aspect of the .edu bonus can create a crucial sense of freedom from the social and academic gender expectations they are used to at home. Matthew's perception that, as a *gaijin*, he was not expected to be familiar with societal norms or conform to normative behaviors in social interactions extends for women to gender expectations. The .edu bonus means they experience being taken seriously as academics, often when local women are not. When Giselle, a biologist, was asked whether she thought it was better, as a scientist, to be an American, an American woman abroad, or a Japanese woman, she vividly recalled her experience:

> I spent time in Japan. . . . The situation for Japanese women in science is miserable . . . I could do whatever I wanted because I was *gaijin*, I'm a foreigner. . . . *Gaijin* are weird, and we all understand that *gaijin* are weird and they're different, so that if a woman wants to be a scientist, we will sit and talk to her because she's a *gaijin*. But, if I had been speaking fluent Japanese, and had been Japanese, it would have been a real issue, a real problem.

Although Giselle felt empowered and at liberty to do her academic work in a context where she was seen as a foreigner rather than a woman, she understood from her female Japanese colleagues that she was treated exceptionally well by their Japanese male peers. Cultural differences allowed her to shed the negative implications of being a woman in academia. As foreigners, U.S. women academics can thus find new ways of being, in which they liberate themselves from gendered expectations, at least temporarily.

In encounters with local cultural expectations, women often experienced being seen as gender-neutral foreigners rather than either women or foreign women. Judy, an Earth scientist who spent her sabbatical with her husband in Japan, described how she and her husband were accepted as foreigners who were not expected to fit in:

> Well, in Japan the research climate is . . . I mean people work all the time. Like people work every night, and they're in the office on weekends and stuff, working in the labs. And I didn't do that. I mean, I was sometimes there in the evenings when I saw them, but since I was on sabbatical, I don't think they held me to the same standard as they would hold their own faculty or grad students. So I see that the culture is really different, and I see that they viewed us as like foreign visitors, and so therefore they didn't expect us on that same schedule of work. . . . They thought the same with my husband. He wasn't in the office every night either.

The Japanese cultural expectation of long working hours applied to neither Judy nor her husband, so she did not perceive gender difference in this reaction. Terry, a full professor of geology, also found that being a foreigner was more salient than gender, when local men perceived her and her team as a threat while conducting research in a rural area in an African country:

> Safety and things like that are never gendered for me in the field. . . . In some of these rural areas . . . I used to just wander into and get into trouble; sometimes you find yourself surrounded by a group of guys with spears, and you're going, "Ooops." And the [men] will say, "Well, they saw you wandering on their land, and they thought you were from the government, and they didn't understand and thought you were trying to do something secret, because if you had not been trying to do something secret, you would have come to the village and announced yourself to the village president." . . . I'd be just as threatening as a foreign female as I would if I were a foreign male. They don't distinguish at all.

The .edu bonus can also shield women from the inequities of gendered division of labor. Gwendolyn, an associate professor of natural sciences, noticed that, when working with her international collaborators, she was not trapped into gendered tasks, such as taking notes or making coffee, as the local women were. Her collaborators listened to her attentively and took her contributions seriously. Ironically, she was used to being expected to take notes in meetings at home. The .edu bonus thus became a privilege that allowed her to escape normative gendered expectations operative both at home and abroad.

The .edu bonus for U.S.-based women academics can also be seen in their access to networks and resources local women lack. Early in her career, Ethel, a social scientist and full professor, received invitations to workshops and conferences abroad, where she gained access to networks of European academics with high status in her field. Although she knew European women professors, she noticed their absence at these high-powered meetings. It seemed easier for the men to open the door to a U.S. woman than to women from their own countries. Similarly, Carolyn, a professor of engineering working in French research labs, felt she had an advantage over local women because she came from the United States. She pointed out, "There are issues with being a woman in the French society and being successful and having to fight for getting the resources that you need. But I was nowhere near that kind of fight." Being a foreign woman with an .edu bonus provided both Ethel and Carolyn with an edge up in comparison to local women.

The .edu bonus thus lets U.S.-based women abroad sidestep the gender disadvantages local women confront. Where U.S.-based women benefit from the .edu bonus and its associations with competence, legitimacy, and academic leadership, domestic women are perceived as less competent. U.S.-based women academics have more status and are seen as expert foreigners and thus become more attractive collaboration partners than local women and perhaps even local men.[39] The .edu bonus may also trump gender because, if women are perceived as foreigners, they do not challenge the local hierarchical gendered order and thus do not threaten it. They are seen more as passersby who will not compete with men for local resources, funding, or positions.[40] This allows them to be treated as exceptions, free from the (at times exclusionary) norms applied to local women and to perceive themselves as academics rather than as women.

Who Are You? The Salience of Race, Ethnicity, Rank, Age, and Gender

Like gender, race and ethnicity become less salient in academic work settings abroad, where the .edu bonus trumps being Asian, black, or Latino/Latina. Several academics from minority groups explained that they felt able, essentially, to pass as American when abroad, where their minority status was less salient than their status as a U.S. academic. Rodrigo, a Latino scholar, observed, "I think the places I went, the emphasis was more that I was coming from the States rather than being an underrepresented minority." At home, an African American or Latina woman academic might experience less status than men of her racial and ethnic background or women from other backgrounds because she is seen as less academically competent and not a legitimate leader on account both of gender and of race and ethnicity.[41] The .edu bonus becomes especially powerful for such women, as it counterbalances both negative status beliefs with the powerful positive status markers of U.S. education and institutional affiliation. Hence, for academics from underrepresented minority groups, but especially women, travel outside the United States for international research can lead to more open doors and higher appreciation than at home.

Faculty from international backgrounds who are based in the United States also experience the .edu bonus as a privilege. Approximately one-third of U.S. faculty members in the STEM disciplines have international backgrounds.[42] Like Latino and black U.S. academics, international academics based in the United States who travel abroad notice the effect of the .edu bonus, which makes their institutional association with perceived U.S. academic power and reputation more salient than their citizenship or country of origin. For example, as Sophia remarked, she gained status back home in a European country because she had a faculty position at a U.S. institution.

For U.S.-based women professors, going abroad means reaping the benefits of both the .edu bonus and the status that comes with rank and age, which can additionally be more salient than gender abroad and garner U.S.-based women further respect. The status of professors varies across countries, as does the highly contextual association of that status with age, rank, and gender, which depends on the hierarchal structures of national academic communities. In general, U.S. academic culture is more casual and less hierarchical than others, particularly in European and Asian countries. U.S. academics are less accustomed to being treated with deference at home, where students might casually greet them with "Hi, Prof," and research teams, including graduate students and technicians, function on a first-name basis. The more formal hierarchical structure of transnational contexts, where academia carries higher status and academics are addressed habitually as "Doctor" or "Professor," is highly visible to U.S. faculty members, who may feel more valued and treated with higher respect than in U.S. settings.

These hierarchies become especially visible when cultural expectations attached to age, gender, and rank intersect, and it becomes impossible to tease out whether women are treated as lower status because of their gender, their rank, or both. This intersection is particularly acute for graduate students, who hold higher status in the United States than in many other countries. At a conference in Japan, Jim, a natural scientist, noticed the gendered division of labor:

> You go to the registration desk, and the registration desk is staffed by attractive women in what I might call sort of disco-ish clothing. And they're serving you coffee and tea and cookies. And I come to discover they are female medical students. You go inside the lecture hall and the audiovisual and the computer equipment are run by handsome Japanese men in nice clothes. And they're the male medical students. If I asked my female graduate students to serve coffee at a conference, they would kill me!

In the United States, this gendered division of labor—enabling men to listen to the talks while assigning a subservient role for women graduate students outside the lecture halls—would be inappropriate.

Philip, a social scientist, described another incident that illustrates the intersection of age, gender, and rank hierarchies. At a conference in Switzerland he attended with a woman graduate student from the United States, a male European senior professor asked the graduate student to get him a coffee. When she asked Philip what she should do, he told her he would take care of it, and he decided to serve the coffee to his colleague himself. Gender becomes especially visible when women are asked to do gender-stereotyped tasks, such as serving coffee to men. Philip resolved the situation by performing the subservient task himself, which did not threaten his own status, as it could be interpreted as a favor between colleagues.

If rank and gender work together to support Philip's status, the salience of rank becomes particularly noticeable for U.S.-based women professors abroad who found that rank and age were more salient than gender. When Molly, a U.S. social scientist, was a visiting professor in Germany, she was about to pump up a large exercise ball to use as her office chair when a secretary told her she could not do this task, insisting it was her job as secretary. Molly was amazed, as she has no support for any such tasks at her home institution. Gender was not explicitly at stake in this interaction between two women, but the professions secretary and professor are clearly gendered. The German secretary had a clear understanding of the division of labor between herself and the visiting professor, as inflected by her gender and both women's ranks. The U.S. professor experienced the intersectional nature of her status, as rank trumped gender.

Academics who visited Asian countries described numerous instances in which rank and age figured more prominently than gender, creating situations that were not always comfortable. Both men and women explained that titles and age were important markers for treatment with respect and deference. Brian, a middle-aged full professor of chemical sciences from a top U.S. research university, noted, "When you go to Korea and you have titles like mine on that business card, everything is done for you. You are taken to the finest restaurants, and you are entertained. They treat you like a king when you have gray hair and a title." Generalizing from his own experience, Brian pointed out how the intersection of age, formal position, and foreignness generates high status and corresponding treatment. However, like other U.S. scholars, Brian felt awkward about this treatment: "It's a role I'm not particularly comfortable with." For U.S. academics, this discomfort stemmed in part from the fact that they were not used to such treatment in the United States, as well as from their inability to reciprocate, given different academic and cultural expectations. In addition, although there are workarounds, federal grant regulations limit resources for hosting international colleagues at home.

Age tends to correlate with academic status, and several women attributed their positive experiences abroad to a combination of age, rank, and their own or their institutions' reputations. Sherry, a full professor of engineering, compared her international experiences in her highly masculine field today and as a graduate student: "If I were a grad student, I guess they wouldn't take me seriously. I think that I had that in the past." Today, when she feels valued by her Korean colleagues she believes it is because she is seen as "a faculty member and, especially coming from [Ivy League university], people don't usually distance me." Despite the respect she receives, Sherry recognized that women are undervalued in this particular cultural setting:

> Korea would be the worst case just because it's still [a] male-dominated society and especially in the area I'm talking about, but they were really nice. When I went there, they listened to me, and they really valued my input. But culturally, I think a lot of females just don't continue. I don't know. It's a societal thing.

Similarly, Cindy, a professor in the life sciences, felt that age was an important status marker. She had been treated differently when she was younger, although she saw gender and age as intertwined:

> [My experiences abroad] definitely had something to do with gender. But, at that time, I can't say that it wasn't a gender plus young age. The pharmaceutical companies are still very male dominated. . . . But also especially in [European country], at the time, I remember meeting with the Health ministers. And of course I didn't say anything. It was clear who got served dinner first. I felt I had to watch my p's and q's, you know, who's this little girl you are bringing along. . . . It was almost like, "I'll carry your suitcases, and you take me, and I get to hear these and attend very high-level meetings," so I just sort of said, "I'll do it."

Cindy's description of feeling she had to focus on her manners reflects her lack of confidence; she later contrasted her insecurities as a young woman with her sense of herself today as a recognized scholar. It is important to recall that status beliefs trigger self-fulfilling mechanisms, as it is easier for those who feel more competent to participate in such discussions.[43]

Although status differentials also exist in U.S. academia, U.S.-based women are less used to age, title, and rank serving as such obvious, important status markers—or to receiving respectful treatment because of them. However, they did believe these markers played a significant role in how well they were treated in international settings. Tatjana, a full professor of biological sciences, explained that when she worked in the laboratory of her collaborator in India, "It was very easy for me to be the senior guest, welcomed guest of this lab, so that was fine." She felt that being a high-ranking academic from the United States was more salient than being a woman academic. Madeleine, a full professor of geosciences, found that her academic reputation superseded gender as she built relationships with collaborators in China:

> I've always felt very respected by my Chinese colleagues. So I haven't felt there was any discrimination because I'm a female. . . . But I guess I was fairly prominent by the time I started working in China. And that may have had an influence. If I had been somebody who was just starting their career at the time, it may have been different. I am an editor of a journal where we get tons of submissions from China. So I'm well known just because of that, as well in China.

For women like Tatjana and Madeleine, the .edu bonus combined with rank and age and the status attributed to seniority were more visible abroad than in the United States. Not surprisingly, then, in a quantitative survey of 100 NSF Principal Investigators, seniority predicted level of comfort.[44] Senior women and men both felt more at ease in international collaborations than their younger colleagues; this is probably in part an outcome of experience, access to resources, and general professional comfort level, but it also reflects the status associated with seniority, which leads to being valued and treated with more respect, especially abroad.[45] The privilege produced by this combination of the .edu bonus, age, and rank is even more important for those who are not used to being treated with respect and taken as seriously as collaborators at home, especially women.

Expecting the Best

The benefits women derive from the .edu bonus have interesting historical precursors. U.S. women academics went to Europe for their advanced degrees in the nineteenth and early twentieth centuries when they did not have access to all-male U.S. universities, and some of them founded U.S. women's colleges.[46] Barbara Czarniawska and Guje Sevón argue that nineteenth- and early twentieth-century European women scientists were seen as "double strangers" and allowed to succeed as scientists and transgress narrowly defined gender roles. Women like Marie Curie who did not have access to academia in their home countries could pursue scientific work in a new host country, even though local women were not accepted as scientists. The statuses of "woman" and "foreigner" canceled each other, enhancing the success of women abroad.[47]

For U.S.-based women abroad today, the status of "foreigner" also has fewer negative connotations. Indeed, my findings suggest that the .edu bonus overpowers possible negative status beliefs that adhere to gender, race, ethnicity, or non-U.S. background. This might be the exception-making status for U.S.-based women academics, as it shows how important U.S. status is—to the point that it elides any other differences.

The myths of universalism and meritocracy in academia obscure important dynamics of inequality within and between countries (see Chapter 2). Although supposedly neither gender nor nation is salient in how competent academics are considered, my research shows that both remain crucial categories that produce and reproduce inequalities in status, power, and access to international research collaborations. Despite claims that academic communities are spaces in which only ideas and skills matter, the .edu bonus shows otherwise. In the creation of transnational scientific spaces nations still do matter. And the .edu bonus that benefits U.S. academics abroad demonstrates that academic nationality is an important status marker that emerges from and reproduces a hierarchical global system that creates inequalities. Ironically, although this bonus enables U.S. based women to find collaboration partners and succeed abroad and creates privileges for them, it can also reproduce inequalities among women of different academic nationalities.

These experiences of elite-U.S. based women who have access to resources and networks, as well as opportunities to overcome fences, demonstrate how academic privilege is produced. When these women leave their own (national) academic context and enter a transnational one, they experience a shift away from the most salient U.S. status markers of gender, race, ethnicity, class, and institution to the status markers that matter abroad: academic nationality, age, rank, and, to some extent, institutional reputation.

As academic work becomes more international, we need to explore the consequences for U.S.-based women and gender relations. Although much research shows how gender matters for women in academia at the national level, we see here how international—as well as national—processes shape career paths today, and gender is implicated in the ways these relationships emerge. Studying these dynamics from a gender perspective offers insights into how the internationalization of work can benefit women and others marginalized in the United States,[48] providing them important opportunities for career advancement.

The .edu bonus provides crucial access to global networks that can enable women to circumvent exclusionary networks at the national level. For example, Kelly, a professor of physical sciences, found colleagues abroad crucial for her research: "There are closed circles in this country," she said, and "It's easier to just expose your research or sell your research and market it in Europe than here." This exchange with international networks can have positive career aspects (see Chapter 2), including important exchanges with colleagues and increased citation counts (see Chapter 1). For Kelly, like other women, expanding networks from home to abroad can translate into valuable academic capital. By allowing women to tap into international networks and collaborative relationships, the .edu bonus can have concrete career advantages.

The .edu bonus works similarly for individuals from minority groups, who also can benefit from going abroad, where race and ethnicity, like gender, become less salient and the status of U.S. academic in a foreign setting more so, generating respect and prestige. It is important to note, however, that the analysis of this chapter has downplayed potential differences based on race and ethnicity, discipline, institution, and national origin in the experiences of U.S. academics. More refined measures for the salience of the .edu bonus in comparison to other status markers and in more specific contexts will require detailed comparable data, which future research could fruitfully produce.[49]

Although the .edu bonus has powerful positive effects for women academics abroad, they cannot escape gender entirely, and they do face fences. In particular, gender tends to trump the .edu bonus in social settings, where women experienced their status as woman overshadowing that of U.S. academic, for example, when hosts are overprotective with general safety concerns; that is, gender is indeed important in various settings *outside the university*. In these spaces, U.S.-based women academics have a different experience of the intersection between foreigner and woman, for when the .edu bonus does not work, fences appear. The .edu bonus therefore does not entirely shield U.S.-based women from gender-stereotypical expectations and gendered interactions, as we will see in the following chapter.

4 Glass Fences

Gendered Organization of Global Academia

PAMELA, A CHEMIST AT AN EAST COAST UNIVERSITY IN THE United States and a parent, was eager to collaborate with colleagues abroad. She felt comfortable bridging cultural differences, as she had studied Spanish in high school and done a study-abroad program in Spain. However, she found it difficult to apply for international fellowships that required her to leave the United States for a year at a time during graduate school and as a professor. She also had not met suitable collaborators because she was not invited to high-level small workshops. Her U.S. colleagues with international reputations were able to attract graduate students and postdoctoral fellows from abroad, but she felt she did not attract such students and scholars because they expected that, as a mother, she would not be as serious about her lab as her male colleagues were. Pamela ultimately found an international collaborator serendipitously, when he was visiting one of her colleagues as a postdoctoral fellow. When he returned to his country of origin, they became collaborators.

Pamela's experience with initiating international collaboration is typical of the experiences of the women interviewed in this study, who found themselves in less advantageous positions than men for participating in international collaboration. We saw in the previous chapter that the .edu bonus can trump gender, race, and ethnicity, but gender is nevertheless an organizing principle in academia. This chapter explores glass fences, obstacles that show contexts where gender remains salient because (global) academia is organized in gendered ways. I argue that fences are embedded in the international collaboration policies and practices of nation-states, funding agencies, universities, professional associations, and researchers themselves.

(Global) science and more broadly academia are gendered at their very access points and also in specific practices of international collaborations and conferences, including resources, opportunities, and the concept of safety abroad. International science is organized around a narrow image of the hegemonic male scientist who has resources, can take risks, and has the power and status in his university and among his peers to obtain institutional and grant support.[1] He has no trouble asking for that support, maintains academic and social networks that can introduce him to colleagues abroad, and can draw on former students and postdocs around the world. This stereotypical image is self-perpetuating: Because he looks like the ideal global scientist, he becomes even more so. But this image does not fit many women like Pamela; in fact, it does not fit all men. And although an individual encounter with a fence might seem a small setback, missed opportunities to collaborate internationally can multiply the disadvantages for women in particular to participate in the ongoing expansion of international collaborations (see Chapter 1).[2]

Fences are gendered challenges that particularly women face when engaging in international dimensions of science and academia, including international research collaborations and mobility. I developed this concept of glass fences to render visible the otherwise unobservable barriers that both reflect and create gender inequities in the globalization of scientific and engineering knowledge. Approaches to science and academia more generally as gendered organizations[3] provide a useful framework for studying how gender operates in them through formal and informal rules and in embedded practices such as the division of labor. Globalization processes can reproduce and intensify gendered inequalities by amplifying burdens already in play at the national level. In this chapter, I map the variations in international research and collaborations and explore specific work settings and research practices that create fences that impede women's inclusion.[4]

Paradoxically, the very institutions that work to encourage international collaborations and research—including universities, funding agencies, professional associations, and government agencies—also establish or perpetuate these fences, which are structurally embedded in the organization of academic work. When universities and funding agencies build access to resources, policies, and procedures around national research but not around international collaborations, they can create a variety of obstacles with material, structural, legal, social, or cultural dimensions.[5] For instance, bureaucratic policies and practices can constrain international faculty collaborations by regulating exchange of ideas, materials, or travel across national boundaries. At times, international work does not fit into nationally oriented procedures and requires acting "outside the box," differently or unconventionally. Obstacles emerge through organizational processes and practices, such as evaluations, that devalue international research or even render it invisible. As we saw in Chapter 2, these obstacles reflect a deep cultural devaluation that can have material consequences when it influences institutional support, as when funding agencies and universities provide insufficient resources, such as time, money, or flexibility, for international collaborations. At the same time, however, some of these obstacles are not as high as we might expect. And whereas these obstacles can concern all academics, some create gender fences.

Business literature uses the terms *glass ceilings* and *glass borders* to describe barriers in women's paths to leadership positions that prevent women managers from participating in a globalizing business world.[6] The notion of "glass" usefully reminds us of the invisibility of many of these barriers, but I argue that the notion of ceiling or border is too fixed, for it suggests that these gendered barriers cannot—or will not—change. The "fence" imagery maintains the geographical connotation of movement through space, but fences can be of varying heights and are not impossible to scale, though to do so takes effort. My notion of fences also underscores the fact that women can and do find ways to climb or jump over some obstacles to international engagement. Fences thus better illustrate the flexibility in these international dimensions of science and academia. Fences are demarcated by the national organization of science and academia, but they also allow some access, especially for U.S. women academics. As we will see, they are socially constructed, and social networks can be helpful in overcoming them. Mentors and colleagues can provide boosts or ladders, or simply open gates, which may be just the help someone needs for his or her career (see Chapter 6). University and agency internationalization and funding policies and practices can lower fences, install gates, open gates wider, or even dismantle fences altogether.

Gendered Structures and Fences

Women have less international collaborations than do men for some obvious reasons: Women faculty compared to men are in institutions with fewer resources for research, they spend less time on research, and they are in less secure positions and in fields where international coauthorships are less common.[7] Material obstacles, including financial costs and dealing with budget rules, can be a consequence of institutional status and rank. And the ability to engage in research collaborations varies according to the resources U.S. academics have in their home institutions and their ability to access external funding.

As we saw in Chapter 2, because international collaborations are often costly, access to material resources is crucial. When faculty host international graduate students or other visitors from abroad, public grant money cannot officially be used to pay them a salary or costs of living, though there are some workarounds. When institutions do not provide housing, start-up costs, and so on, they expect that their guests will bring funding or that faculty will use overhead or slush fund accounts; however, faculty with smaller and fewer grants can accumulate less slush fund money from overheads, and women tend to have less than men.[8]

Another crucial resource is time, and there is a well-documented gender gap in time commitments that I argue creates fences. As international collaborations can be time costly, gender difference in ability to devote time to do research gets amplified in international research. Compared to men, U.S. women professors spend less time on research and more time on teaching, mentoring, and service, creating gendered inequalities. Although some of these gendered time inequalities in academia are related to work–family conflicts, a body of literature shows that women are also overburdened with service because there are simply often fewer women available for committees, for leadership roles, or with mentoring for the same reason.[9] Thus, gendered differences of time allocation can create gendered inequalities in international engagements. Because academic work is organized in stratified ways that reinforce gendered inequalities and to privilege elite men in research universities, leaving many women academics with less access to resources of all kinds, thus producing fences.

Fences can also emerge due to persistent gendered inequalities in science. Compared to funding resources for existing collaborations, agencies, professional associations, and universities do far less to support building inter-national networks, assuming that faculty already have collaborators through their own networks. However, finding suitable collaboration partners can be a particularly gendered issue. The Women's International Research Engineer-ing Summit (WIRES) has been an exceptional initiative that has convened women engineers in networking events supported by the European Centre for Women and Technology (ECWT), the U.S. National Science Foundation, the Georgia Institute of Technology, and the Ohio State University. A survey among the participants found that the number one barrier, a fence to interna-tional collaborations, was finding partners.[10]

Women's challenge to find collaborators is that, due to persisting gendered inequalities in academia worldwide, there are simply fewer women professors to collaborate with, making it difficult for women to find women collabora-tors abroad.[11] This matters because women are more likely to collaborate with women than are men.[12] Homophily is the concept that explains why faculty tend to work with people who are like themselves.[13] We might, however, also expect that women in some specialized fields might be the only women na-tionally, but the chances to find collaboration partners of course increase if they seek collaborators worldwide.[14]

Fences can emerge from the social imagery of faculty who engage in in-ternational collaborations.[15] Universities and funding agencies deploy gender when they operate on the assumption that faculty members are flexible, un-encumbered, and independent, fitting the ideal of the internationally mobile academic entrepreneur who is socially networked to academics in high-status positions across the globe. He—most definitely a he—chooses to work with the best people in his field in the United States and internationally, gets in-vited abroad or has resources to pay for his own travel, and can easily engage in international travel for research purposes. This cosmopolitan, entrepre-neurial U.S. academic has the resources to handle any obstacles he encounters and far better fits the ideal of the neoliberal university system, with its empha-sis on individual success and output orientation, than do most professors—especially women but also many men. In other words, he is a figment of the neoliberal university's imagination (a cultural imaginary) on which agencies and universities base their policies for the highest-level academic elites, an ideal that is unrealizable for many academics. For instance, most U.S. grants and fellowships assume high flexibility for mobility and do not cover extra costs for families (see also Chapter 5).

Gendered Opportunities Abroad

How Does It Matter Where You Go?

Globalization processes raise questions about how professors perceive the universality of academic work environments, what working abroad means for academics, and how gender shapes motivations of faculty to engage internationally. On the one hand, Saskia Sassen's theory of globalization supports the idea that national differences matter less and less today, with elites in major cities around the globe living in similar worlds compared to their compatriots in rural communities.[16] University libraries and laboratories look very much alike across continents, supporting scientists' continued insistence on the *universality of science*.[17] Yet national and local spaces and contexts continue to matter. Indeed, I argue that the way we construct differences of space and context, and of local and academic cultures, has gendered implications. Stereotypes about the safety and effectiveness of women in specific environments can create fences; academic and societal differences mean that a U.S. woman anthropologist who goes to Uganda has a very different experience from a Ugandan woman physicist who goes to the United States. Similarly, culture matters: Although anti-Americanism might hamper U.S. faculty experience abroad, interviewees in this study did not mention it as a serious barrier for collaborations; rather, most had positive experiences because of the .edu bonus, as the reputation of U.S. science helped them successfully conduct research in other countries (see Chapter 3). Clearly, then, both scientific nationality and gender are important for understanding how faculty experience research abroad.

In general, the meaning of going abroad for U.S.-based faculty—both women and men—depends on the national and cultural contexts of their destinations, the kind of scientific work they do, and who they are. As we saw in Chapter 2, U.S. professors find a range of occasions to engage with colleagues abroad, which create varying opportunities and challenges vis-à-vis mobility, funding, and administrative support, along with personal comfort and safety. These vary with the type of work, as they do at home, but also create additional challenges and opportunities.

To begin with, destination matters for all faculty. In interviews and focus groups, faculty members distinguished countries along several axes of resources that could determine their ease and comfort, including their own cultural familiarity; language (and potential language barriers); travel conditions such as food, water, and degree of Westernized comforts; and importance in the academic world. Not surprisingly, many considered travel to Western European countries easier, due to relatively short flights (for those on the East Coast in particular) and easier communication, and more desirable, due to the status associated with European research institutions. Interviewees often portrayed Asian, Latin American, African, and Middle Eastern countries as more difficult to navigate. Brian, a full professor of natural sciences, admitted, "Next month I have to travel to India and to China, and I am scared!" Brian was excited about visiting countries he had never been to but uneasy about putting himself in situations where he had little knowledge and less control. By contrast, Tanya, a U.S. woman professor originally from India, had fewer concerns about traveling "home," because she spoke the language and knew how to navigate the environment. Brian and Tanya show how generalizations about the accessibility of overseas environments for U.S. academics risk oversimplifying the diversity of experiences U.S. academics bring to—and have in—other countries.

It is also important to differentiate between academic and societal cultures. Gender norms may differ in different realms. Societally, they may be based on traditional gendered expectations (for example, division of labor, or male breadwinner models), even as scientific environments in the same contexts can be more egalitarian, with fewer family–work conflicts for women than in the United States. A number of women in the study remarked that some academic environments abroad were friendlier toward mothers, with less expensive and more readily available child care and more women colleagues. Indeed, some countries stereotyped for their traditional gender relations also have surprisingly high numbers of women in academia, especially in comparison to the United States. In Turkey, for instance, 37 percent of university physics faculty are women, compared to 5 percent in the United States.[18]

Managing International Collaborations: Bureaucratic Obstacles
Marissa, a full professor of natural sciences, explained how she manages her collaborations, including her experience with some typical fences. In her daily work, Marissa brings together teams of colleagues, postdoctoral fellows, and graduate students from various countries in Europe. Their collaborations happen in person in the United States and abroad, at conferences, and via Skype. The major obstacle she has encountered is finding U.S. funding that will pay expenses for her collaborators when they visit her. She has also learned a lot

about visa regulations for visitors to the United States, as well as national regulations regarding intellectual property and exchange of samples, as her work involves transferring biological samples across national borders. Marissa handles language difficulties and intercultural challenges in the team while trying to promote a collaborative team-based work style. Although these obstacles may not appear gendered, they can be harder for women to overcome, especially because women are more likely to be at resource-poor institutions, and even within the same institutions women have less access to administrative support compared to men.[19]

The work Marissa describes resembles the image of a global managerial scientific entrepreneur, as in Raewyn Connell and Julian Wood's model of the transnational modern global manager, which values diversity for facilitating innovative, creative thinking.[20] This image could open more space for women as global scientists, given that women are presumed to possess strong soft skills, language capabilities, intercultural competencies, and leadership styles that lend themselves to international engagement (stereotypes, but possibly useful ones).[21] However, many women lack the material and structural foundations for achieving such a role, given their positions in the highly stratified U.S. academic system, including access to resources.[22]

Collaborations across national boundaries can include myriad complications with laws, regulations, and dealing with authorities; therefore access to administrative support and bureaucratic knowhow is another crucial resource. Coordinating data collection and exchanging materials across countries can require time-intensive negotiations for legal and customs permissions. If research includes humans, different institutional ethics boards are also involved, which means additional (sometimes contradictory) rules. Keeping up with visa and immigration requirements for both U.S. scholars and international visitors requires expert legal knowledge and presents challenges for university administration.

National security protections come into play when collaborators exchange knowledge in sensitive fields like nuclear energy or work with hazardous samples that pose potential threats. Since September 11, 2001, heightened concerns about security have posed challenges for cross-national exchange of research materials, as Edward, a full professor of biological sciences, explained:

> Homeland security is an issue, and dealing with biological samples there's a lot
> of extra regulations and issues that you have to deal with. I just sent samples to

the UK, and it was a nightmare. And you know I don't want to go to jail [laughter], and so you know you have to follow the letter of the law; it's very strict; you know people used to just get on the plane with things—like you could carry proteins on the plane, and you can't do that anymore. That's a challenge.

Marissa's and Edward's experiences illustrate how research administration across national boundaries is complicated by myriad laws, rules, and practices. International collaboration often requires enormous coordination and tacit knowledge about negotiating for resources in a department and university. It is particularly difficult for faculty members without sufficient administrative support, as well as those excluded from internal and external networks with colleagues, which often means they lack crucial information about navigating more costly collaborations with more complicated bureaucratic hurdles.

Although on the surface these obstacles might seem gender neutral, women often have less access to tacit knowledge, resources, networks, and administrative supports than their male colleagues.[23] This in turn creates fences, as women in less secure positions (untenured, non–tenure track, in resource-poor institutions) feel they can take fewer risks.[24] This fear keeps them from venturing abroad, potentially keeping them from moving their careers forward, which ultimately amplifies and reinforces academic status hierarchies. Thus we see how the foundational structures of academic institutions produce a wide range of fences, many of them self-perpetuating.

Working Abroad: Research Institutions, Laboratories, and Fieldwork

International collaborations often require U.S. academics to travel abroad to conduct fieldwork or work at research laboratories and institutions. Culturally, we tend to imagine these expeditions in gendered ways. Stories and documentaries[25] often cast traveling scientists as explorers and risk takers who can handle adversity and potentially dangerous natural and political conditions. Driven by the quest for adventure in unknown territories, academics who take expeditions along the Amazon River, sample polar ice on research ships in Antarctica, work on rigs after oil spills near Japan, or conduct fieldwork on HIV transmission in Ethiopia possess optimum self-confidence and self-assurance. This image fits our traditional images of the explorer and our stereotypical depictions of men, not women.

However, these stereotypes risk exaggerating gendered differences and making invisible that such work settings might not be desirable for men as well as women (or, indeed, might be amenable to some women). The stock explorer image also erases the rigor and repetitiveness of fieldwork, which, in fact, often requires skill sets, such as patience and detail orientation, that we tend to associate with women.

There is also great variation in the feasibility of research locations for women and men, with or without children or other family responsibilities. Alexandria, a full professor of oceanography, remembers working on a research vessel where the ship staff provided cooking, cleaning, and laundry services because male researchers were not expected to be able to accomplish these tasks themselves. Although Alexandra observed how convenient life was, she also noted that the ship had no accommodations for family members. The setup of the ship was organized on the basis of gendered assumptions about its inhabitants. Researchers were expected to travel on their own, without responsibility for reproductive work or concerns about leaving their partners, children, or other family members behind for months at a time. The research ship did not provide opportunities for men or women who enjoyed cooking and spending time with their families to have a balanced life.

Of course, many field sites today are far less adventurous and remote and more suitable for visitors, allowing partners and families to accompany academics on longer research stays. At the Max Planck Institutes and the DESY center in Germany, the CERN center in Switzerland, and cities and towns with infrastructures, accommodations for visitors are largely suitable for families. Facilities accustomed to hosting international guests offer temporary apartments, handle visa arrangements, and support visits in other ways. By supporting academics with families, these facilities help remove obstacles that are otherwise fences not only for women (see Chapter 5). Of course, these accommodations pose varying (gendered) opportunities and challenges, depending on faculty members' language skills, cross-cultural competences, and fluidity in adapting to a foreign environment.

Attending Conferences Abroad

Fences can also be found at another crucial site for international collaboration: the international conference. Robert, a full professor of security studies, explained that he had twenty-four conference and workshop meetings lined up for the following academic year. Like Robert, top-level academics are expected to travel regularly to present papers and discuss their work with colleagues around the world. Long flights and jet lag can make such travel uncomfortable for everyone, but for those with sufficient funding, first-class hotels and conference centers that cater to the international academic elite eliminate much of the discomfort. As Charles, a full professor of civil engineering, remarked, a Hilton in California does not look very different from a Hilton in China, India, or Australia. When workshops and conferences take place at research institutes or universities and include well-organized programs for leisure activities and sightseeing, faculty need to do little planning aside from booking flights and hotel rooms.

Although these conferences are a key place for faculty to make new contacts and maintain or reestablish old connections, our survey of 100 NSF PI revealed a gender gap in the importance of conferences for establishing collaborations.[26] Half the men in the study met their collaboration partners at conferences, but only one-third of the women did. Women were more likely than men (42 versus 32 percent) to draw international collaboration partners from existing networks.[27] These networks include established mentors, as well as former graduate students and postdoctoral fellows who work outside the United States and provide a natural pipeline for building international collaborations. However, in interviews, many men revealed that attending international conferences, in particular smaller invitation-only workshops and meetings, was a key means of meeting future collaborators, starting projects, and maintaining international professional networks.

Not surprisingly, the expectation of intensive conference travel assumes a (gendered) ideal of a hyperflexible academic entrepreneur who can engage in international travel at any time. But although such travel may be necessary for some research, it is worth asking how many conferences faculty really should be expected to attend. International conferences are a highly visible form of academic practice that represents and creates prestige and status for invited participants. However, this model is problematic on multiple fronts. Several interviewees insisted that even though face-to-face meetings were important for establishing new collaborations, including creating trust, highly effective practices of international collaboration offer alternatives. Furthermore, although many women and some men discussed the challenges of international conference travel, for women in this study conferences were particularly challenging.[28] Thus, continued insistence on face-to-face contact in the internet age is itself a fence.

The expectation of frequent conference travel not only is gendered, failing to meet the needs of people with care commitments, largely (but not exclusively) women, but also does not fit many academic work lives for both women and men. Faculty who have responsibilities for laboratories with student researchers, experimental subjects, or time-sensitive experiments and trials often cannot leave their facilities frequently or for extended periods of time, making it hard to meet expectations for international travel. Yet the powerful myth of the hyperflexible traveling academic persists, imposing normative expectations and ignoring obstacles for all academics, because of their diverse work and family lives and other commitments.

The organization of international meetings has gendered repercussions that reproduce fences by making access and social dynamics especially difficult for U.S. women academics. Gendered issues include who gets invited, who has access to resources to participate, and who can easily travel. If no general calls for papers are circulated, for instance, faculty must be visible to colleagues who can invite them to workshops. Several women in the study mentioned how difficult they found it to get invitations to speak on panels and at symposia or to give keynote addresses because international elite networks are often organized along old-boy lines. They found that male colleagues of equal status received invitations although they did not. Even when individuals receive invitations to conferences, if organizers do not pay for their expenses, participation depends on grants or personal budgets. And, as we saw before, because women tend to have fewer and smaller grants they have fewer resources for expensive travel.

The smaller international conferences and workshops, however, bring especially good opportunities to initiate and maintain networks and collaborations. For example, Anthony, an associate professor of physical sciences, found small workshops particularly helpful in building connections to colleagues; for example, staying in the same hotel and having breakfast at a small table allowed him to have a one-on-one conversation with a long-admired senior colleague in his field. Coffee breaks, lunches, and dinners at these smaller conferences provided crucial ways for junior faculty to talk to more senior people who at home would have been more preoccupied.

The timing of international conferences can also be a challenge, for it is rarely in sync with U.S. academic or school schedules. Although bringing children to conferences is an increasing option in the United States, conferences abroad rarely provide child care, limiting the feasibility of bringing children along as a solution for work–family conflicts.[29] Moreover, international airline tickets and hotels are generally costly, and funding agencies do not usually pay travel expenses for families, leaving these costs to be absorbed privately.

The ability of faculty to travel extensively abroad also depends on their care responsibilities—for children, but also for partners and elderly or disabled family members—and other local commitments. Care commitments are still gendered, so it is difficult to tease out whether they are simply obstacles for everyone or fences that influence women in particular. Vanessa, an associate professor of biology, remembers that her mother got seriously ill, and, instead of traveling to an invited workshop in Japan, she flew to visit her mother in the hospital and take care of her in the United States. She could have gone on a shorter U.S. conference trip, but the international travel was impossible. As Chapter 5 demonstrates, these family responsibilities no longer solely concern women, as men are increasingly called on to share responsibility for care duties, especially in dual-career couples. Academic couple James and Haley, both associate professors of physical sciences, have divided the conferences in their field; their rule is that one parent will always stay with their children at home while they each take part in every other conference. This alternative, more egalitarian model of parenting and partnering demonstrates how care commitments and responsibilities do not have to remain gendered. In more traditional arrangements, however, in which women are the primary caregivers, the ability to engage in conference travel, particularly longer international trips, is likely to contribute to a gender gap in conference attendance.[30]

International conferences often create time and space for socializing in heavily gendered ways that can have professional effects. Several women professors said they were acutely aware of being seen as women when socializing with foreign colleagues, more than with U.S. colleagues. They reported doors held open for them, expectations that they would flirt to get help from technical personnel, pressure for intimate sexuality from foreign hosts, evening conference programs for men only, and other gendered forms of socializing. Both women and men recognized the importance of the personal aspects of collaboration, as friendships can provide a foundation for academic collaborations. Thus collaborations start not only during the official part of conferences but over dinner and drinks, taking faculty outside the more formal academic setting and into the more informal social realm, where norms of behavior and interactions between women and men, including sexuality and drinking, are more obviously gendered.

Socializing over lunch and bonding with colleagues after hours are important practices among academics during visits and conferences. After a long day of presentations, socializing often involves alcohol. In these situations, women can feel conflicting pressures: to be "one of the boys" but also to be moderate in their alcohol intake. Some hosts organize men-only evening events, such as visits to karaoke bars in Japan, which include women dancers and heavy drinking. Although not all men enjoy heavy drinking, drinking with male colleagues can pose an extra challenge for women, who may encounter uncomfortable situations when drunken colleagues make sexist jokes, flirt, or proffer unwanted sexual overtures.

Natalie, an associate professor of engineering, recalled a professional meeting to discuss plans for a research collaboration at the home of a Japanese collaborator, who went on to organize an evening out with only the men at the meeting:

> After my visit there, his driver took me back, and [my collaborator] joined us. And it was clear that when I was in the car, he was on the phone, making arrangements for an evening activity for people [from the meeting]. I knew the faculty he was calling to go out with; he dropped me off at my hotel, and they went off and did their evening thing.

Natalie found the visit isolating and lonely because her hosts did not include her in any evening social activities. She concluded she would not return on her own. She had a similar experience of exclusion at a conference in South Korea:

> I was more comfortable with the U.S. folks who went . . . I wasn't waiting for the invitation, I had no problem walking up to one of them and saying: "What are we doing tonight?" And I was told, well, there's a group being arranged, but you are not going to be included. And I said, "Oh, one of those," and they said, "Yes." And another senior female faculty member and I went shopping at the twenty-four-hour market, while the others did whatever they were doing . . . I think they went to . . . a karaoke place [with a] private room for the group, and you can order food and so forth, and sometimes a hostess will join you and stay with the men . . . I've been in a group of men and women where the Asian men and sometimes the U.S. men will dance with the hostess . . . I know karaoke places are capable of creating privacy. It was something they didn't want me to see.

Not all men enjoy these normative forms of male bonding through objec-tifying women. However, exclusion from such socializing means women miss out on potentially important opportunities to build and deepen professional networks. Most examples of sex-segregated after-hours socializing in South Korea and Japan involved heavy drinking in bars, where it was considered unsuitable for women to witness their colleagues getting drunk. Yet women also talked about pressures to drink at conferences in Europe. Maria, an as-sociate professor of social science, believes that her success in initiating and carrying out international collaborations with European partners is due to the fact that "I go out drinking beer with the men." Katelyn, a full professor of engineering, explained:

> You really can't do anything in France or Spain without going to dinner or something like that. I mean, you just have to. So there's this whole . . . that whole other component of just being friendly. And I think that's the best part of col-laborations anyway. I hate to go out there and not go to dinners and all that. That seems like the best part.

Although both Katelyn and Maria felt comfortable joining male col-leagues in these forms of socializing, many other women shared stories of feeling excluded, socially isolated, or simply uncomfortable when groups of men engaged in heavy drinking during workshops and conferences.

In general, interacting with colleagues outside the more formal structures of academia (for example, laboratories, conference panels, and discussions) posed challenges for women, even those in senior positions. When visiting a British university, Laura, a full professor of biotechnology who held a distinguished chair, noticed that her local hosts took male visiting professors to lunch, even though they had less scientific standing, and did not take her. She resorted to socializing with graduate students and postdocs, although British professors of equal status would have been more appropriate companions. It seemed clear to her that the reluctance of the male hosts had to do with her gender.

Negotiating the Minefields of Being a Woman Abroad

Can Women Be as Effective Abroad?
Another fence is the persistent cultural stereotype that women professors might be less welcome and less effective in different cultural environments

abroad. A few women professors did express concern about how they would handle a cultural context with few women colleagues. Given the sexist local climate, Sara, a Japanese-born associate professor of engineering, explained that she would make sure to choose wisely among potential Japanese collaborators:

> I would be very cautious about whom I could collaborate with. Unless I know that person really well, I don't think I'd want to collaborate. Whereas if I'm a man, I don't have to really worry about it. As a guy, you don't get the sexist things that females do.

U.S. academics often assess whether a particular environment will be welcoming for women by the number of local women in academia. But although local women are only marginally represented in academia and academic leadership in some countries, U.S. faculty can be surprised to find that in other countries women's representation in science and academia more generally is higher than at home, as discussed earlier. Overall, the numbers of women faculty, postdocs, and students depend on the field, institution, and country. Women seeking collaboration face diverse options, not simply a monolithically unwelcoming male world of science abroad.[31]

Outside the university setting, women professors encountered some challenges to their authority. Erin, an assistant professor of archeology overseeing excavation workers in Egypt, found it difficult to be recognized as a "leader." She explains that the Egyptian men were not used to working for a woman and resisted it, as her status as a U.S. scientist had no impact on the threat she posed to their sense of masculinity. They viewed Erin as a woman first and an American second, which led them to challenge her leadership. This particular situation occurred in a setting with powerful societal beliefs about the gendered leadership. Interestingly, however, none of the women professors in this study found that their legitimacy as a supervisor was questioned in laboratory and university settings abroad. In those contexts, I would argue, the .edu bonus as their status as U.S. scientists maintained their authority.

Several interviewees expressed concerns about whether women would be respected as scholars and in leadership positions in particular countries. Most concerns reflected gendered and racialized stereotypes about "Arab countries," which faculty members and administrators believed would be hostile to women and have difficulty taking women seriously as professors.[32] Women might also receive fewer invitations to collaborations from their male colleagues if these colleagues share such concerns. Scott, a full professor of biomedical engineering, demonstrates this reasoning, as he believes that to ensure the success of his team he might not take women abroad: "Having women in certain parts of the world, like [country in South Asia], having women on the team is sometimes difficult to deal with because of the male-dominant society." His concern is that the lack of women's acceptance abroad would be a distraction and ultimately undermine the research project. These concerns are also prevalent in global business, where widespread gendered stereotypes hold that women find it difficult to be accepted as negotiation partners or effective leaders, especially if there are no women peers in the other country. Although Adler found that these stereotypes are most often unwarranted, they do raise concerns for supervisors who resist sending women abroad.[33] Even though my data do not speak to this directly, in the academic context the parallel is that women in U.S. universities might receive fewer invitations and opportunities to collaborate or teach abroad or themselves shy away from going overseas out of fear of not being effective there, as Erin did.

Can Women Be "Safe" when Abroad?
Undoubtedly, women can encounter sexism, sexual intimidation, and harassment such as unwanted flirtatious behavior when conducting fieldwork abroad.[34] However, we know little about whether they encounter more or less such behavior at home or abroad, nor do we necessarily know whether this makes travel abroad in general more or less dangerous for women than for men.[35] Thus, it is important to explore how academics discuss safety issues. Safety is another realm in which fences operate, especially when the safety of fieldwork and travel abroad is constructed in gendered ways, as an issue that influences only women. Fieldwork abroad that seems to offer adventurous men an opportunity to prove their manhood through risk taking and exploration can be represented as dangerous for women. Gendered constructions of safety can thus limit women's international opportunities by depicting foreign countries as dangerous. At the same time, they can create a false sense of women's safety in the United States by distracting them from gendered problems within teams, among U.S. colleagues, or at home institutions. Furthermore, these constructions can undermine reasonable and legitimate considerations about men's safety. Indeed, although interviewees raised concerns about women's safety and often implied or directly depicted local men as the

source of unsafe conditions for women, they rarely discussed safety concerns for men.[36]

Although gendered depictions may represent fieldwork as dangerous only for women, it may actually present both women and men with challenges to comfort and safety. Wandering for months to explore geological formations in remote areas, studying volcanic activity, interviewing armed fighters in countries mired in political conflict, and conducting research at the origin points of epidemics require different kinds and degrees of preparation and risk tolerance from working in a library or one's own laboratory. These images of dangerous work fuel the myth of the masculine risk taker and explorer and vulnerable women who have to be protected.

Safety issues are just as likely to concern both women and men. Recall how Terry, a full professor and geologist (in Chapter 3), found that her gender was not salient when local people brought her to the village president because they had caught her walking through their land. She reasoned that "I'd be just as threatening as a foreign female as I would if I were a foreign male. They don't distinguish at all. And that is a safety issue, but, again, it is not gendered." Although Terry's point is that outsiders would be considered threatening and gender is not at work here, it is quite possible that her gender might have helped her be seen as less threatening, which meant she provoked less aggression in this situation, leading to less danger for her team. Similarly, being a woman can be an advantage when conducting fieldwork, when local people are more comfortable working with or talking to women than with U.S. men whom they might find more intimidating.[37]

Several women faculty mentioned situations in which they felt that their gender was highly visible and that being a woman was more salient than being a foreigner or an academic. Women academics also face the same concerns as any women traveling abroad. Gendered dress codes are a particularly illustrative example of gender salience and the interaction between gender and nationality. Foreign women may not be expected to wear the same clothing as local women, but they are still expected to wear gender-specific garb, that is, different clothing from what men wear. Gary, an associate professor of chemistry, explained that when he traveled with his wife in the Middle East, she was expected to wear gender-appropriate clothing:

> Although it seems that in most of the Middle East, there's an understanding that you don't expect the visitors to behave quite the way folks around here

would behave . . . most of the native women were pretty much completely covered . . . But for Americans who are there or Westerners . . . they were allowed to be full faced, otherwise everything else was covered. So when my wife and I visited, the same rules applied to my wife; she had to make sure that she was covered.

Being a woman and a foreigner both come into play, as a dress code specific to foreign women reflects cultural expectations. In her tips for how to be a successful woman scientist abroad, Kaitlyn, an associate professor of Earth science, suggests a delicate balancing act between conforming to local dress codes and presenting scientific competence:

I think that you have to, in many ways, whether you like it or not, accept their culture. So for example, if women there don't wear tank tops and bikinis, don't do that. I mean, adjust to their local culture. It will help in many ways. On the other hand, be confident and such that they realize that you are as competent a scientist as anyone. So you have to play the game, kind of . . . Get the respect and don't challenge their culture, . . . [and] be clear that your science is as good as anyone's, or better and that the fact that you are a woman has nothing to do with the quality of your science, your research, and your abilities.

Kaitlyn points out the complicated dance between "doing gender" in culturally appropriate ways and insisting on one's scientific competence as a woman.[38] Also, regardless of whether they actually felt or were safe, women academics perceived their hosts' concern for their safety as a signal of the salience of gender. Although Allison, a full professor of engineering, felt highly respected academically, she perceived her hosts as overly protective:

Where it became clear that it mattered that I was a woman was [when] I was told that it was not safe to be out after dark alone. I was treated as an honored aunt, auntie. [The lab director] was worried that I would get sick or have an accident and . . . tried to control everything that I did, which drove me crazy.

We do not know whether the hosts would have treated a male visitor similarly, but Allison experienced their overprotection as a consequence of the intersection of being a woman and a foreigner, which laid on her a vulnerability she did not feel. Several other women also felt their hosts exaggerated safety concerns. In other words, regardless of whether women academics are actually safe abroad, the perception that they are not reflects the salience of gender in their international experiences. Not surprisingly, then, women welcome the opportunity provided by the .edu bonus to put gender on the back burner.

Do Women Need Special Protection Abroad?

Foreign hosts were not the only ones who tried to protect women academics. Our interviews described various preventive or "protective" considerations at their home institutions. A university administrator interpreted sexual harassment laws in the United States in such a way that the university would need to warn women faculty about attending international conferences if incidents of sexual harassment occurred there. Given the prevalence of sexual harassment throughout the academic world, of course, this kind of measure would stop women's travel to both international and national conferences. Furthermore, it is difficult to imagine how a court in the United States would uphold travel bans for women faculty. Faculty, however, expressed protective concerns with regard to women students. Despite his overwhelmingly positive experience with collaborators abroad, Scott explained that he had used caution before:

> There have been times where I've had to make a decision that this isn't a trip that I can have female students go on. There are trips where they do go, but they have to be well thought out. I am not going to put them in a situation that is really not productive. And it's not helpful to the project, it's not helpful to them, it's not helpful to their collaborator. So you really just have to evaluate on a case by case basis.

As noted here, Scott believes the extra efforts it would take to take women as students or colleagues on research teams would undermine the productivity and success of the project. Similarly, Daniel, a full professor of Earth sciences who was invited to a conference in a Middle Eastern country, noted, "I'm thinking that I probably wouldn't take a women graduate student with me . . . There are things that you need to do and be sensitive to where you are. There are probably some places that you wouldn't send a female graduate student or postdoc." This statement is surprising because Daniel expressed pride that his daughter spent time learning Arabic and working in several Middle Eastern countries; although he supported his own daughter, he still generalized about unsuitable environments for his female students and postdocs.

Some faculty concerned with safety of women students purposely avoid placing them in uncomfortable situations abroad. Angela, a full professor of biology, explained that she always made sure to send women students to foreign labs in pairs, whereas she sent men by themselves. Although this strategy could help women graduate students feel more comfortable, it denies men the same benefits. The double costs of sending pairs might also lead to unintentional discrimination against women graduate students; that is, the act of removing one fence (safety) could create another (cost).

Sharing rooms on trips also raised gender-specific concerns. Although some professors thought it was appropriate for same-sex students to share hotel rooms or apartments on longer trips, they provided women students with housing separate from male students. Of course, this assumption reinforces heteronormative ideas that men cannot be victims of harassment and sexual violence by other men. Thus, some strategies for protecting women can inadvertently undermine gender equality by limiting their access and opportunities to research abroad and reproducing gendered ideas about safe and unsafe relations.

Gendered concerns and constructions around safety create fences that impede women but not men and therefore can influence women's opportunity and ability to do academic work abroad. Such cautions and preventive measures constrain women from explorations of international research opportunities. We need to critically examine what kinds of places are deemed safe for women, by whom, and why. The cultural biases in U.S. academia's perceptions of women's risk outside the country fuel stereotypes about environments constructed as unfriendly to or unsafe for women, particularly Muslim-majority countries in the Middle East. Interestingly, however, none of the women in this study who visited Middle Eastern countries perceived them as hostile, unsafe, or threatening.

Academics of color also had positive experiences when they ventured abroad. Both men and women from underrepresented minority groups reported very few negative experiences. The only exception was Mark, an African American professor of physical sciences, who encountered racist incidents, including racial remarks and one racially motivated physical assault, in an Eastern European city where he traveled with his family:

The only bad story I have to tell is when I went to [Eastern European country] in 2000. There were overt racial remarks made, including sort of gestures where someone saw me walking down the street, and they were pretending they were a monkey. And I was in a restaurant, and it was a woman about twenty-two who assaulted me.

In another situation, he was called "nigger" and told he "should go home." His experiences illustrate that context matters and that race relations are locally constructed. The .edu bonus does not always work for African Americans, and in this case Mark's status as a black person was more salient. That these negative experiences occurred not in a university setting but in a restaurant and on the street, in interactions not with colleagues but with local people, demonstrates that the experiences of women and people from minority groups can vary according to whether they are perceived as foreigners or visiting academics. We can see that gender, race, ethnicity, and (academic) nationality can work very differently in local and academic cultures. Similarly, homosexuality might be outlawed in the country but accepted in the academic context. Generalizations about safety thus erase differences in foreign cultures, making them an even more problematic frame for assessing the viability of international collaboration for women and minorities.

Is It Safer for Women at Home Than Abroad?

The assumption that traveling outside the United States is particularly unsafe for women also creates an image of U.S. academia and society as safe for women. Interestingly, William, a full professor of engineering, remembers how a U.S. job candidate described the concerns of her Iranian colleagues about her safety in the United States:

> We interviewed a U.S. woman who was doing work in Iran. And I asked her if it was dangerous or if there was a lot of anti-Americanism that she ran into in Iran. And she started to laugh, and she said, "Well, the Iranians had begged me not to come back to the United States because they watch American television every night and they see Americans shooting each other every night." They felt very protective toward her and felt she just wouldn't be safe in America. You watch American TV with all these rapes and all the rest of it.

The construction of the dangers lurking abroad ignores the fact that women and some men throughout their careers encounter danger in their U.S. academic workplaces from sexual harassment to sexual assault; perpetrators can be supervisors, colleagues, or students. Indeed, a recent pioneering study of field researchers suggests that women and men should fear their own supervisors and team members more than local men in the fieldwork environment.[39] In particular, women graduate students were more likely to experience sexual harassment from direct supervisors or fellow graduate students than from local people. Men can also be victims of sexual harassment, most likely, though, from other men and peers than from women supervisors.[40] Sexual harassment thus should not be used to discourage women from going abroad; rather, we need to find ways to discourage U.S. perpetrators from taking advantage of situations away from home.

Strategies for Women Working Abroad

Awkward, potentially uncomfortable, and unsafe situations demonstrate how women perceive that their gender is salient in negotiating mixed-sex socializing on research trips and conferences. And although some women might choose not to travel at all, others do, and they shared strategies they use. Whether they were responding to constructed images or experiences of travel abroad, women interviewees did take precautions to avoid situations in which they risked exposure to danger or discomfort. Some traveled with their graduate students, which created not only a sense of safety in numbers but a more professional space for interactions with hosts and colleagues at conferences and also important networking and professional opportunities for their students. Others actively presented themselves as heterosexual married women by displaying wedding bands and bringing photographs of husbands, even if this meant making up a nonexistent husband. Women with actual husbands sometimes brought them along on conferences or research visits for safety reasons.

The safety concerns these strategies addressed were aimed at both the broader society and potentially uncomfortable situations with colleagues, as Julia, a full professor of social science, explained:

> When I was younger, yeah, [feeling comfortable socializing with colleagues] was an issue. It was one of the reasons I often took my husband with me. I found that . . . as I got older there were many more options to have all-women groups or equally combined groups, where you didn't feel you were being targeted as the woman of the evening, whatever that might have meant. But yeah, yeah, I was very uncomfortable. And what I found, that answer for me, was to bring my husband with me.

Similarly, Caitlin, a full professor of physics who visited Germany for a semester, found that while she had interesting professional interactions with colleagues and felt part of the research institute, she did not have access to socializing opportunities while she was on her own. Indeed she received dinner invitations from colleagues only when her husband visited, perhaps, she reasoned, because a single woman was not considered a suitable dinner guest. Her husband's presence thus helped her overcome social exclusion. Mariah, an assistant professor of geosciences who was stalked by a local man, found that only her male partner's visit put an end to his advances because it showed him she was already in a relationship. Of course, for women and men in same-sex relationships, bringing partners along means outing themselves in potentially hostile work or societal environments, so the accompanying partner strategy cannot serve as a shield for all women.

Academic work that takes place across national borders is organized in gendered ways, as these fences reveal. Fences make it more difficult for women to engage in international collaborations and conduct research abroad. Gender becomes salient for women in terms of access to conferences and research institutes, important resources and administrative supports, but also practices such as cultures. Unfortunately, colleagues and professional organizations can create inaccessible, uncomfortable, or unsafe environments for women when they organize conferences and social events with exclusionary practices. These practices, and the stereotypical image of the global scientist on which they are based, need to be nuanced to make the image and reality of global academia more inclusive for women.

The variation in international research collaborations and locations demonstrates that fences are not inevitable, but human made. Fences can be socially constructed through myths, stereotypes, and misperceptions. Some cultural fences emerge from stereotypes about women's safety or effectiveness abroad. Even as these fences may be founded on myths and stereotypes about how other cultures treat women, they can be powerful, limiting women's access and, in effect, creating their own reality. It is therefore essential that we critically interrogate these fences and dismantle these myths.

Glass fences allow us to explore how global academia reinforces gendered inequalities. As we have seen, the organization of conferences, resources, and opportunity structures for international collaborations is gendered. When academic organizations internationalize academic work on the basis of an imagined male norm of a global scientist, they create global academic work structures and practices that fit the lives of a specific subset of already privileged men and are exclusionary for many women. However, these gendered ways of organizing international research and collaboration can be challenged and changed, as I argue in the conclusion of this book.

We also need to challenge the belief that international collaborations require extensive international travel. Although one's own mobility may be necessary for some types of research, alternative if less visible practices of international collaboration include emails, phone calls, videoconferencing, exchanging information online, sending students and postdoctoral fellows, or hosting collaborators. These strategies can better fit the diversity of academic work and personal lives, which I explore in the following chapter.

5 Families and International Mobility

Fences or Opportunities?

ASKED WHAT SUGGESTIONS SHE WOULD GIVE OTHER WOMEN academics who wanted to do research abroad, Jenna, a full professor of biological science, advised travel first, then kids: "I would definitely encourage women to do it. Do it before you have kids! Get it started at least, because it is hard." Jenna's perspective is widespread. Although many changes have occurred for women in academia, faculty, university administrators, and policy makers still share the assumption that family commitments limit women's international academic mobility. Isabella, an associate professor of biology, explained her decision to stay local while on leave: "I could have gone to Europe; I could have gone to Africa and researched the animals that I wanted . . . But that's not going to happen. I am married, and I am going to have a family. I did not get married to leave him alone and go to Africa." Similarly, Rafaelle, an administrator, shared her view of the realities of international travel by contrasting two women faculty members: Jane, who has children and has not been involved in international collaborations, and Susan, who does not have children and has extensive international contacts and travels abroad for research every summer.

In this chapter, I look more closely at the assumption that family responsibilities create barriers for women academics, preventing them from engaging in international research and collaborations. Although the literature provides mixed evidence that marriages, relationships, and children, in particular, hamper women's international scientific involvement, many interviewees expressed this view. Their actual experiences, in fact, painted a more complicated and notably shifting picture. For academics today, family and its responsibilities mean much more than women and children: Men also make decisions on the basis of their children, parents can be another care responsibility or an invaluable support, and gay and lesbian families have their own legal and practical issues, to name just a few. The ramifications of this extended definition of family bring both challenges and opportunities. Traveling abroad can magnify work–family conflicts, in what I call the "amplification of family burdens." At the same time, international research opportunities can bring exciting family opportunities, depending on the research sites.

Academics live in diverse family constellations and have local commitments that shape their mobility; when it comes to working abroad, these can be potentially constraining but also motivating. Many faculty members with family responsibilities are mobile and engaged in international collaborations, and family as well as institutional support can be crucial to their efforts. Ultimately, then, families in all their permutations prove to be not permanent barriers but fences: With effort, academics do surmount them to their professional and personal benefit. Yet women still bear more of a burden for family responsibilities than men—and, perhaps even more important, feel more of a burden. Those fences do, on the whole, remain higher for women, a fact that has important policy implications.

Do Children Prevent Women from Going Abroad?

I think for a short time you can work it out. If you go away for a long time, probably you can work it out. If you have young children or babies, it's hard. But when you don't have young children, that's different.

Diana, assistant professor of health sciences

Diana's comments foreground the complexity of determining whether children serve as a barrier to women's participation in international research collaborations. Despite the common wisdom among academics and policy makers alike, which holds that children universally impede women's international mobility, I argue that much in fact depends on context—family and institutional supports, particular family commitments, the distance and length of the travel, and the nature of the research, as we will see in the following discussion. The literature is similarly equivocal. One branch suggests that family status, and foremost having children, explains the underrepresentation of women among the professoriate. Children challenge women's success in academic careers in general and have a negative influence on (international) collaborations and international travel because mothers are more likely to be burdened by domestic work and caring for children.[1] Nancy Steffen-Fluhr and her collaborators conclude that women tend to orient their careers locally and establish collaborations closer to home because they lack supports to be mobile temporarily or in the longer term.[2]

Other studies suggest that family status might have less influence on participation in international collaborations or in more nuanced ways than we might expect.[3] In our analysis of NSF survey data on PhD recipients, Lisa Frehill and I found that the differences between faculty who had children and those who did not were very small: We found that 19.9 percent of women with children collaborated internationally, as did 21.7 percent of women without children; 28.6 percent of men with children and 27 percent without had international collaborations.[4] Although children made a negative difference for women and a positive difference for men, both gaps were small. For academics who had international collaborations, the patterns were similar: Although faculty with children, women and men alike, traveled slightly less than their childless peers, the larger gap was between women and men in general (41.5 percent of women with children, 42.7 percent of women without children, 49.4 percent of men with children, and 51.8 percent of men without children traveled abroad).[5]

It is important to note, however, that children are not the only familial factor that influences international travel. Partners may be even less portable than children, and their employment status and perhaps consequent ability to support—or lack thereof—can play a significant role in faculty's international collaborations. Katrina Uhly, Laura Visser, and I found in an analysis of ten countries including the United States that the constellations of employment status of partners were at times more important than having children. In particular, for women and men with academic or part-time employed partners, the presence of children matters less. And, interestingly, the gender gap in international collaborations is smallest for women and men who are single or who have an academic partner. By contrast, the gender gap is larger when women and men have full-time employed nonacademic partners.[6]

Similarly, Louise Ackers points out that parenting and partnering are separate but interrelated issues, particularly for parents in dual-career couples:

In her study of Marie Curie postdoctoral fellowship recipients in Europe, she discusses how partners have been underestimated compared to children to explain gendered patterns of mobility.[7] Partners are thus an important predictor of how both women and men handle children and international research and mobility commitments.[8] Family responsibilities do matter, however, pointing to how postdoctoral fellows are embedded in social relations; as Regula Leemann puts it: "Complex formations related to gender, partnership, children and dual career constellations, as well as to social class and academic integration, are resulting in inequalities in the accumulation of international cultural and social capital."[9] Interestingly, having a child decreased the odds of going abroad for both women and men.

Together, this research suggests that family status is an important factor to explain persistent academic gender inequalities. However, we need to consider the effects of children in the context of partnerships, and the role of partnerships themselves, as dual-career couples in particular can bring challenges but also supports to women's academic careers.[10] And the support, employment status, career (academic or not),[11] or nationality of their partners might better explain the international research engagement of women and increasingly that of men, too, rather than their children alone.

Building Fences: Diverse Challenges for Families

Despite the nuances of the literature, faculty and administrators continue to believe that family is the most common issue that keeps women from international engagement. This notion is supported by the discourse of amplification of burdens with regard to combining family and international research. This discourse often focuses solely on the challenges faced by women, who are already burdened with responsibilities for their children, as they try to arrange international work. It tends to neglect not only the challenges faced by men who desire to be actively involved in their families but also the diversity of family and personal commitments that constrain international mobility. Furthermore, this discourse fails to recognize the variation of fences, depending on the destination and how diverse families are themselves.

This discourse of family as the key problem for women in international engagement resonates with the motherhood myth across academia, which promotes motherhood as the key and sometimes only reason for women's underrepresentation in the STEM fields.[12] A similar idea of the "family plan thesis" developed by Erin Cech explains different career choices of women and men.[13] The flexibility stigma then becomes attached to faculty who are seen to deviate from the ideal-worker norm, which in the context of academia of course means being considered as less committed to research and straying from the ideal of full devotion.[14]

The discourse on families as barriers for faculty is deeply gendered, centering almost wholly on motherhood, with little if any mention of fatherhood. Both women and men administrators and faculty discussed international research as a pursuit fundamentally incompatible with motherhood. Abigail, an associate professor of computer science, contended that "this kind of face time [for international collaborations] that is needed is harder for women to get to if they've got a family at home and they don't feel like they can be away." Similarly, Dennis, a full professor of engineering, believed that "it's easier for men to leave the family and spend time internationally than the woman." Katie, an assistant professor of Earth science, pointed to the experiences of her colleagues: "And I know a lot of other women who have worked internationally, and then when their kids came along, it's suddenly like, 'Oh! Now what am I supposed to do?'" For Emma, a professor of natural science, the issue was personal, as family commitments were her major qualm about taking on international projects: "It's difficult logistically, just with all the issues that you have to deal with relating to being away from here for a long period of time. That would be my main hesitation, just dealing with family issues. Otherwise I think it's great working internationally."

Colleagues give well-intentioned warnings to women, as future mothers, to think ahead, but they do not give such warnings to men, who are just as— if not more—likely to be future fathers; this reproduces the perception that women, more than men, need to get international travel out of the way early, before having kids. Kevin, a full professor of mathematics, was even more discouraging: His advice to women colleagues was, "Don't get pregnant. Sorry." This biologizing take on women's prospects implies—and creates—extremely high fences for mothers, while suggesting that for fathers, parenting might be inconvenient and less than ideal but not something that should be avoided altogether. The discourse about the globalization of science thus depicts families as a special burden for women, while disguising the facts that men have families too and that family demands vary for everyone. Furthermore, it implies that, if women choose not to have children, they will not face any fences, a myth I dismantle in Chapter 4.

If we look more closely at the logistics for parents bringing their children on trips abroad, we find that while they certainly can be challenging,[15] their feasibility depends greatly on the destination, the institutional contexts, and the family itself. The nature of the international travel itself can also make a difference, depending on what kind of research is being undertaken, where, and for how long. For example, Alexandria, mentioned earlier, a full professor of oceanography who spends months at a time on a research ship, explained that she was not only the only woman on the ship, but it was also not possible to bring her children with her. Although the ship catered to the well-being of the scientists on board, providing food and cleaning services, it had no child care facilities or access to schools. Similarly, Aili Tripp, a full professor of social science, writes about how she conducted fieldwork in a politically unstable country with her son.[16] Academics in such situations or in remote regions may deem the risks calculable for themselves but insurmountable for their children. But beyond these clearly prohibitive situations, international locations vary in how challenging they are, what opportunities they provide for parents and children, and what fences exist, also depending on the specific situations in specific countries.

Fences and other challenges related to caregiving also depend on the families themselves as well as their (institutional) resources. How portable children are depends on their age, individual needs, and personal adaptability, as well as how they and their parents deal with challenges like time changes, language barriers, and different cultures and foods. As we will see later, parenting styles make a difference: What some parents consider impossible, others find exciting. And, finally, support systems and infrastructure also come into play, from the availability of support from partners and grandparents to day care and schooling options.

As with Diana, mentioned earlier, who felt that "if you have young children or babies, it's hard," discussions usually focus on taking young children abroad as more burdensome than taking older children. However, some parents find that older children are more complicated because they are more self-determined about their needs and expectations for schooling, activities, and friendships. When her daughter was young, Sydney, a single mother and associate professor of social science, took her on multiple trips to rural villages in Asia, but, as the daughter grew older, she began to resist because she did not like falling ill on these trips: "Eventually she told me, 'I do not want to go to do research with you.' So now I am writing a proposal for what I can do and also bring my daughter. I had to try to stay away from impoverished areas because she gets sick all the time, and now that she's older, she can say 'no' to me. When she was younger, she had to come." Another single mother could not convince her fifteen-year-old son to go abroad with her. He insisted on staying in school with his friends, so he lived with his aunt, while she arranged to shorten her research stay from a year to three months. This mother also remarked that if her son had been younger, he would not have had as much choice.

The more complicated reality of traveling with children of different ages is just one way in which the discourse about family as a burden for mothers of young children (usually assumed to be heterosexual and married) overlooks the ways today's families, relationships, and personal commitments are increasingly diverse and construct multiple barriers to mobility. When we examine this broader notion of families and further dissect what it means for faculty mobility, we identify a wide range of potential (often unaddressed) familial barriers that concern all kinds of faculty members. In short, the conventional discourse leaves out how family burdens can matter even for those who do not fit into the stereotypical heteronormative nuclear family with young children.

The legal ramifications of crossing national boundaries are another issue for faculty, one that concerns men and women alike, as well as extended family members. Although travel arrangements for married couples and their children are relatively simple, visa regulations are often not amenable to more complex relationships, including unmarried couples, other adult family members, or friends.[17] Faculty who intend to bring nonmarried partners or other adults with them as companions or caretakers for children often encounter cumbersome legal barriers. Jacqueline, a full professor of natural sciences, explained that, although her mother was willing to travel with her for a year in Africa, she had to fly back to the United States several times during the year because she could get only a three-month tourist visa. Along with the hassle, this workaround increased the costs of the trip, including the time and money for visa applications, alternative child care when the grandmother was gone, and transportation back and forth.

Custody arrangements can also create legal challenges. To bring her daughter on a two-month research trip to a European country, Alice, a full professor of engineering, had to petition the court for permission to override the father's refusal to let her leave the country with her child. Parents without formal custody rights, like some parents in same-sex relationships, can have difficulties taking children abroad. These examples suggest that the amplified burdens of parenthood apply not only to women in heterosexual married relationships but to many other parents whose identities and experiences must be considered when talking about the family as a factor in international travel.

The experiences of lesbian, gay, bisexual, transgender, and queer (LGBTQ) researchers in same-sex relationships, with or without children, further show the diverse legal and cultural familial challenges of international mobility. Some countries prohibit homosexuality altogether and actively target homosexual individuals. Even when homosexuality is legal or accepted, crossing borders can raise complicated legal and bureaucratic questions about recognizing partnerships or children's custody and adoption papers. Other countries—along with different regions, cities, or neighborhoods—can vary greatly in how welcoming they are for LGBTQ individuals and families. Living abroad might thus impose extra challenges but also opportunities to seek more inclusive, progressive places to live, especially for diverse families.

If we go a step further and consider that faculty have a variety of relationships and ties, we uncover further limitations to any simplistic discourse of family as barrier. Studying U.S. expatriates in global businesses, Tina Starr and Graeme Currie have argued that singles have families, too, beyond the nuclear family.[18] Single faculty also have social network ties and community responsibilities that may be even less portable than children or partners and which they may not—or may—be inclined to leave behind. In addition, faculty can have broader care issues—for themselves or other family members, friends, and neighbors—that may keep them from engaging in international travel. Larissa, a full professor of engineering, explained that she refrained from traveling because her mother was ill, while Donald, an associate professor of chemical sciences, noted that his wife's illness kept him from going on a sabbatical abroad. In this context, as well, such responsibilities concern both women and men. Although women do the lion's share of caring for relatives, men are also involved in these activities, albeit often in gendered ways, say, shoveling snow rather than cleaning or cooking.[19]

One final barrier that intensifies burdens for academics organizing personal and family commitments for international trips is finance. Taking a family abroad can entail expensive travel, language courses and translation, international health insurance for children and other dependents, and additional costs for housing, food, and other domestic expenditures. Unlike businesses, which tend to cover such costs to entice employees to go abroad, U.S. universities and funding agencies vary greatly in how they support faculty travel and research in general and international travel and research in particular. Few pay directly for travel and living costs for another adult or children, and many academics must thus depend on private financial resources.[20] Of course, this is not possible for everyone. Although senior professors generally earn relatively comfortable salaries, international mobility imposes financial burdens on many, constraining their options to combine family and work and thus reproducing differential access to such opportunities. For faculty with lower salaries, the financial obstacles can seem insurmountable. Gender comes back into play here when we recall that women, in general, tend to be concentrated in lower-paying academic ranks, fields, and academic institutions. Therefore, the lack of financial resources for faculty with care commitments should be considered a key fence.

For all academics, international travel requires resources of time, money, energy, and logistics. When work takes parents abroad, these needs and challenges converge with standard work–family conflict in a discourse of amplified burdens. These literal and figural costs are then framed discursively as gender-specific barriers because of the assumption that a conventional nuclear family with prescribed gender expectations is making these decisions. This assumption also erases the fact that institutions shape the contexts that constrain individual decisions. Funding agencies and institutions that regulate things like immigration and health insurance are not particularly accommodating when it comes to supporting the international mobility of academics with families, let alone academics with diverse families.[21] When they do try to address family issues, their focus on the heterosexual nuclear family with (young) children perpetuates the mother-centric discourse of barriers and negates the varied kinds of challenges and family models that, as we have just seen, actually characterize the experiences of faculty who undertake—or choose not to undertake—international research.

Making It Work: Gender, Strategies, and Guilt

Despite the familial challenges detailed in the previous pages, many academics with care commitments still choose to engage in international research and collaborations. In doing so, they face many real choices. Amy Lubitow and I found that the simplest choice is whether to go or not to go, a decision that of course can come at the expense of important research opportunities.[22] Once parents do decide to go, the next choice is whether to take the children with them or leave them at home to be taken care of by others. Some parents bring their whole families on trips abroad, including partners or other adults who can take care of the children.[23] Although many men can rely on partners to travel with them or stay home to take care of the children, many mothers recruit an array of people to take over their care work, either at home or when they travel, including partners, grandparents, other relatives, friends, neighbors, and nannies; they also supplement these caretakers with extended hours in child care. When these options do not solve their work–family conflicts, parents may compromise their research by changing fields or limiting international travel.

Still, mothers in particular make it work, even when they have to modify their research agendas, sabbaticals, and travel plans because of their families. For some women (and, notably, none of the men), the solution, sometimes temporary, was to stop international travel altogether when they got pregnant and their children were young.[24] Gabrielle, an assistant professor of Earth sciences, explained the adjustments she made:

> So I went over to [Asian Country] four times when I was a PhD student for my research and actually stopped going when I got pregnant. And took seven years off from research over there and then just this past year applied to get funding to go back and continue that research. After I had my son, I didn't go back for seven years. And I had another son in the middle of there. So basically I didn't apply to start this project back up again until my youngest child was old enough that I could leave him for a few weeks. I went in August for four weeks, and that was a really long time. I don't think I'm going to do that again. This time I'm going to be gone two weeks because I think that's more reasonable.

Gabrielle first waited for her child to be old enough, then limited her time away. Interestingly, though, in both strategies, she perceived motherhood and international research not as incompatible but as something to be worked out carefully. She did not decide to end her international research; rather, she decided when and how she could travel. Still, while some women explained their choices as temporary breaks, others, looking back, felt that having kids took them off the trajectory of international research for good.[25]

Some women also chose to reduce their overall time away from home by switching fields or shifting from field to experimental work; these changes allowed them to be closer to telephone access, take shorter trips, or work on local projects. Marine or geoscientists, social scientists, and other field researchers identify research topics and plan new projects that do not require long absences from home. Researchers conducting fieldwork try to organize shorter trips rather than going away for months at a time. Instead of multiple month-long field trips, for instance, several women discussed how a maximum of two weeks away seemed more doable. Sending graduate students and postdoctoral fellows or collaborators to do the observations, data collection, or other fieldwork is another strategy faculty reported. Other scholars mentioned how they moved to analysis of easily shared data aided by advances in computer technologies of data communication.

Although many scholars adapt their international research and conference commitments to make them more family friendly, there were some gender differences in how faculty talked about limiting their international travels.[26] Both mothers and fathers limited the length and frequency of their travels because of their children and/or partners, but men in general seemed more at ease with staying longer—five days or a week—for international conference travel and short-term visits. Several mothers, especially those with younger children, mentioned that they kept to a two-nights-away rule, which maximized the benefit while limiting the disruption at home. However, this was not feasible if the travel involved longer international flights.

As already noted, study participants shared the assumption that children have very limited portability and prevent their mothers, but not their fathers, from traveling internationally. Mothers talked about work–family conflicts as more burdensome than fathers did. This is similar to Mary Ann Mason's and Marc Goulden's findings in a study of University of California faculty that women with children were more than twice as likely as men with children to report that doing research away from home and attending conferences causes stress (about 46 versus 22 percent).[27] However, a few men did limit their travels because of family concerns. Jose, a full professor of engineering, found himself turning down an invitation to spend a semester in Japan in large part because of his family. It is important to note, however, that the data do not reveal the full extent to which mothers and fathers differ in accommodating their work to family considerations, in good part because it is not clear whether men did not have these experiences, women were simply more conscious of them, or the focus group and interview situation made it more legitimate and socially acceptable for women to point to family responsibilities as a research constraint.[28]

Parenting and Guilt

Although the strategies mothers developed to maintain at least some degree of engagement in international research and collaboration involved compromises, adaptations, and cutbacks, women still expressed more work–family conflict than men. Lara, an assistant professor of biology, explained that work–family "balance" is a myth: "You think that the balance exists, but there is no such thing. I do have a family and do have a life, so I must do it. But it is extremely challenging." As other studies have found, mothers used much stronger language than fathers in pointing out the effects of their family commitments, the hardships they felt, and the heavier burdens they bore.[29] Beatrice, a social science assistant professor, explained how difficult international travel would be for her:

> So it wasn't as though I could say to my husband, "I'll be away for three days, can you take care of this?" What I would do is take care of it all. He will be picked up by this person; he will be dropped off by that person on these three days . . . So while I was away, I accommodated for all my usual activities and didn't impinge on my husband at all.

This mother worried about the potential stress even a brief trip would cause for her family. She felt responsible for making alternate arrangements for her child's transportation to and from day care so as not to "impinge" on her husband. The ways in which women themselves frame these issues provide important insight into their beliefs about the causes of these burdens and their limited mobility. In turn, identifying these factors can highlight potential solutions to these challenges, which I address in Chapter 6.

Martha, a full professor of physical sciences, pointed out that even though her children are now in high school and college she feels still that traveling is a burden on them:

> My kids are older, but still it's there . . . I'll tell you I'm a little nervous about doing this. It's the longest I've ever been away since they've been little. Men do this all the time, but I'm not comfortable in doing this, and I'm doing it because

I thought once they were older it was OK . . . But even the nineteen-year-olds need you. So that's always going to be a problem. You do the best you can . . .

Contemporary U.S. child-rearing practices set the context for the expectations mothers and fathers place on themselves about good parenting. Gendered ideologies of parenting create a discourse of guilt for absent parents that seems to be felt more strongly by women than by men, in particular because mothers are expected to be omnipresent whereas fathers can be absent at times and still be good parents. Like Martha, other mothers talked about guilt for leaving their children behind when they traveled because they felt their children needed them. They also felt they could not burden their partners and other family members with their absence for too long. Martina, an associate professor of social sciences, described her situation with her three-year-old son and husband as a no-way-out situation:

I can't carry him as a package, yet I also can't dump him on my husband, who's also an academic and works seven days a week. So, if you ask me how children and international collaboration works, I have no answer to it. I think it does not work. Unless you're super rich and you have five nannies whom you can travel with or you can leave them at home day and night, . . . otherwise no. I can't abandon my child; when I abandon my child for a couple of weeks for research trips, it's a major life crisis. . . . Yeah, this part of the question, I have no answer to it; I'm sure some other people are doing a better job than me, but I'm failing.

Fathers did not express such guilt, perhaps because they did not have the same internalized sense of responsibility for being physically present with their children or perhaps because their social environment does not hold them accountable as it does mothers. Petra, an associate professor of geosciences, described how her neighbors challenged her when she took a two-week trip to a European country that she had put off for years. Although she had arranged for the grandparents to stay with her family in her absence, the neighbors were stunned that she would leave her husband in charge of the kids for so long. But when her husband went on frequent trips and she stayed home with the children alone, none of her friends, family, or neighbors complained about her husband's behavior or pitied her for being left with full responsibility for the kids.

These feelings of guilt and mothers being held accountable by others illustrate what Sharon Hays calls "intensive mothering," in which women equate good motherhood with being present in their children's lives to the largest extent possible.[30] The discourse of intensive mothering frames experiences and interpretations of everyday mothering and fathering in families.[31] The idea of intensive motherhood is an example of gendered cultures around parenthood, one that brings particular expectations of physical proximity for mothers. It is also a class phenomenon, closely related to today's "helicopter parents" of older children, similarly reflecting trends in middle-class child-rearing practices described by Annette Laureau.[32]

It is important to note that mothers varied in how much guilt they expressed about being absent from home. Some mothers enjoyed "time off" from their children and partners, although also admitting that it could be considered less socially acceptable. For example, while spending an evening with friends at conferences, Ariel, an associate professor of social science, admitted after having a drink or two that she considered getting a good night's sleep in the hotel without her children waking her up at night a form of bliss. So spending time on an overnight work trip, away from duties at home and lives organized by family schedules, can also be a (guilty) delight.

Fathers face quite different expectations. One dominant discourse of fatherhood is the responsibility of the breadwinner to pursue his career and work wherever it takes him (including abroad), even if this means having to be away from his family.[33] This makes the discourse on absent fathers quite different from that on absent mothers. The discourse of guilt based on social expectations also applies less to fathers than to mothers.[34] When James, an assistant professor of chemical sciences, asked his department chair to support his travel to an international conference because he did not have the funds himself, he framed his reasoning in the context of his family: "Otherwise [without the departmental support], I am out on my own, and so, I'm a young guy, recent family, new family, you know, I'm worried about being about to pay for it. I'm willing to go still because I want to represent [my university] internationally, so I think the financial support is a huge barrier." Being with his children was not an issue; rather, his family created a financial barrier that he was determined to overcome to do his work.

Although physical proximity is not an expectation for fathers, some fathers did talk about making arrangements around their families as part of being a good partner and father. Craig, a social science associate professor whose wife works full time as a university administrator, took his family into account in his travel plans: "This trip, even, is short because I can't be away from my family, too long. . . . So if you have young kids and a partner, you can't strand them with the young kids for long periods of time." Although he was aware of his obligations to his family, Craig noted that he still had more liberty to travel for work than his wife did, demonstrating that gendered structures persist. Karl, an associate professor of natural sciences, also acknowledged that he felt the severity of parental guilt differently from the way his wife did: "Ideally, [an equal partnership] would be our goal. We don't live up to [it]. I don't live up to it. Because I can get away with being less good than I should, and my wife does not. I am sure she would agree that she does more than I do. But I still . . . I'm at least cognizant of it and do not try to exploit it."

Whereas fathers experience less pressure to feel guilty for being gone, active fathers do feel desire as well as pressure to spend more time with their children and be good partners to their wives. Daniel, a full professor of physical sciences, frequently had family issues on his mind:

We are all in that boat basically. So it's really hard on my family whenever I travel. I have five kids, so when I'm gone for a couple of weeks it's really, really tough on my wife. And one of my graduate students has a son who's about a year old, and so we went to Seattle for a meeting last month and that was kind of tough arranging things with his wife and getting it all set up because it was rough on her. So, yeah, we deal with those kinds of issues pretty frequently.

Some fathers noted that they missed their families when they went away, whereas others said they felt guilty for not being home. Kevin, a social scientist and associate professor, explained that "I do want to spend time with my kids, and I would aspire to be that perfect kind of dad, and the perfect academic, and then reality sets in. So, yes, I miss . . . I talked to my son on the phone from the airport this morning." Similarly, Marian, a full professor of natural sciences, observed how one of her international visitors found it difficult to be away from his family: "He had children at home whom he said he missed terribly over the five weeks here. He talked to them on Skype with a computer camera every night. So he was able to leave, but it was still painful."

Given the different sets of gendered expectations for parents, it is not surprising that the discourses of fatherhood, particularly that of fathers as breadwinners, are more compatible with international engagement than the discourses of motherhood, particularly that of intensive mothering. Mothers clearly felt the pressures on them, as evident in the ways they shifted their professional practice once they had children and the guilt they expressed about their absences. Yet fathers did seem to be increasingly attuned to their parental responsibilities, both in their choices about travel and in the feelings they expressed. Interestingly, though, while most faculty members talk about children as an issue that can stand in the way of their research, few point out how the ideological expectations of intensive mothering or institutional factors, like limited funding and support, are also significant reasons that they feel constrained in their mobility.

Partners Matter

The difficulty of international research collaborations for parents depends in large part on whether they have supportive partners and networks to help them take care of their children and household tasks. Since the elimination of nepotism rules in the 1970s, more academics have sought to combine two career paths in one family. Dual academic couples are quite common, especially for women in STEM fields, who are likely to be coupled with other academics and sometimes even with academics in the same discipline.[35] Navigating both expectations and opportunities for international mobility, whether for conference travel and short-term research visits or for visiting positions and long-term appointments, poses challenges for all couples.

Keeping the Fires Burning:
Gendered Divisions of Labor in the Home

Family responsibilities are not unchangeable facts that inevitably burden women and mothers but depend on how couples arrange parenting and housework. In other words, whether and how much women and men perceive family responsibilities as a burden with regard to international travel varies according to how couples divide caregiving and other domestic duties or outsource them. Although research suggests that these divisions have shifted to a slight degree, studies show that the gender division of labor in families of women faculty remains uneven: More mothers than fathers are primary caregivers for children, women often carry the responsibilities for children, and they do the lion's share of domestic work.[36] As Scott Coltrane and others have found, whereas men have increased their share of playing with children, women continue to take on the major responsibilities of organizing the household, doing the everyday time-consuming care of laundry, cooking, feeding, bathing, and bedtime, and arranging other types of care, schools, doctor's appointments, and the like. Men tend to get involved in tasks that are of a periodic and less essential nature, like maintenance, that include changing the oil in cars and yard work, that is, activities that *can wait*. By contrast, women carry the responsibility for urgent and frequently reoccurring tasks that *cannot wait*, like drop-off and pickup at child care or activities.[37] Women have, however, decreased their overall time spent on housework, largely by outsourcing it as paid work to others.[38]

When parents travel internationally, their absence makes the division of labor more visible; not surprisingly, the absence of a parent who handles crucial tasks is felt heavily by the other parent. Richard, a full professor of chemical sciences and father in a dual-career couple, described how he can manage during his wife's absences only by working part time, whereas when he travels, his duties and responsibilities can wait until his return:

> We have a pretty even split in terms of how we manage the family. But, the split is, she manages the kids a lot more, and I manage the house a lot more, like getting stuff done around the house. When I go on a trip, the stuff around the house can sort of sit, but the biggest issue is who drops off the kids at daycare, who picks them up, who gets the boy to the Cub Scouts. And that's really, really hard—it's really hard. So when I go, she takes over, and when she goes, she's going to a conference this week, and I'm taking three days this week. I'm going to be working half days because, if I drop them off, if I pick them up, there's only four hours in between that time that I actually do anything, so it's a little bit more than an equitable balance.

As well, couples need to negotiate the extra work that accompanies international travel, such as arranging child care (whether the kids are left at home or come along), handling schooling issues, and temporarily organizing two households. Given the persistent gender division of labor with regard to regular duties, it is not surprising that women felt that these planning and organizing tasks—including leaving long to-do lists for their partners and others who cared for the children and household—fell mostly on them. By contrast, several men felt they were dispensable, because they primarily saw themselves as helping out at home. Timothy, a full professor of Earth and atmospheric science, explained, "Well, to be honest, they're both older now. . . . Even at the time they were both in school. My wife works full time as well. But it was not a big imposition. I mean if it was for a month or so, yeah, that would be a problem. But a week here and there is not a big deal." His sense that his absence was not significant was closely related to seeing himself as replaceable in caregiving duties, by his partner or others. Walter, a father and associate professor of engineering, explained that he felt comfortable with his mother jumping in and covering for him, although he noted that his wife did not feel that way when she went away.

Those in dual-career couples can rely less than those with stay-home partners that their partners pick up the slack, though women whose partners are also academics feel more supported than women whose partners are employed in businesses.[39] Commuting relationships are especially common in dual-career academic couples, leaving some women faculty de facto single during the week or even the entire semester. Kristen, an assistant professor of social science, explained:

> For me, that's huge. When you have a partner who has a job that is also extremely demanding, I can't count that he's going to be home for a week, and especially since he's working out of state right now. So I'm literally taking care of the kid on my own and seeing him on weekends. So it's even more difficult right now to imagine doing that. Thankfully, I have good child care—my parents can help out—so it's doable. But it's not—I can't sort of drop everything and go tomorrow if something interesting pops up. I imagine there are people in similar situations who are much more restricted in the ease with which they can try these things out.

Commuting relationships thus create extra challenges and constraints for parental mobility, constraints that are again gendered. Parents with primary responsibility for their children have to rely entirely on outside help to organize their family commitments when they travel, or they need to take their children with them. Although some women commute back and forth to their families, more often women are the temporarily single parents. These gendered structures of the division of labor in the home create gendered inequalities in the ease with which mothers and fathers can go on international trips.

Portability and Support:
How Partners Make a Difference

Having a portable—or at least supportive—partner is an important factor in faculty mobility. What I call "portable partners" are partners or spouses who are in a situation in which they can and are willing to adjust their lives to travel with their partner for short-, medium-, or longer-term stays.[40] Challenging the conventional thinking that children are the main hindrance to travel, I argue that, although children are clearly one factor that shapes international mobility, particularly for mothers but also for fathers, partnerships, which can re-create gendered inequalities, are often underestimated as shapers of mobility for both women and men. Whereas portable partners easily accompany an internationally traveling academic, supportive partners are willing to stay back and continue to provide emotional support while managing the household, family, and social life in the traveler's absence. Both kinds of partners can be crucial to enabling faculty mobility and collaborations. Although having a portable partner has always been an issue for women, today it is also a concern for men, who can rely less on their partners' short- and medium-term geographic mobility—or on their ability, due to their own careers, to function effectively as stay-at-home supportive partners. Hence, partner portability needs to be considered a changing, gendered variable. Indeed, although having children makes international travel more complicated for dual-career couples, children themselves can be more portable than partners. Patrick, a full professor of biomedical sciences, reasoned:

> And then there are family issues. What do you do with the children when you go abroad for a year? I mean I'm talking about long term, like for a sabbatical. . . . It's difficult to find a research opportunity for both husband and wife. We increasingly see that we have husband and wife getting the faculty positions in universities.

Gendered expectations for partnerships clearly persist. When men talked about their wives, they expected them to be accommodating, deferring their own needs and expectations to support the mobility of their husbands, which they saw as crucial for their own career. Peter, an associate professor of engineering, pointed out:

> If it is only one week or something, most of the time these trips are about a week or so, so I guess they are used to this pattern. I mean, they are used to the pattern of me disappearing two or three days when I go to the domestic conferences; it is only a little bit longer than that, so they're fine with it. I mean, they know that this is part of the job, and it happens frequently.

Similarly, Harold, a full professor of Earth sciences, explained that his wife was supportive and reasoned: "I do have kids, but my family is quite understanding because I keep it to a minimum. I try and be realistic about it. So no, I would say no. Most of my trips are just to meetings and conferences. So I would say my usual trip is one week to ten days."

By contrast, women who mentioned partners expressed gratitude and cast them as providing exceptional support that was not taken for granted. Indeed, when women discussed their decisions about conducting research abroad, those who talked about being able to leave used a discourse of grateful appreciation toward their supportive partners. Joan, an associate professor of natural sciences, emphasized her husband's support: "I have one son and a very supportive husband with a very full-time career. At times, it was hard, but having a really supportive partner is the crucial thing."

A few women had portable partners whom they could bring along on trips, which they clearly appreciated. Cara, an associate professor of social sciences, recalled, "My husband has a very flexible job. And so, in that respect, when we had children, it was very easy for him to accompany me if he wanted to, which was not always the case." Like Cara, some women noted that, although they were lucky to have such supportive partners, it was also work to negotiate that supportiveness. Hanna, a full professor of social science, explained:

> Well, first of all, I was in a very unusual marriage. I had a feminist husband long before the word was even used. So, and I think; by the way, that is an important point . . . that you have to work this out case by case. That's how they deal with it. There is no normative; there is no collective; there is no expectation. Everybody has to figure it out themselves. And that's why it's so time consuming. That's why it's so burdensome. Because there are no rules for this. And I just lucked out. Or however you want to put it. So that I was able, first of all, my husband traveled with me. He was able to do so.

Hanna's comments reveal an awareness that her situation was exceptional, which in turn points to the ways institutional supports are missing for women's travel, and neither logistics nor ideologies are favorable toward women who travel.

Indeed, many women clearly felt that it was not legitimate to leave their kids under the charge of their husbands for long. As Martina reflected earlier, it was hard for her to leave her child behind. Similarly, Mary, a full professor of Earth sciences, explained that she could not ask her husband to cover for her at length "because I have kids at home, and my husband kind of runs out of patience." Internalizing the intensive mothering ideology, women expressed deep ambivalence about the effect of their absences on their children and partners. And Martha, who previously had explained how her travel was a burden on her children, pointed to the guilt she felt even though she had waited to travel until her children were older: "When my kids were younger, I just didn't travel. And at a point when they were teenagers, which I think they needed me quite a bit, I didn't travel. But now, I'm traveling way too much and thinking it's OK because they are older, but I don't think it's OK, if you want to know the truth. I think I'm traveling too much."

Constructions of gendered partnerships underlie these notions that mothers cannot be gone, leading to the discourse that blames the presence of children for mobility challenges, while rendering partner support—and lack thereof—invisible.[41] The gendered discourses and constructions of what it means to be a good partner and what women can expect from their partners make it difficult for them to imagine that their partners will go with them, make career sacrifices to be with them, or stay home and take care of the family while they are gone.

An important shift is taking place, however, producing an alternative discourse, one that holds that men with families have responsibilities that go beyond being the breadwinner and might impede their 24/7 dedication to career, flexibility, and mobility. Especially among younger men, this discourse signals a change in attitudes, as men engage more actively in their families and, even more, seek to be good (egalitarian) partners. Men felt less at ease leaving their wives at home with the children, as shown earlier, especially when the wives had their own careers. Academic partners talked about taking turns attending conferences or deciding to limit their travels because they perceived the high burden their absence placed on their partners. Kevin, an associate professor of natural science, explained:

> I very seldom travel internationally; she goes to more U.S.-based conferences. It's basically more a function of time away from work than it is time away from family. She knows that I'll manage. And she knows that I would support her to go wherever she needs to go, but I think it's pretty clear, in terms of, I don't like to go on business travel because I don't like straining her because she has all these pressures, the same kinds of pressures I have. I don't like it when she dumps it on me, and I don't like to dump it on her for the same reason.

In a subtle way, men in dual-career couples are becoming more like women, as neither are guaranteed to have stay-at-home partners. And although some women and men continue to take gendered inequalities for granted, international travel raises awareness of gendered discrepancies, which has the potential to create more room for couples to negotiate.

Discourse and Its Discontents

Constructions of motherhood and the gender division of labor at home create gendered expectations that continue to constrain mothers' choices about international travel and contribute to the discourse that mothers, especially those with young children, cannot be expected to engage in international travel. By contrast, constructions of fatherhood combine with the same gender division of labor to position fathers as secondary caregivers, which makes their travel choices more flexible. Those who see themselves solely as breadwinners can feel more at ease about being gone and leaving their partners to take care of the children and home. The data here do not tell us to what extent fathers or mothers accommodate their families; there are some indications, however, that fathers today are taking their children and partners into account when making choices regarding international travel and mobility. Still, mothers seem to feel a more extensive set of pressures, both ideological and practical, and the constraints felt by men remain invisible in the discourse that families are a burden only for women with children.

There is no doubt that there are fences for mothers and that individual mothers may perceive international travel as more cumbersome. Mothers *and* fathers should be free to cut back on travel to accommodate families without being punished professionally. However, my concern is that the focus on family as a fence, that is, the discourse of family as a specifically maternal burden, can influence the opportunities offered to women, including invitations to workshops and conferences abroad, as well as important international collaborations. For, despite these complications and burdens, many women are making family, work, and travel happen, and they should have opportunities to engage in international research. The other significant effect of this discourse is that it renders invisible both the role of partners, positive and negative, and the deeply problematic lack of institutional support. In other words, it flattens a more complex social and political landscape into a simplistic view of individualized gendered burdens and choices.

Choosing (Family) Mobility:
Professional and Personal Benefits

Although the discourse of family as a burden is clearly powerful, it does not take into account the ways families can be a motivating and supportive force for faculty traveling abroad. Indeed, international mobility provides parents with multiple opportunities to pursue their goals and values. Taking children and other family members along on international travel can be a personally rewarding experience for everyone. Having a portable family can even make it easier for researchers to go to distant, remote areas that single people might perceive as too socially isolated, especially if the local communities are organized around families.

Of course, parents vary in how feasible they consider international travel and living abroad. Like Isabella at the beginning of the chapter, who decided earlier in career not to go to Africa for her research because of her husband and most recently chose to spend her sabbatical with shorter trips to California rather than a longer stay in Latin America because of her teenage children, some interviewees explained that sabbatical stays abroad were impossible because of their family commitments. For others, children were a motivating factor because they wished to give their children the experience of living abroad. They saw international travel and research as enriching experiences for themselves, their partners, their children, and other family members. In this discourse, international research appears as a perk of academia and a privilege academics can share with their families.

The discourse of family as a burden also leaves out the ways children can be helpful in building relationships with colleagues and even research participants and others abroad. Ruth, a full professor of health sciences, noted that bringing her family along created strong ties with her collaborators, who housed her and her family in their home. When the collaborators came to the United States, she returned the favor, and their family stayed with her. Ruth credits the bonds created through these family visits with deepening their professional relationships and contributing to a positive collaboration. For Carla, a full professor of biological sciences, traveling to India with her children opened doors, as people felt at ease interacting with her via her children. Tripp points to studies of women anthropologists who took their children along on their fieldwork, which enabled them to build a different quality of relationships with local people, families in particular.[42] Being a mother can garner legitimacy and respect in some communities; it can also serve as a commonality to help build rapport.[43]

Although social ties can prevent faculty mobility, for some faculty, familial and social relationships are driving forces behind spending time outside the United States. Faculty who have spent time abroad might relish showing their families places where they have ties from previous visits, and international faculty based in the United States enjoy taking their partners and children back home. In this discourse of transnational lives, extended research trips abroad allow academics to immerse themselves and their children in other cultures and languages, often while closer to extended families and friends. Rodrigo, a Latino full professor of engineering, felt that living abroad in a Spanish-speaking country was an important experience for his children: Living in an environment where they shared the dominant language and belonged to the dominant culture enabled them to be in the majority for at least that summer. In addition, Paul, a full professor of Earth sciences, who is white and whose wife is Southeast Asian, explained that he preferred to go on sabbatical in a city that promised a multiracial, multicultural environment for his children, rather than a neighborhood with a predominately white population. These concerns show how families and ties matter in faculty mobility.

Some faculty valued the unique educational experiences international mobility provided their children. John, a full professor of social sciences, married to another social scientist, said that they chose to go on their international sabbatical before their kids finished high school, so they could take advantage of a high school year abroad. Middle-class values place a high estimation on cultural competencies gained from exposure to other cultures in other countries where children can learn about the world.[44] This is in line with Pierre Bourdieu's notion of cultural capital: International (educational) experiences are seen as symbolizing taste, a cosmopolitan worldview, and a sophistication associated with the upper middle class.[45] Top-tier U.S. colleges expect young people to speak multiple languages as part of being cultured.[46] For parents, then, and especially academic parents, strategic exposure to different cultures makes children better rounded while also serving to maintain class status.

On the practical side, although child care arrangements abroad can be as cumbersome and costly as they are in the United States, in some European countries parents can rely on cheaper, high-quality, publicly funded child care. International parents benefited from kinship networks abroad that took care of their children while they conducted research. In countries where domestic labor is less expensive than in the United States, parents were able to afford privatized care for their children, though these decisions could also be fraught, entailing discomfort with language barriers or cultural differences regarding child-rearing practices.[47] Although international mobility is often depicted as expensive, lower costs for child care abroad could sometimes offset extra expenses. Furthermore, for academics whose care commitments are abroad because their families do not live in the United States, combining research and family commitments can be enabled through international research stays. In all these benefits, we see the practical limits of the discursive construction of family as a burden for international travel and international travel as a burden for families.

Family ties might also be a motivating factor as something to escape from. Annett, a full professor of engineering, reasoned that she chose to go on her sabbatical year in Europe away from her husband as a way to figure out whether she still wanted to be with him, and they did get divorced the following year. Before being certain about whether to leave an unhappy intimate relationship, being far away allows faculty to consider the next steps in their personal lives, sometimes enabling them to mend these struggling relationships or serving as the precursor to separation or divorce.

Furthermore, family responsibilities, especially in extended families, can be perceived as a burden. Evelyn talked about how temporarily living abroad allowed her to escape what she perceived as too protective and demanding extended families, with expectations of closeness, frequent contact, spending all holidays together, and so on. Although financial commitments might persist vis-à-vis families, for women like Evelyn, being on another continent, with more expensive, longer flights, time differences, and a sea in between shielded them from intrusiveness of family members they did not appreciate at home. Cecilia Manrique and Gabriel Manrique argue similarly that women academics migrating to the United States were also driven by the desire to break away from confining gendered cultures in their home countries.[48] Families at a geographic distance will have less opportunity to use social control and hold women accountable for norms and expectations of certain "gendered" behaviors. Hence, in these cases, family responsibilities did not stand in the way of mobility; instead, mobility brought the opportunity to retreat from these imposed commitments, creating incentives to overcome fences and other obstacles.

Fences Are Not Equal

The gendered discourse about family as a barrier for academics engaged in international research depicts family—and more specifically children—as on the one hand, primarily a barrier for women, a glass fence, and on the other, the key barrier women face. As a result, children are viewed as obstacles that prevent women from engaging in international research and collaborations. When work takes faculty abroad, the work–family conflict can certainly be amplified by the extra burdens international research imposes on caregivers. However, there is a huge variation in how individuals handle these challenges, and many faculty members find ways to manage them and continue with their international collaborations and travel. Rather than barriers, then, families can constitute challenges for both women and men, albeit to different gendered degrees. And the diversity of today's family arrangements means that these fences can be more or less difficult for women to climb over. Contrary to the conventional discourse as well, families can provide opportunities for faculty, offering crucial support and motivation for international mobility, or, to continue the metaphor, serving as ladders with which to scale fences. It is safe to say that the fences are slowly becoming lower for women and higher for men, although women continue to do the most climbing.

Today, the institutions of family, kinship structures, and gender relations are undergoing profound transformations, becoming increasingly diverse and shaped by globalization, which for academics increases the viability of leading transnational lives.[49] These changes add to the complexity families have long brought to academic mobility. The diversity of living arrangements is gradually eroding the model of the male breadwinner. Single parents and dual-career couples challenge the assumption that men—and women—can rely on partners at home to hold down the fort or portable partners to accompany them. And family demands include not only child care but also caring for disabled, ill, or elderly family members and friends.

Still, when faculty members and policy makers alike discuss family as an issue, they usually refer first to how children limit women's mobility and then, more recently, to the concerns of dual-career couples. This discourse of family as a problem for women with children obscures the diversity of families and the different issues at stake in family mobility. Instead of lumping all domestic social bonds under the rubric of family, separating issues of children and partners, while also recognizing the profoundly gendered nature of both, will enable individuals both to identify and legitimately embrace solutions and to better inform policy decisions.

This chapter finds that familiar and other social commitments for both women and men faculty create situations in which they face challenges in meeting the needs of their research and other expectations of academic mobility. In the absence of institutional supports with regard to both funding and flexibility, the individual strategies couples adopt to meet these challenges can reproduce and amplify gendered inequalities in both families and academia, creating one more reason for the underrepresentation of women, especially in internationalizing STEM fields.

This chapter thus shows that families must be a crucial consideration as universities and funding agencies devise internationalization strategies. Faculty who are less mobile because of family responsibilities may be put at a further disadvantage by not being able to engage in promising research and career opportunities abroad. If funding agencies and academic institutions do not provide institutional help for academics with families, the conclusions drawn in this chapter suggest that these obstacles will keep more women than men from participating and benefiting from international research collaborations and more generally the globalizing world of science. Thus, families indeed can constitute fences; which institutional supports could address more to reduce these fences, as we will see in the next chapter.

6 Toward an Inclusive World of (Global) Academia

I live my life in widening circles that reach out across the world.
Rainer Maria Rilke[1]

ACADEMIA IN THE UNITED STATES IS IN A PERIOD OF TRANSI-tion that can be read as threatening, exciting, or both. As scientific and technological knowledge production becomes increasingly globalized, U.S. academia both faces challenges to its dominance and has opportunities for repositioning itself. The pressures to compete globally have brought international research collaborations into the spotlight, especially as a way for U.S. institutions to maintain and improve their own profiles. As the nature of academic work more broadly shifts toward increased collaboration at both the national and international levels, international collaborations expand the pool of experts with specialized knowledge, skills, and access to local resources who can work together. In the increasingly competitive academic world, internationally coauthored articles are published in higher-ranked journals and receive more citations than other publications.

In this book, I have explored both the effects of these global dynamics on U.S. faculty and universities and how faculty negotiate these changes. I argue that because international collaborations are the next frontier for faculty—women in particular—they must be approached consciously and strategically, as the globalization of academia is a deeply contradictory process structured in gendered ways.[2] Internationalization entails both glass fences that reproduce gendered inequalities, and opportunities, like the .edu bonus, that allow faculty to escape and challenge them. Given the intertwined status inscriptions based on both gender and specific academic nationalities, international research collaborations carry gendered meanings, and the globalization of academia (re-)creates the stratified organization of academic work. Yet the globalization of academia is an ongoing process that stakeholders—including policy makers, funding agencies, universities, research centers, professional associations, and faculty members—are continually shaping and reshaping. This is particularly visible in the push for further corporatization and managerialism of higher education, which threaten to exacerbate inequalities and discriminations in academia while providing some tools to tackle with gender inequalities, thus creating paradoxes for the promotion of gender equality, as Myra Marx Ferree and I discuss elsewhere.[3] The stakeholders can create global academia in exclusive ways—or seize the opportunity to create a new world of inclusive academia.

Some of these stakeholders are crucial gatekeepers who provide the intellectual, personnel, financial, and logistical supports, resources, opportunities, and networks that make international collaborations possible. The ways they shape these supports can provide crucial incentives and disincentives for international collaboration overall, and for women and minorities in particular. If they use a gendered ideal of the hyperflexible, international, elite academic entrepreneur to design these supports, they risk re-creating gendered inequalities. My research provides two key lessons for funding agencies and universities who want to promote international collaborations and gender equality in academia and thus to create a more inclusive world of global academia.

- First, identifying, eliminating, and supporting faculty in overcoming obstacles is crucial for promoting faculty research collaborations abroad and moving U.S. research institutions and funding agencies toward a more globally oriented academic world.
- Second, funding agencies and universities could shape this globalizing world in more inclusive ways and promote the participation of all faculty in international endeavors by creating internationalization strategies that tackle obstacles and glass fences and by ensuring that diversity policies promote engagement in international research and academia.

Eliminating Obstacles

International collaborations are an inherently diverse form of faculty activity because they involve multiple people, places, and forms of knowledge production and exchange. They thus pose challenges for organizations that are oriented toward locally or even nationally based research. As a result, despite their privileged position in the highly stratified world of academia worldwide, U.S. faculty face obstacles when they attempt to collaborate internationally. Although their relatively low international engagement can be explained partly by the sheer size and research capacity of U.S. science and academia in general, I argue that obstacles for all faculty keep them from greater involvement in international research collaborations.

Although funding agencies and universities express a commitment to promoting scientific knowledge, internationalization, and gender equality, they nevertheless create—or reproduce—obstacles that impede these aims. I argue that these obstacles reflect an organizational context characterized by an absence of consistent internationalization strategies, which in turn creates contradictions, including a national academic environment that undervalues international collaborations. The resulting obstacles are material (pertaining to financial and other resources), bureaucratic, cultural, and even symbolic. Funding agencies and universities need to review their policies, eliminate unnecessary rules that create barriers to faculty mobility and collaboration, and develop internationalization strategies that recognize the diversity of both research needs and the needs of the scholars who conduct that research.

Promoting Gender Equality through Diversity and Internationalization

Fences make international research and collaboration particularly difficult for women and so reveal the gendered nature of globalization of scientific and engineering knowledge. This should not be surprising to those familiar with gender critiques of academia, for universities as organizations have long been criticized for having deeply gendered practices, cultures, and structures. My research reveals that global academia has similar structures. But it does not have to. Some of these fences are based on the conventional ideas that family is a barrier to women's careers and that women's competence and leadership skills are not accepted in other countries. My research reveals the limitations of these assumptions. Family is not necessarily a fence solely for women, especially when we recognize the diversity of family constellations in which faculty live today, and many women—and men—are actively engaged in scaling

that fence. When they reach the other sides of fences, women can be successful abroad, especially when the .edu bonus comes into play.

Still, the power of these assumptions, combined with the gendered organization of scientific work, means that funding agencies and universities risk
inadvertently perpetuating existing gender inequalities if their strategies do
not take those inequalities into account. But although tearing down fences
should be their goal, they should not push faculty to succeed internationally
in ways that create undue additional burdens.

It is important to keep in mind that, as a result of the .edu bonus, which
makes academic nationality more salient than gender for U.S. scholars, international collaborations can provide women with important openings for
intellectual engagement, advancement of their scholarship, and professional
and personal empowerment. As Vincent Larivière and his collaborators
reason, "Because collaboration is one of the main drivers of research output and scientific impact, programmes fostering international collaboration
for female researchers might help to level the playing field."[4] Ironically, then,
certain inequalities in (global) academia can help women escape gendered
inequalities. Opportunities for visibility and career development through international collaborations can thus be especially meaningful for women and
others marginalized at home, including individuals from minority groups in
the United States.

Moving Forward

Stakeholders who are aware of both international opportunities and fences
can devise inclusive institutional strategies for internationalization that contribute to the goal of broadening U.S. participation internationally, which
in turn can contribute to increased gender equality in academia both at
home and abroad. In the following sections, I discuss strategies to promote
a more inclusive international scientific world, using key insights from my
research to offer specific suggestions for how funding agencies and institutions can promote internationalization in ways that are more inclusive while
also internationalizing gender equality and diversity strategies in academia.
Existing equality efforts frequently do not consider the international aspects
of academic work, while internationalization strategies of funding agencies
and universities frequently do not take gender or diversity into account. My

research suggests some concrete steps stakeholders can take to integrate gender equality, diversity concerns, and internationalization strategies.

The key findings of this study also have implications for future research. Although I have been able to answer some of the questions that have driven my research, there remains much to learn about gender and the globalization of scientific and engineering knowledge more broadly, and I provide suggestions for future study. I conclude by arguing that the project of integrating women into STEM fields and academia more broadly needs to be conceived globally rather than nationally, international dimensions of academic work have to be taken into account, and internationalization and diversity efforts must move forward hand in hand, as part of a larger effort to create a truly inclusive academic world.

Strategies for Eliminating Obstacles

Funding agencies and universities have the capacity to create internationalization strategies without fences if they are purposefully mindful of the implications of program design and implementation.

Focus on Faculty

Faculty are the central actors who build international connections and networks, contributing not only to knowledge and scientific innovation but also to meaningful long-term institutional relationships.[5] These relationships benefit their own research and teams, as well as the work of postdoctoral researchers, graduate students, and undergraduate students across the university. Their efforts thus educate future scientists and academics while contributing to a more broadly skilled U.S. labor force. When institutional internationalization strategies focus on support for faculty, they take a crucial step toward sustainable long-term dynamics, not only in research but also in the university teaching mission, contributing to increased global competencies of all participants.

- Institutions could support faculty-introduced and -driven initiatives.[6]

Provide Resources

Faculty perceive funding and time as primary obstacles that prevent engagement in international collaborations.[7] Funding agencies and universities often fail to offer sufficient resources, including funds for research, travel, or even hosting collaborators. Faculty also often perceive funding for international projects as limited and the application process and administration cumbersome. When funding agencies and universities hesitate to support international research projects or make it difficult to obtain that support, only high-status faculty in privileged institutions have the resources—funding, administrative support, autonomy—to engage in high-risk but potentially high-reward international projects. Because women often occupy less privileged academic places, gendered inequalities are particularly likely to be reproduced when it is difficult to gain access to the resources to participate in international research and collaborations. In sum, lack of resources for international research leads to significant equity issues and perpetuates existing hierarchies.

To create more equal access to international research, universities and funding agencies should consider how they can best support the necessary competencies and infrastructure for international collaborations, from compensating faculty for their (extra) costs and time to increasing administrative staff allocations and reducing teaching loads—all moves that would help overburdened faculty at less-resourced universities create and manage international opportunities. In designing these supports, U.S. funding agencies can learn much from European agencies, which have more experience in overcoming national administrative obstacles and have created more mechanisms for facilitating cross-national collaborations.

- Funding agencies could increase incentives and financial supports for collaborations.
- Funding agencies could reduce opportunity costs for proposals for international research funding through measures such as joint review processes with international funding agencies, which would reduce the complexity of planning, budgets, and regulations faced by international research partners.[8]
- Costs for international collaborations could be covered through add-on or supplemental agency funding mechanisms that add international components to existing grants, thus reducing opportunity costs for faculty and institutions.
- Universities could provide faculty start-up funding specifically dedicated to international projects. This would help minimize risk for

junior faculty and allow them to start on a more equal footing with established colleagues.

Promote Inclusive Networks

Finding appropriate collaboration partners can be a difficult task.[9] Building and maintaining the networks that enable collaborators to find each other often requires effort and mobility. Conferences, especially smaller invitation-only workshops and meetings, are key sites for nurturing international collaborative relationships. These events allow faculty to meet prospective collaborators, maintain international professional networks and relationships, and initiate and work on joint projects. However, women and men from underrepresented groups can find conference participation more challenging for a number of reasons: lack of resources (money and time), professional and personal discomfort, or simply absence of invitations. Institutions can take steps to make these networks more inclusive of all faculty members.

- Professional associations and workshop organizers should create structures that visibly include diverse participants. These can range from open calls for participation, to free child care, to social events that appeal to all.
- When distributing money and resources for international projects—such as conferences, seminars, symposia, and workshops—universities, funding agencies, and professional associations could insist on diverse participation and ask for demographically diverse rosters of participants, including key speakers of different gender identities, races, and ethnicities and full participation by graduate students and postdoctoral researchers.

Increase Supports for Family Flexibility

Flexibility is a crucial factor for ensuring equitable participation and increased mobility of faculty members. In instituting flexibility, institutions need to take into account the diversity of family constellations and commitments; policies that focus solely on women with young children will not meet the needs of all faculty members. Universities and funding agencies could recognize that faculty have diverse family responsibilities and live interdependent lives that can include care commitments; institutions could support them in meeting those commitments. Although U.S. funding agencies and universities tend to set these issues aside as private, European agencies are increasingly paying for dependents (partners and children) and offering leaves or grant and fellowship extensions for child rearing, and the United States can take a lesson from their successes.

- Funding agencies and universities could provide flexible support for faculty with family responsibilities, including the timing of funding.
- Research funding could include financial support to bring families on international travel and longer stays, including costs for international health insurance, child care, and school fees. One way to fund these costs is as supplementary or add-on awards to existing grants.
- Institutions could provide help with restrictive visa regulations and other bureaucratic business that concern family members.

Recognize Diversity by Increase Funding Flexibility

Because of the variation in international research collaborations and the diversity of faculty who engage in them, certain obstacles are more of a challenge for some than for others, and fences concern women in particular. There are different issues in different disciplines and contexts, and different countries present specific burdens. A one-size-fits-all model is inadequate for addressing these issues and challenges, especially for women and for men from minority backgrounds.[10] Flexible supports are thus crucial to encouraging broad participation, especially for those who face more obstacles and fences. Once again, European agencies can provide a model, for they have been embracing notions of flexibility that include considering individual circumstances, alternative concepts of mobility such as virtual and shorter-term mobility, and flexicurity (portable social security benefits in the EU).[11]

- Institutions could create fellowships, funding opportunities, and institutional supports that fit the diverse paths of academic careers.
- Funding agencies and universities could revisit and broaden eligibility criteria, for example, criteria that privilege quantity versus quality of publications, or broaden definitions of excellence to include contributions to diversity (such as mentoring or service).
- Funding agencies could create more frequent or flexible deadlines for grant and fellowship applications, along with their start times, to improve coordination of schedules with international collaboration partners and family members.

- Universities could create more flexible expectations for proposals, merit, tenure, and promotion, including timing, teaching schedules, publications, research trips (length and number), all of which are interconnected. It should be easier, for instance, to rearrange teaching schedules so that faculty can travel internationally for conferences and research.

- Funding agencies could design programs to fund and support frequent, shorter visits, instead of only a fixed time period. For example, the German Alexander von Humboldt Foundation now provides funding for a maximum of eighteen months over three years, with minimum stays of three months, rather than the previous one-year fixed term.

Value and Recognize International Research

Obstacles also emerge when faculty and disciplinary expectations for international collaboration are out of sync with U.S. university and funding agency evaluation practices, which still tend to undervalue international research.[12] European and Asian institutions value international research experiences and collaborations with U.S. colleagues in particular, but these U.S. faculty efforts count less at home—unless they translate into U.S.-centric metrics of scholarly excellence like grant dollars and U.S. publications.

- Universities could include measures for international activities in transparent evaluation criteria for proposals, merit, tenure, and promotion. International reputation, reach of research, or building global competences in others could be included as broader criteria of excellence, recognizing international engagements and rewarding faculty for the often challenging, time- and resource-intensive efforts of building and maintaining international networks.

- The goal of preparing a globally ready workforce could be included in criteria for evaluating proposals and faculty accomplishments to support and reward faculty who involve students and postdocs in international research.

- Institutions could develop informed standards based on reliable information from international peers to evaluate the reputation of international collaboration partners to demystify research and research capacities abroad, so that they can be better assimilated into U.S. expectations and understandings of academic work.

Create Inclusive Institutional Partnerships

The existing structures of (global) science are not perceived as inclusive by women in particular; indeed, women talk about how difficult it is to find collaboration partners and gain access to networks.[13] Because initiating, organizing, and maintaining international networks are labor, time, and cost intensive, and therefore daunting, funding agencies and universities can support network creation in multiple ways rather than relying exclusively on individual faculty to initiate and maintain them. Furthermore, because funding for international projects is so competitive, agencies and universities can increase incentives and supports for collaborations and mobility of students, postdocs, and faculty by furthering and monitoring equal access to institutionalized partnerships, workshops, and exchanges that reduce risks and costs for all faculty.

Institutionalizing administrative and faculty-driven collaborations across universities and countries in the form of institutional partnerships can ease the risks and burdens on faculty members. It can also promote more internal visibility and rewards for faculty engaged in this work. Funding for institutional collaborations that are inclusive for women and minority academics can offset some of the structural disadvantages they face.

When supporting networking workshops on specific themes, funding agencies can explicitly reward research areas in which women and individuals from minority groups are represented or stipulate that, in areas in which they lack representation, network events will overrepresent their participation. A successful example of such an effort to build networks for women is the Women's International Research Engineering Summit (WIRES), which brings women engineers together at international workshops funded by multiple U.S., European, and other universities; funding agencies; and nongovernmental organizations.[14]

- Institutional partnerships could provide faculty with infrastructure to identify and conduct successful international collaborations.
- Funding agencies could expand cross-university partnerships and ensure their continued financial support.
- Universities could support such partnerships by providing seed money to apply for larger grant funding, research assistants to assist in proposal preparation, administrative supports for faculty-driven partnerships, and travel costs for collaboration partners.

- Funding agencies and universities could support network creation by funding and hosting international working meetings organized in inclusive ways.
- Professional associations could support networking events at conferences that create more inclusive ways for socializing and exchange, with the goal of bringing U.S.-based women and individuals from underrepresented groups together with international colleagues. These might include theme-specific "speed dating" exchanges and up-to-date directories where members can make their specific expertise visible to assist in broadening the search for collaboration partners.

Strategies for Helping Faculty Succeed

Besides creating and supporting international research opportunities, funding agencies and universities can create more access for diverse faculty by mentoring and training faculty to work abroad. As we have seen, although U.S. institutions do not always expect an international presence at the assistant professor level, an international reputation is a more common expectation for promotion from associate to full professor.[15] Thus, younger faculty are often advised to work toward a national reputation for tenure and shy away from risky international collaborations until they attain it.[16] This pattern creates an unfortunate contradiction for those whose research agendas require research abroad to demonstrate the scholarly achievement that is, of course, a key tenure expectation, not to mention being essential for their own scholarship and contribution to knowledge.

- Institutions could be transparent about expectations for international work at all stages of the tenure and promotion process, including how to fulfill those expectations.
- Mentors should be aware of and help junior faculty navigate contradictory tenure expectations.
- Mentors could also be prepared to provide information on how to deal with obstacles and climb over fences.

Provide International Grants Training
As we have seen, international collaborations require resources and administrative supports. Obstacles can emerge when faculty lack access to infor-

mation, resources, and strategies for handling bureaucratic obstacles. Women and others excluded from internal networks in departments and universities often do not easily pick up this shared knowledge from their colleagues, so they benefit most from transparent and fairer procedures of resource distribution and information that dismantle these fences.

- Mentoring and career-advice structures could provide information about funding opportunities within and outside the institution, including travel funds.
- Universities could provide information and training sessions and institutionalize dedicated pre- and postgrant support on how to apply for internal and external international grants, navigate international grant management, create and manage budgets, and the like.
- Universities and funding agencies could increase transparency about their own administrative procedures and policies. Rather than expecting faculty to negotiate individually with chairs, deans, or other administrators, a process that benefits the already established and powerful, they could establish clear policies and programs for research leaves and course buyouts.
- Universities could facilitate interdisciplinary exchange on campus; for example, colleagues from the humanities and languages could help prepare visits abroad.

Support International Visitors at Home

Although U.S. faculty can feel treated like rock stars abroad, they often lack funding and supports to host collaborators. For faculty members with limited mobility, bringing partners to the United States or sending students abroad can be important alternatives to traveling. However, although there are some workarounds, public funding agencies usually do not cover expenses for international visitors, and universities vary in the extent to which they provide funds and physical space for visiting collaborators. Indeed, in this era of strained budgets, it is not uncommon for U.S. universities to charge international visitors fees of several hundred dollars for administrative support for visa, library, or computer privileges. Some visa regulations do not support international partnerships; for example, visitors on "business visas" are explicitly not allowed to do "collaborative research" on campus. Embarrassing regulations, like the visa requirement that universities must ask hosts to verify sufficient English language capabilities of international visitors, from graduate students to full professors, add further cultural and practical impediments. Universities and funding agencies can take steps to mitigate these barriers by creating a more welcoming environment, financially and administratively. Such an environment will have gendered implications because limited mobility can be a concern for women in particular, so their prospects for engaging globally will be enhanced by the possibility to do so at home.

- Funding agencies and universities could create a supportive administrative infrastructure for receiving foreign visitors and traveling abroad, including information on visa regulations, health insurance support, temporary housing facilities, and office space.
- Universities could provide support for technological equipment, such as phone and video conference calls, electronic whiteboards, and so on, to expand international research contact.
- Funding agencies could find more ways to help cover costs incurred by non-U.S. collaborators.

Provide Training in Cultural Competences

Intercultural knowledge and skills are critical for successful international collaborative activities. Given the varying levels of comfort faculty express about venturing abroad for collaborations, it is surprising how little preparation graduate students, postdoctoral researchers, and faculty receive for conducting research with international partners at home and abroad. By contrast, global businesses expend significant effort training managers and skilled workers in effective global skills and intercultural communication and sensitivity. Although many faculty work in internationalized teams at home, they receive little guidance in how to lead teams across cultural and national boundaries. Although some funding agencies and professional associations have codes of ethical conduct regarding international partnerships, universities rarely do. Effective international collaborations and partnerships require faculty to have information and cultural competence. Cultural competency skills would also improve working relations at home in international teams.

Information about and support for developing cultural knowledge and skills would also help eliminate myths about the effectiveness of women in international assignments, which have plagued the business world.[17] Mentoring and career advising for women and individuals from minority groups could also include skill sets and information about opportunities for extended stays abroad.

- Universities could provide venues for sharing expertise and knowledge among faculty about how to work abroad and collaborate. These efforts could address specific national contexts and could also involve a greater availability of foreign language courses.
- Academic institutions could provide information about research systems and academic and societal cultures in other countries to give U.S. scholars a more nuanced sense of these as well as a more critical understanding of U.S. science and academia and their own cultures. A sophisticated understanding of cultural norms and expectations in daily life and research environments will enhance their ability to work in a more collaborative way.
- Universities and funding agencies could create, monitor, and enforce ethical standards, including transparency, open communication about goals, clear expectations about how collaborations work, and what partnerships mean. This framework will help create space for less exploitative collaborations.
- Training could be provided for women and men on how to handle risks to personal safety, including sexual and gender harassment, and individuals from minority groups could be provided with strategies to obtain knowledge about local environments and navigate potential xenophobia, racism, Islamophobia, homophobia, or other prejudices.

Dismantle Myths and Stereotypes about Research Abroad

Existing policies on gender equality miss their mark when they do not address the fences. Fences based on the wide range of gendered myths and stereotypes about women's ability to take part in the international world of academia need to be dismantled. My research shows that women with children should not be categorically excluded (or excused) from international opportunities but rather supported. Similarly, protective attitudes of faculty members toward their own students, especially women students, perpetuates myths and stereotypes that, as we have seen, may not be warranted. Dismantling these myths while providing support, information, and training will benefit both women and men by supporting a positive experience abroad and also create wider access and broader opportunities for women.

Faculty need opportunities to build cultural competency, language and other soft skills.

- Universities could provide information and support to women in recruiting top international talent for their research teams and labs and provide assistants to host visitors to their institutions.
- Universities and mentors could provide information, opportunities, and support strategies about dealing with family responsibilities during international collaborations.

Start Training Early

Not surprisingly, faculty who have had previous international experiences are more likely to be involved in international research collaborations than faculty who have not left their own country.[18] And, although this book has focused on faculty, it is crucial to build these competences throughout undergraduate, graduate, and postdoctoral education. Funding agencies and universities need to support international activities at all these levels to develop skill sets and provide opportunities to create networks that future faculty members can build on when they get academic jobs. Obstacles for students are well documented: funding, of course; also the science and engineering curriculum, which often does not allow time for study or research experiences abroad; as well as the fact that, as studies reveal, the social background of students predicts who has access to foreign language acquisition and international travel experiences. That is, students of color and students from economically disadvantaged backgrounds participate less in study-abroad programs than white students.[19] Institutional support can provide necessary resources to overcome these barriers while also signaling the value and importance placed on such experiences and collaborations early on.

- Universities could create immersion experiences abroad for undergraduate and graduate students, as well as postdoctoral researchers, to prepare future faculty for building successful international teams.
- International opportunities could be integrated into existing undergraduate and graduate programs, through summer programs and semesters abroad, to build interest and skills.

A Word of Caution:
International Collaboration as Normative Expectation

Even as funding agencies and universities need to design internationalization strategies that support international research collaborations in all the dimensions outlined in the preceding pages, including alignment with individual career advancement, they need to avoid replacing one set of constraining measures for success with another, that is, promoting a new normative idea that all faculty could collaborate internationally. Although we need to create inclusive strategies to promote international collaborations, we also need to be careful not to have a negative impact on those who cannot participate in them—or on those for whom international collaboration is not academically necessary or worthwhile. Universities and funding agencies in Europe are moving toward requiring international mobility for academic careers.[20] When institutions raise the bar by setting expectations for faculty to demonstrate international reputation, collaboration, and mobility, scholars with mobility restrictions can be disadvantaged. In fact, in her study of the Marie Curie Mobility fellows in Europe, Louise Ackers argues that mobility as a career requirement is discriminatory to those who are less mobile.[21] Thus, international activities should not be required but rather supported in ways that do not disadvantage faculty—women and men—who have limited mobility.

Given the many reasons for nonengagement in international collaborations, especially activities that require travel should not be used as the norm. Academic cultures in both the United States and Europe would benefit from clearer criteria for the kinds of international scholarship and outcomes they expect. There are various forms of faculty international engagement, and not all of them require mobility, especially in an era when it is so easy to share data and communicate research findings online. Depending on research-specific needs, which vary widely, scholarship does not necessarily require or benefit from intensive face-to-face interactions, nor does it have to be produced via coauthored grants and publications.

Finally, we need to make sure that simply spending time abroad does not become the default criterion for international engagement. This would simply increase the hoops academics have to jump through—hoops that some highly qualified and talented faculty will not be able to reach. In addition, merely spending time abroad will not necessarily develop cosmopolitan outlooks, broader views, cross-cultural competences, or skills, nor is being abroad the only way to become involved with other academics around the world. Rather, if scholars are supposed to collaborate both nationally and internationally, they should be able to demonstrate their efforts with multiple forms of evidence, such as serving as reviewers for or on editorial boards of international journals. In short, while increasing the value of international research in U.S. academia can surely benefit the United States, it will be misleading and exclusionary to equate excellence simply with international mobility.

Future Research Directions

In the emerging field of study, *international gender, science, and organizations*, we need research that looks systematically at the intertwined processes of globalization of scientific and engineering knowledge, the internationalization of universities and funding agencies, and the integration of women into STEM fields and other disciplines. Understanding how gender matters in the globalization of scientific and engineering knowledge is crucial to planning for the future of women in science and academia more broadly around the world. This study considers only one locality, the United States, and one modality, sending academics abroad (most other studies have focused on the United States as the receiving side). My data are thus limited to the perceptions of U.S. academics, both women and men, about their international collaborations and reception abroad. Studies are needed to show how scholars elsewhere perceive collaborations and partnerships with scholars from the United States and other countries.

I have focused on STEM fields, although I included social sciences in my study. My research aimed to identify the larger patterns in faculty experiences of and institutional supports for international collaborations. I did not find any striking differences among disciplines, though the nature of my data does not allow for detailed comparison by disciplines, fields, and subfields. Future research on an even larger scale could study field-specific gendered inequalities and cultures by comparing not only disciplines but subfields in specific practices of research, international collaboration, and degrees of internationalization. Such a study might reveal variation in departmental evaluation practices, though accountability and managerialism are moving toward more standardized evaluation practices, allowing less room for field-specific metrics.

I caution before an expectation to find a theory that predicts simply more or fewer fences in one discipline compared to others because patterns of glass fences are likely to depend on various factors. For example, such patterns do not fall simply along the lines of so-called soft and hard sciences because even subfields vary greatly in the scale and practices of collaborations that may or may not include international research sites and laboratories. A distinguishing feature, of course, is how scholarly work gets done and how academics collaborate, which is profoundly different for experimental laboratory science compared to more theoretical work.

Additionally, my study cannot shed light on how inclusive or exclusive international research networks are for women. Research is necessary to compare, for example, how gender works in international recruitment processes and competitions and how women are represented in international professional organizations and on international journal editorial boards. From U.S. studies, we know that it matters whether organizations rely on self-nominations or nominations by others and whether women are on award committees as members and chairs.[22] We need to explore whether these processes also work in international scientific and academic organizations and to systematically consider whether and how gendered barriers and burdens at the national level are amplified, creating fences when work takes researchers abroad.

In-depth analyses of the effects of U.S. funding agency and university internationalization strategies on diversity and gender equality could also provide best-practice models for understanding the complexities of promoting gender equality in the globalizing world of science. With the qualitative data of my study, I have been able to shed light on the gendered meanings faculty associate with collaboration. However, my data cannot speak to the frequency of collaboration for women and men, whether they benefit evenly from international activities, the quality of research produced, or whether gender differences are significant. We need more quantitative data that can allow us to document the prevalence of fences and trends of gender in collaborations, including cross-national data to analyze specific national and organizational contexts.

Finally, my research has focused on faculty from U.S. research universities, where faculty have opportunities to accrue academic, social, and human capital to attract international collaborators and have better chances of getting resources. Additional research could consider less well-funded institutions—including minority-serving institutions, teaching-intensive colleges, and community colleges—and investigate their strategies for building international collaborations and how their faculty perceive their opportunities and barriers. This research is particularly important because these institutions are key to training and retraining the U.S. workforce and creating global competence among U.S. students.[23]

Beyond the farthest parameters of my research, professional societies and organizations could be studied more thoroughly, as they are important gatekeepers and partners for effecting change. Their academic work and recognition processes can play a key role in supporting internationalization and gender equity through organization and management of conferences, journals, and the like.

Researchers should also investigate university internationalization practices on the teaching side, in particular to ensure that women and men can take part equitably in these educational opportunities. When universities build satellite campuses around the world, including in countries that have gender exclusionary policies and antihomosexual legislation, can faculty, staff, and student exchanges be inclusive? What are the gender implications of MOOCS? Will there be a gendered division of labor where women are hired as local teachers and high-status U.S. men do the big lectures? Or might such new education modalities provide opportunity for reaching students globally and making education more inclusive, especially for women? As these new forms of teaching demonstrate, internationalization is a continued ongoing process, and new research areas and questions about access, equity, and gender will continue to arise.

Promoting Gender Equality in Global Academia as an International Effort

The United States cannot create an inclusive (global) academia on its own. We find exclusionary processes not only on the U.S. side but also in other countries and transnational research endeavors. Making science and academia more inclusive of U.S.-based women without addressing gender and other forms of inequalities across the world will not go far enough and will ignore the interconnectedness of science and academia. There is a promising historical lesson about how women can open doors for each other that extends to today and possibly into the future. When U.S. women pushed open doors to study at German universities in the nineteenth century, their presence inspired German women who were excluded from the German universities to demand admission.[24] And this interactive dynamic is still at work today. Closed doors for women in one country encourage them to seek research opportunities abroad. U.S.-based women have a powerful incentive to climb over fences, and the .edu bonus open doors abroad. In turn, they might provide role models, networking, and research opportunities for women and underrepresented men in the countries they visit, thus opening doors for these students and colleagues in the United States. And in turn these open doors in the United States might be crucial for these academics' advancement back home, especially because the United States has such high status in the world of science and academia.

Only tackling issues of gender, science, and academia globally will create a more inclusive world of science. This work is already underway. An international effort of gender and science advocates has produced a series of international reports and cross-national comparative analyses.[25] Since 2011, the Gender Summits, beginning in the European Union, have already included the United States and South Korea. These meetings provide opportunities for crucial joint discussions and efforts to address women's participation and representation at senior and leadership levels nationally and internationally and to provide opportunities for the United States to learn from programs that have worked in other countries. Integrating women and individuals from minorities into STEM is no longer a separate process from globalization of science and internationalization strategies in academia. Structural barriers that hinder engagement of women faculty mean that women will be less involved in international research collaborations and mobility, and science will benefit less from their contributions. Internationalization strategies must include furthering international networks and shaping academia in more inclusive ways. If the globalization of scientific and engineering knowledge continues at current rates, creating a more democratic academia with open participation will not be one country's project alone. We must eliminate gendered structural barriers—the fences I have discussed at length—so that women can play an active role in international science, contributing their expertise to advancing research and reaping the personal and professional benefits of travel and work abroad. The United States has an immense opportunity to live up to its own image as a model for scientific progress and use its (still) powerful position in the science by working with other nations in creating an inclusive, innovative, productive world of science and academia.

REFERENCE MATTER

Methodological Appendix

Sample Characteristics N = 121

T HE SAMPLING STRATEGY OF THE STEM FACULTY SOUGHT to maximize diversity of fields, age, rank, gender, and race/ethnicity background. The sample of 121 interviewees and participants of focus groups includes faculty from thirty-eight research universities across the United States; twenty-three of these universities are public whereas fifteen are private institutions, and at least thirty-seven of the interviewees received National Science Foundation grants to conduct research abroad (see Frehill et al. 2010). This sample also includes twenty-one faculty members who occupy administrative positions such as director of an interdisciplinary research center, chair of the department, (associate) dean, or other administrative positions.

The largest group of faculty are in the fields of engineering (thirty-nine professors, or 32 percent), biology and other life sciences (twenty-six professors, or 22 percent), and social sciences (twenty-one professors, or 17 percent) (see Table A-1). Almost half of the interviewees are of the rank of full professor, associate professors were 26 percent, and 19 percent of the professors had the rank of assistant professor (see Table A-2). Not surprisingly, therefore, the average age was approximately 50.5 years old.

The sample included fifty-one women (42 percent) and seventy men (58 percent) (see Table A-3). One hundred and three faculty members (85 percent) identified as white, and eighteen faculty members (15 percent) identified as racial/ethnic minorities, including seven Asians (6 percent), six Hispanics (5 percent), four African Americans (3 percent), and one Native American

TABLE A-1. Number and percentage of faculty by field.

	Number	Percent
Biology and other life sciences	26	21
Chemical sciences	10	8
Earth, atmospheric, and ocean sciences	10	8
Engineering	39	32
Mathematics/computer sciences	10	8
Social sciences	21	17
Other	5	4
Total	**121**	**100**

TABLE A-2. Number and percentage of faculty by rank.

Rank	Number	Percent
Assistant	23	19
Associate	32	26
Full	60	50
Other	6	5
Total	121	100

TABLE A-3. Faculty by gender and country of educational degree in percent.

Country	Men (n = 70)	Women (n = 51)	Total (N = 121)
U.S. educated	37	27	64
International degree	21	15	36
Total	58	42	100

TABLE A-4. Number and percentage of faculty by racial/ethnic background.

Race/ethnicity	Number	Percent
White	103	85
Asian	7	6
Hispanic	6	5
African American	4	3
Native American	1	1
Total	121	100

TABLE A-5. Number and percentage of faculty by country of degrees.

Country of degree	Number	Percent
United States	78	64
Central/Eastern Europe	6	5
Western Europe	6	5
China	5	4
United Kingdom	5	4
Central and Latin America	4	3
Turkey	4	3
India	3	2
Middle East	3	2
Canada	2	2
Israel	2	2
Other (Japan, Australia, East Africa)	3	2
Total	121	100

(0.8 percent) (see Table A-4). Sixty-four percent of the faculty were educated in the United States, while at least 35 percent of the faculty had at least one international degree (BA or higher) (see Table A-3). The most frequent other countries/regions include six faculty each from Western Europe and from Central/Eastern Europe, five faculty with degrees from China and the United Kingdom, and four faculty with degrees from Central and Latin America and Turkey (see Table A-5).

Although most of the faculty and administrators had some experiences of international engagement including participating in international conferences, having international collaboration partners, and having coauthored grants or publications, not all of them did.

Notes

Chapter 1

1. To protect the confidentiality of my interviewees, the story of Thelma is a composite of aspects of many interviewees. Throughout the book, to disguise the individual faculty members and administrators, I have given pseudonyms to respondents and changed their fields if it was necessary and when the specific fields were not relevant.

2. See also Hogan et al. 2010.

3. My data do not allow me to study the prevalence of women's and men's international collaboration, nor do I study how women and men might differ in how they conduct international research collaborations.

4. Globalization is also a controversial concept in sociology of science. Although some maintain that science has always been global, others argue that over the past decades global science has become a new phenomenon due to the increased scope and intensity of the flow of ideas, knowledge, people, and norms and values.

5. Among many others, Xie 2014; Xie and Killewald 2012; Teitelbaum 2014; and Stephan 2012.

6. For example, "Effective international S&E partnerships advance the S&E enterprise and energize U.S. innovation and economic competitiveness, but they also have great potential to improve relations among countries and regions and to build greater S&E capacity around the world" (NSB 2008: 1). Among the strategic goals for 2011–2016 is to "keep the United States globally competitive at the frontiers of knowledge by increasing international partnerships and collaborations" (NSF 2011: 8).

7. This book focuses on international research collaborations; however, mobility is one of the key predictors for international collaborations of faculty (see discussion later). See also Childress 2010 and Altbach and Knight 2007 for the importance of faculty in internationalization strategies of universities. How high-skilled labor

mobility contributes to globalization processes is widely recognized (see Sassen 1988). And the notion that mobility in general is not gender neutral has also been established (see Cresswell and Uteng 2008).

8. See data later in the chapter and Scellato et al. 2012.

9. Leemann 2010 and Costas, Camus, and Michalczyk 2013.

10. Key questions for this meeting are how to "make international collaboration successful and sustainable" as well as the "responsibilities of researchers, entrepreneurs, educators, and policymakers in global scientific endeavors," (AAAS 2016). See also National Research Council 2014 for a summary of a workshop on international research collaborations.

11. See also my work on globalization of higher education and its implications for gender equality projects in higher education (Zippel et al. 2016 and Ferree and Zippel 2015).

12. See, for worldwide, Ramirez and Kwak 2015 and Ferree and Zippel 2015; for Scandinavian countries, see Nielsen 2014; for Germany, see Zippel et al. 2016; for the United States, see National Academy of Sciences et al. 2007, 2010, and Institute of Medicine et al. 2007.

13. Executive Office of the President of the United States 2013: 4.

14. See Freeman 2010: 393.

15. I am building on Altbach and Knight (2007), who developed an important definition to distinguish internationalization and globalization in higher education. My research, however, focuses more on the research than on the educational side of universities.

16. The American research university serves an ideal for the pursuit of excellence around the world; see Ramirez 2006.

17. I use the broad definition of the U.S. National Science Foundation for what constitutes a STEM field. These fields include chemistry, computer and information technology science, engineering, geosciences, life sciences, materials research, mathematical sciences, physics and astronomy, psychology, social sciences (including archaeology, anthropology, economics, and sociology). Although there are variations of collaboration patterns among fields, Leydesdorff et al. 2014 find that patterns of international coauthorship are surprisingly similar for social scientists and other scientists, although Mosbah-Natanson and Gingras 2013 find that for sociology the United States and Europe continue to form the key centers of collaboration.

18. See Cummings and Finkelstein 2012a; around 50 percent of U.S. faculty in STEM fields (agriculture 67 percent, life science 54 percent, physical sciences 52 percent, and engineering 47 percent) say they collaborate internationally, whereas this percentage is much lower for non-STEM fields—only 14 percent in law and 25 percent in education and the humanities and arts fields. Most researchers use coauthorship data from science and other databases to measure collaborations and to map collaboration networks among scientists. Despite some limitations, these available data are one of the best sources to conduct research on the prevalence and patterns of collaborations. Coauthoring means at a minimum some engagement among scientists over

research and thus is a form of collaborative activity. The limitations include, for example, inconsistent coverage of journals across databases and exclusion of non–English language journals. In addition, disciplinary practices vary greatly as to who is listed as an author in which positions and so on (Glänzel and Schubert 2005).

19. Jöns and Hoyler 2013.

20. See Ferree and Zippel 2015.

21. And we do not have data that allow us to distinguish faculty by social class background, race/ethnicity, gender identity, or sexual orientation.

22. Although the data of my study allow me to explore this proposition, different methodologies, for example, experimental designs and long-term comparative studies with larger sample sizes, would be necessary to provide the strongest kind of social scientific evidence.

23. Mandelker 1994 invented the concept of glass border to depict the women's underrepresentation in expatriate assignments. She argued that glass borders contribute also to the underrepresentation of women in senior management (see also Adler and Izraeli 1994).

24. Rosenfeld 1981 argued already gender differences in academic careers are due to gender differences in mobility among institutions. And Shauman and Xie 1996 found gender differences in geographic mobility of academics. Similarly, Cañibano et al. 2011 investigate how important temporary international mobility is for academic careers of Spanish PhD holders. But, so far, there are no theories or studies of U.S. faculty to explain the intersection of international (short-term) mobility and career success.

25. Childress 2010 discusses two exemplary cases of universities that focus on faculty international research collaborations as part of their broader internationalization strategies, Duke University and the University of Richmond. Each institution developed faculty seminars to support faculty's pursuit of international scholarship, which were sponsored by well-regarded university centers, included an interdisciplinary focus, and considered the balance of timing and other faculty commitments. Additionally, the University of Richmond paid for faculty's visa and passport fees, showing faculty that their engagement was valued and helping to motivate it, and Duke related its internationalization plan to its reaccreditation process.

26. I draw on the gender theory of gendered practices advanced by Connell and Wood 2005 and Martin 2003.

27. Wildavsky 2010; Altbach and Salmi 2011; and Kauppi and Erkkilä 2011.

28. Merton 1979.

29. In the United States, for instance, at a National Bureau of Labor conference in 2005, former Harvard University President Larry Summers notoriously stated that the lack of women in top science leadership positions might be due to differences in innate mathematical and logical skills, re-igniting a public and academic ongoing debate about the causes of women's underrepresentation in many STEM fields.

30. Forty years of interdisciplinary research on gender and science literature has pointed to organizational and institutional factors, along with unintentional biases,

that contribute to a lack of women in STEM fields (for a good overview, see Institute of Medicine et al. 2007). These factors include gendered inequalities in access to networks, institutional resources (space, grants, and fellowships), and other opportunities for advancement; a lack of a "critical mass" of women; and a lack of mentoring and role models for women. Explanations for the small numbers of women and lack of advancement in STEM fields also include their "chilly climate"; lack of institutional support for a work–life balance; and gender bias and cultural schemas that contribute to discriminatory (evaluative) practices in hiring and advancement.

31. Bailyn 2003; Britton 2010; Fox 2010; Roos and Gatta 2009; and Smith-Doerr 2004. However, for more regional perspectives on the EU, see Husu and Cheveigné 2010.

32. Institute of International Education 2014.

33. For the European Union Ackers 2000, 2004 and Vinkenburg et al. 2014; for Switzerland Leemann 2010; and for Australia White 2014.

34. Jöns 2007, 2011 and Leung 2014.

35. At the International Congress of the International Mathematical Union, Seoul, South Korea, August 13–21.

36. The concept of a gender gap means that a woman academic in the identical position as a man would be more or less likely to be involved in international collaborations. Many large-scale studies measure collaborations by coauthorships. Because there are other differences in the propensity to collaborate or coauthor, for example, based on rank and discipline, and women tend to be in lower ranks and under- or overrepresented in particular disciplines, studies control for these other factors (Smykla and Zippel 2010 and Frehill and Zippel 2011). Many non-U.S. studies find significant gender differences in collaborations and coauthorships, especially in international collaborations; see Abramo et al. 2013; Kyvik and Teigen 1996; Larivière et al. 2013; and Nielsen 2015.

37. Bozeman et al. 2013; Bozeman and Gaughan 2011; Cummings and Finkelstein 2012b and 2012c; Glänzel 2001; and Melkers and Kiopa 2010.

38. Many studies find significant gender differences in collaborations and coauthorships; for example, Bozeman and Corley 2004; Steffen-Fluhr 2006; and Sonnert and Holton 1995.

39. Fox and Mohapatra 2007 make an important distinction between collaboration that is cooperation among peers and teamwork that includes scientists who collaborated with students.

40. Also, Padilla-González et al. 2011 find that U.S. women faculty have more domestic collaborations compared to men, who are more likely to collaborate internationally.

41. Around the world, Larivière et al. 2013 find that for the fifty countries in which faculty are most productive, this is the case. For European countries, for findings that show lower percentages of women's international collaboration and integration in international networks, see Abramo et al. 2013; Jöns 2011; and Leemann 2010. For Canada, Larivière et al. 2011 find that women tended to collaborate within the

same providence. However, German coauthorship patterns found that teams composed of women only are more likely to be international than those of men or mixed teams, though they receive lower citations than those of internationally composed men-only teams (Elsevier 2015: 22).

42. See Smykla and Zippel 2010 for an overview and Chapters 4 and 5 for more discussions. Gender homophily means that women are more likely to collaborate with other women than are men. Because there are fewer women than men in higher academic positions around the world, women might find fewer other women to invite them to collaborate than do men; thus, this explanation finds that the cause for gendered patterns is the gender-segregated academic system (Vabø 2012 and Jöns 2011). Another prevalent explanation is that family commitments and dual-career priorities decrease women's mobility, and less international mobility means fewer opportunities to build international collaborations (see Ackers 2004; Kyvik and Teigen 1996; Larivière et al. 2011 and 2013; and Leemann 2010).

43. See Cañibano et al. 2015, who find no overall gender gap in international mobility among Spanish doctoral holders; however, they find specific gendered patterns. Cañibano 2009 previously also found cohort effects; whereas gender imbalances exist for older cohorts of academics, they are not significant for younger cohorts. Women have fewer and shorter (international) visits; they go abroad at earlier career stages, and they stay in closer geographical range to home. Costas, Camus, and Michalczyk 2013 find that in France and Germany women are not less mobile than men. Ackers 2004 argues that a life course perspective is necessary to study mobility of women academics. See also Jöns 2011 and Leemann 2010.

44. For a discussion of various benefits and pitfalls of collaboration, see also Fox and Faver 1984.

45. Fox and Mohapatra 2007 and others point out that the relationship between collaboration and productivity is complicated. To put it simply, we do not know whether more productive faculty are asked to be in collaborations, or whether faculty are more productive when they engage in collaboration.

46. Larivière et al. 2013: 213.

47. For example, Larivière et al. 2013 and many others find that internationally coauthored publications are cited more frequently worldwide. Freeman, Ganguli, and Murciano-Goroff 2015 show this relation also for coauthorships of U.S. scientists, but they attribute this finding to the fact that international coauthorships involve more authors than domestic coauthorships. However, Hsiehchen et al. 2015 find that having collaborators from more different countries by itself increases the citation impact of articles.

48. According to Cummings and Finkelstein's 2012c survey of U.S. professoriate (including faculty in business and the humanities, in addition to STEM fields) find that international collaborations are a significant predictor for the attainment of senior rank. This could be linked to productivity; indeed, Melkers and Kiopa 2010 find a correlation between international collaborations and productivity for U.S. faculty. Both women and men faculty at the associate level who engage in international

collaborations are more productive in terms of publications than are those without international collaborators (409–410). However, Padilla-Gonzales et al. 2011 analyzing the same CAP dataset that Cummings and Finkelstein used find that international collaborations are a significant predictor for productivity only for U.S. men but not for U.S. women faculty.

49. The jury is out as to whether there is a gender bias in how collaborative work gets evaluated. A recent study of economists shows that women's contributions in coauthored publications do not receive the same recognition as men's contributions, hurting women's chances of getting tenure. Sarsons 2016 found that teamwork pays off less for women than for men because coauthored and solo-authored publications are valued differently for tenure for men and women. Women who published single-authored work were more likely to get tenure than women who coauthored publications. The penalty for coauthored publications is even higher when women coauthor solely with men and decreases when women are coauthors with other women.

50. Acker 1990; Britton 2000; Martin 2003; and Connell 2011.

51. Bird 2011; Ecklund et al. 2012; Jacobs and Winslow 2004; Husu and Koskinen 2010; Misra et al. 2012; Misra et al. 2011; Roos and Gatta 2009; Smith-Doerr 2004; Winslow 2010; Wharton 2015; Whittington and Smith-Doerr 2008; van den Brink 2010; and van den Brink and Benschop 2012.

52. Of course adjuncts and faculty in other fields and institutions with fewer resources face additional structural barriers.

53. Kapheim et al. 2015.

54. Most research studies use broad definitions due to field and discipline and leave it to respondents to define what they consider collaborations. For increases in (international) collaborations, see overviews in Bozeman, Fay and Slade 2013; Glänzel and Schubert 2005; Stephan 2012:73; and Wuchty et al. 2007.

55. Freeman et al. 2015.

56. Wuchty et al. 2007; see also Freeman et al. 2015.

57. Adams 2013; Gazni et al. 2012; Leydesdorff et al. 2013; and Wagner 2009.

58. Adams 2012.

59. Unlike Sassen 2001, who might argue that scientists who belong to the global elite differ less around the world, like high-skilled professionals working in cities.

60. For example, although Germany has stricter restrictions on stem cell research, the UK is more permissive on research on human embryos. Stephan 2012 tells the story of a Chinese American scientist who has a dual appointment at a U.S. and a Chinese university; it allows him to afford large-scale research on mice in China that would be more expensive in the United States.

61. National Science Board 2016: 5–9.

62. Frehill and Zippel 2011: Figure 1, page 41. Among U.S. doctoral degree holders, 27 percent of women in businesses, 23 percent in government, and only 21 percent in educational institutions say they collaborate internationally. The numbers for men are higher: 39 percent in business, 29 percent in government, and 28 percent in

educational institutions. The gender gap is also highest in businesses, with 12 percent more men indicating that they have international collaborators, versus only 7 percent in academia.

63. Finkelstein 2014 and Jacob and Meek 2013. For the EU, see Ackers 2005; Børing et al. 2015; Morano-Foadi 2005; and Musselin 2004; for China, see Leung 2014; for Korea, see Park 2007. Overall, Altbach 2015 reminds us that professors worldwide are not a very mobile group, yet a selected group of scholars and scientists are highly mobile.

64. Women make up a higher proportion of full-time faculty at undergraduate colleges (42 percent) compared to research universities (34 percent) (see West and Curtis 2006). The percentage of women professors by ranks (assistant is highest, full is lowest) decreases even among research universities depending on the type of institution (doctoral, high research, or very high research activity). Although doctoral institutions have 30 percent of women as full professors, very high research activity universities have only 23 percent. And although 53 percent of assistant professors at doctoral institutions are women, only 45 percent at very high research activity institutions are women. See the data on instructional staff with faculty status by gender for 2012 fall, source: IPEDS data center (National Center for Education Statistics 2015). Thanks to Yun Cho for the calculations.

65. See the data later in the chapter; also Adams 2013; Cummings and Finkelstein 2012b; Franzoni et al. 2012; and The Royal Society 2011.

66. Institute of International Education 2014a.

67. According to the National Science Foundation, approximately 27 percent of employees in S&E occupations in the United States were foreign born in 2010, yet among all college-educated workers (regardless of occupational category) only 15 percent were foreign born. At the doctoral level, over 40 percent were foreign born in each S&E occupation except the social sciences (National Science Foundation 2014).

68. According to Franzoni et al. 2012, only 5 percent of U.S. scientists were outside their country in 2011.

69. Altbach and Knight 2007, Stichweh 2009, and others have pointed out that universities have always been international institutions. Universities can be considered simultaneously global, international, national, and local; see also Levitt 2015, who theorizes how local and global are not exclusionary ideas but can constitute one another.

70. Anderson 1983.

71. Fox 2001 and Merton 1979.

72. Merton 1979. Lamont 2009 also points out to the social processes of evaluations in academia.

73. Bozeman and Gaughan 2011; Fox 2001; and Melkers and Kiopa 2010.

74. Ridgeway 2011.

75. Ridgeway 2011; Miller, Eagly, and Linn 2015 found evidence of persistent gender-science stereotypes in sixty-six nations.

76. See also Ramos and Martin-Palomino 2015, who find emancipatory desires in internationally mobile Spanish women.

77. Singer 2003.

78. Rossiter 1982.

79. Miller 2008: 56.

80. Gillett 2013 and Jules-Rosette 2005.

81. See Altbach and Knight 2007 and Stichweh 2009.

82. Adler and Izraeli 1994.

83. Acker 1990, 2006; Britton 2000; and Martin 2003.

84. NSF survey data reveal that those who earned degrees abroad are more likely to engage in international collaborations than those who have only U.S. degrees (Falkenheim and Kannankutty 2012). Cummings and Finkelstein 2012b: 101 find that the odds of U.S. faculty who spent one or two years abroad after their undergraduate degree were three times likelier to engage in international research collaborations than other faculty. See also Freeman et al. 2015 and Franzoni et al. 2012.

85. Leemann 2010, for example, points to the intersectionality of life course, family, class, and gender in explaining why some faculty participate less in international collaborations.

86. Data from the Institute of International Education, the Open Doors Report 2014a show that 76.3 percent of students going on study abroad are white and that black and Latino/Latina students are underrepresented. Studies find that family income, financial support, but also cultural barriers play important roles in explaining the overrepresentation of white students.

87. I draw here on the work of Acker 2006 and others, who have pointed out that globalization is often thought of as gender neutral and that the theorizing of gender in the United States has only recently begun to take it into account.

88. Research on gender and globalization processes depicts them frequently as disempowering for women focusing on low-skilled labor; see Acker 2004, Ehrenreich and Hochschild 2003, and Salzinger 2004. By contrast, my interviewees are high-skilled privileged women (see also Luke 2001).

89. Salzinger 2004 and Collins 2003.

90. See Bozeman, Fay, and Slade 2013, who argue that organizational contexts shape the propensity of scientists to collaborate.

91. Xie 2014: 1 and Jöns and Hoyler 2013.

92. Xie and Killewald 2012.

93. See Stephan 2012 and Teitelbaum 2014, questioning the pervasiveness of the argument about general shortages.

94. Xie 2014: 1 (electronic copy) and Teitelbaum 2014: 173.

95. See Teitelbaum 2014: 172–173.

96. National Academy of Sciences et al. 2007, 2010.

97. Case studies bear fruit on the specificity of countries. Knobel et al. 2013 discuss these developments in Brazil; Robertson and Keeling 2008 compare the positions of various countries.

98. Xie 2014: 1 and Xie and Killewald 2012; see also Teitelbaum 2014 and Stephan 2012.

99. NSB 2016 Figure/Table 4-8. Sources: National Science Foundation, National Center for Science and Engineering Statistics, OECD, UN.

100. NSB 2014; table 4-6.

101. Tuchman 2009.

102. See trends in R&D by agency, AAAS 2015. There was a brief spike in 2009 with the American Recovery and Reinvestment Act.

103. NSB 2014: 4-4.

104. See The Pew Charitable Trusts 2015.

105. Ibid.

106. McMillan Cottom and Tuchman 2015, Kleinmann and Vallas 2001, Tuchman 2009, and Ferree and Zippel 2015.

107. Slaughter and Leslie 1997 and Slaughter and Rhodes 2004.

108. Altbach and Salmi 2001; Jöns and Hoyler 2013; Hemlin and Rassmussen 2006; Espeland and Sauder 2007; and Sauder and Espeland 2009.

109. Jöns and Hoyler 2013; Robertson and Keeling 2008; and Altbach and Salmi 2011.

110. NSB 2014 and NSB 2016, Table 5.24.

111. Clark 1987 and Tuchman 2009.

112. See the earlier discussion of explanations for this underrepresentation—and also Institute of Medicine et al. 2007 for a useful overview of the literature.

113. See Ramirez and Kwak 2015 for a useful cross-national comparison from 1970 through 2010. Comparisons across countries are difficult because of varying career paths and data availability, however, among the countries worldwide that have higher percentages of women among STEM degree holders and academics than the United States are Bulgaria, Latvia, Romania, Finland, Switzerland, Turkey, and Croatia (NSB 2016; European Commission 2016).

114. NSB 2014 and NSB 2012, Figure 5-25. Notes: "Article counts from set of journals covered by Science Citation Index (SCI) and Social Sciences Citation Index (SSCI)." Sources: National Science Foundation, National Center for Science and Engineering Statistics, and The Patent Board, special tabulations (2011) from Thomson Reuters, SCI and SSCI.

115. NSB 2016: Table 5.27.

116. Adam 2012 uses data from the Web of Science.

117. Leydesdorff et al. 2014.

118. Wagner et al. 2015.

119. Franzoni et al. 2012: 1252 conducted this survey in 2011. See also Appelt et al. 2015 for a comparison of how the United States fares among OECD countries.

120. Cummings and Finkelstein 2012b find that having spent time abroad after a BA increases the likelihood that U.S. academics engage in international collaborations; Freeman et al. 2015 find that collaborators spend time together at an institution;

Scellato et al. 2012 also find that immigrants are more likely to engage in international collaborations, create networks abroad, and have coauthors from more countries than the other scientists.

121. Frehill and Zippel 2011; analyzing the 2006 NSF survey of doctoral recipients with sample size $N = 30,800$ respondents found that one-third of STEM PhDs say they collaborated with other countries. See also Adams (2013); Cummings and Finkelstein (2012b); Franzoni et al. 2012; and The Royal Society 2011.

122. Luukkonen et al. 1992 find that cross-country variations of international collaboration can be explained by a range of factors including "cognitive, social, historical, geopolitical, and economic factors" (101).

123. Institute of International Education 2014 and Robertson and Keeling 2008.

124. Teitelbaum 2014 and Stephan 2012. According the National Science Foundation 2014: 3-53, "At the doctoral level, over 40 percent were foreign born in each S&E occupation except the social sciences." Among PhDs in S&E, the five largest countries of origin are China (23 percent), India (13 percent), the UK (6 percent), Canada (4 percent), and Germany (4 percent) (see Figure 3-36, page 3-53).

125. Scellato et al. 2012 find that scientists who are internationally mobile as postdocs or for jobs have the highest rates of engaging in collaborations across national borders.

126. According to the National Study of Postsecondary Faculty 2004, at least one-third of STEM faculty are foreign born (National Center for Education Statistics 2004). Cummings and Finkelstein 2012c find that 21 percent of faculty are foreign born, but only 5 percent are foreign trained (72). This study includes STEM fields as well as humanities and business where foreign born/trained are fewer.

127. For quotes, however, I noted, however, whether faculty were foreign born, if their background seemed relevant to what they said.

128. Clark 1987 points out how important institutional types are for shaping the American academic profession. The definition of research universities is based on the Carnegie Classification of Institutions of Higher Education 2015. About 209 universities are considered to have high or very high research activity; these institutions grant doctoral degrees and conduct research.

129. Cummings and Finkelstein 2012b: 100 find that institutional context is a predictor for research active faculty's international activities, including research collaborations and international coauthorships; this includes research institutions as well as faculty-driven internationalization efforts.

130. However, as we will see in Chapter 2, university tenure requirements, with their emphases on grants and publications alongside rigid teaching schedules, can also impede international collaboration (see also Cummings and Finkelstein 2012b).

131. See Appendix for more details in the sample and sampling strategy appendix. See also Frehill, Vlaicu, and Zippel 2010.

132. Hogan et al. 2010.

Chapter 2

1. The institutional environment, however, is key in fostering or inhibiting collaboration, both within and beyond the institution as Bozeman, Fay, and Slade 2013 show.

2. See, for example, Ramirez and Tiplic 2014 show how in Europe the idealized American research university has become the globally favored model that stands for excellence.

3. See also researchers who point to academic, economic, political, and sociocultural dimensions: de Wit 2002; Knight 1999; and Childress 2010.

4. Schott 1993 and Merton 1973.

5. Traweek 1988 and Latour and Woolgar 1986.

6. Traweek 1988: 162.

7. For economists of science views, see Stephan 2012.

8. He gave a public talk in Boston in 2007.

9. Kato and Ando 2013; Li, Liao, and Yen 2013; Liao 2011; Puuska et al.; and Freeman et al. 2015 argue that this is only due to the larger size international collaborations usually have.

10. National Science Foundation 2011: 8.

11. See Chapter 1.

12. UNESCO 2005; OECD 1996; and Salmi 2009.

13. NSF 2015.

14. Castellani, Jimenez, and Zanfei 2013; Castellani and Pieri 2013; and Qiu 2014.

15. Ledford 2014.

16. NSF 2014c.

17. NSF 2013b.

18. Steven Hankin of McKinsey & Company coined the term *the War for Talent* in 1997.

19. See, for example, Lexington 2009.

20. For example, Chinese scholars are lured back with attractive packages in the hope they will increase "brain circulation" and spur urban development (Zhang 2016). The EU Marie Curie Mobility Schemes cater especially to those who have received training and worked outside the EU. The German Alexander von Humboldt Foundation's most prestigious international professorships have been attracting a few faculty from around the world but even more Germans who have built their academic careers abroad. The German Excellence Initiative and funding of graduate schools are meant to build research and training capacities to attract top researchers and graduate students from around the world. The organization German Academic International Network (GAIN)—underwritten by the main German funding institutions—is organizing annual events alternating between Boston and locations on the West Coast; the goal is to attract academics (back) to Germany and to increase the presence and profile of German universities and research institutions in the United States.

21. See Teitelbaum 2014: 173 and Wildavsky 2010.

22. National Academy of Sciences et al. 2007, 2010; White House Office of Science and Technology Policy 2014; and NSF 2014a and 2014d.

23. Stephan 2012; and Teitelbaum 2014.

24. Institute of International Education 2014b.

25. NSF Science and Engineering Indicators 2014: 2–33.

26. See also Chapter 1. Bozeman et al. 2013 show that institutional environment is key in fostering or inhibiting collaboration, both within and beyond the institution. Franzoni et al. 2012 show that one's own international mobility increases international collaborations. And Freeman et al. 2015 found that many collaborations started with partners working at or visiting the same institution.

27. Liang et al. 2008: 8; Corley and Sabharwal 2007; and Franzoni et al. 2012.

28. Zippel, Ferree, and Zimmermann 2016.

29. Strikingly, *international* as a term is usually used as meaning "outside the United States." Although some faculty do mention differences among continents, regions, and countries, the most prevalent distinctions occurred with generalizations about the United States, Europe, Asia, North Africa, and the Middle East.

30. Beoku-Betts 2004; Katz et al. 2003; and Radhakrishnan 2011.

31. Wagner 2003, 2007.

32. Bourdieu 1984, 1988; Hardill 2002; Leemann 2010; Jöns 2011; Beck and Sznaider 2010; and Kauppinen 2013.

33. Melkers and Kiopa 2010; Moody 2004; Hunter and Leahey 2008; and Bozeman et al. 2013.

34. Jones et al. 2008.

35. However, Cummings and Finkelstein 2012b: 106–107 found that faculty with more senior status are more likely to be involved in international collaborations than assistant professors. But a review of the literature by Bozeman et al. 2013 found that tenure status is not associated with greater levels of international research collaborations; the only exceptions are collaborations that have a mentoring aspect. They also find that, in general, younger professors are more productive than those who are a bit more advanced.

36. See also Chapter 1.

37. See Chapter 1 and de Wit 2002; Lucier 2009; and Pyenson and Skopp 1977.

38. These government regulations include Export Control Regulations that cover the exports not only of goods and commodities but also of information. These regulations can apply to presenting unpublished papers at conferences, carrying a laptop computer or GPS device, or other items related to "controlled" technology or technical assistance.

39. Uhly and Zippel 2014; see also Childress 2010.

40. This survey was conducted by the American Council on Education 2012. There has been little change since 2003 when 5 percent of doctoral institutions had these guidelines to explicitly evaluate faculty's international efforts.

41. Uhly and Zippel 2014.

42. Beall 2015.

43. Uhly and Zippel 2014.

44. Fox and Xiao 2013.

45. For a useful overview of the literature, see Institutes of Medicine et al. 2007, NRC 2010, and MIT 1999.

Chapter 3

1. There is a large body of literature exploring intersectionality of gender and axes of inequality; see Browne and Misra 2003; Cho, Crenshaw, and McCall 2013; Choo and Ferree 2010; Collins 1999; Davis 1981; McCall 2005; Mohanty 2003; Patil 2013; Verloo 2013; Walby 2007; and Yuval-Davis 2006.

2. Compare with Nancy Adler's 1984, 1987, and 1994 classic work on women managers who successfully worked in Asian countries in the 1980s because they were seen foremost as foreigners who happened to be women. Czarniawska and Sévon's 2008 historical study explains how early women scientists were seen as double strangers and allowed to study and work in other European countries than the ones they had grown up in. See also Epstein's 1973 classic study of a positive effect of the double negative African American women managers experience and can turn into an advantage.

3. See Ridgeway 2011; Adler 1987; and Baruch and Reis 2015.

4. Studies based on interviews have shown over and over the isolation and marginalization women experience in (academic) workplaces, particularly in STEM fields, due to small numbers (Britton et al. 2012; Hearns and Husu 2011; Institute of Medicine 2007; Kanter 1977; Kemelgor and Etzkowitz 2001; Smith and Calasanti 2005; and Valian 1998.). This sense of exclusion is also expressed in higher levels of dissatisfaction with the (departmental) climate and professional networks (Belle et al. 2014; Bilimoria and Stewart 2009; Briton et al. 2012; Rosser 2004; Settles et al. 2006; Sheridan et al. 2007; Sonnert and Holton 1995; Smith and Calasanti 2005; and Wharton 2015). See Chapter 1 for how research on a quantitative gender gap in research collaborations is inconclusive.

5. Rankin et al. 2007 show how exclusion from networks also limits women's access to tacit knowledge.

6. Fox and Xiao 2013.

7. Gutiérrez y Muhs 2012; Pasupathy and Oginga Siwatu 2013; and Ridgeway 2011.

8. Fox 2010; Cantwell and Taylor 2013; Espeland and Sauder 2007; Sauder and Espeland 2009; Hazelkorn 2011; and Jöns and Hoyler 2013.

9. Gaughan and Bozeman 2016 investigate how rank and gender shape experiences of international collaborations.

10. Ridgeway 2011: 37.

11. Ferree and Zippel 2015; Lamont 2009; Ramirez 2006; and Ramirez and Tiplic 2014.

12. Gaughan and Bozeman 2016 also find how both rank and gender also matter in how U.S. STEM scientists interpret experiences with collaborations.

13. See Chapter 1; Ecklund et al. 2012; Roos and Gatta 2009; and Misra et al. 2011.

14. Dietz and Bozeman 2005.

15. Adler 1987 and Baruch and Reis 2015.

16. Adler 1987.

17. Heilman 2001.

18. Merton 1968.

19. Fox 2010.

20. Merton 1968.

21. Ridgeway 2011: 37.

22. Connell and Wood 2005; Ecklund et al. 2012; Hearn 2001; Krais 2002; Rossiter 1982; and Smyth and Nosek 2015.

23. Wajcman 2004.

24. Ridgeway 2011.

25. Frehill, Abreu, and Zippel 2015 and Charles 2011a, 2011b.

26. Charles and Bradley 2009.

27. Miller, Eagly, and Linn 2015.

28. Institute of Medicine et al. 2007; and Smyth and Nosek 2015.

29. Ridgeway and Correll 2004; and Ridgeway 2011.

30. Ridgeway 2011 does not develop an explicitly intersectional approach to gender, as she believes that gender is the main status category; I find her concept of salience useful to show how gender and academic nationality also intersect as a "process" in the .edu bonus. Choo and Ferree point out that "intersectionality as a process highlights power as relational, seeing the interactions among main effects as multiplying oppressions at various points of intersection" (2010: 129).

31. Gazni et al. 2012 find the United States to be a core country in scientific productivity with researchers from other countries seeking out U.S. researchers for collaboration, and it is a major producer of multinational collaborations.

32. Miller et al. 2015; Smyth and Nosek 2015; Gutiérrez y Muhs 2012; Pasupathy and Oginga Siwatu 2013; and Ridgeway 2011.

33. See Chapter 4.

34. Gazni et al. 2012.

35. For example, *Nature* has used a double-blind review process only since 2015.

36. The top twenty universities include sixteen U.S., three UK, and one Swiss university, according to the Shanghai Academic Ranking of World Universities from the ShanghaiRanking Consultancy 2016.

37. Berger et al. 1977 and Wagner and Berger 1993; all direct quotes from Turco 2010.

38. Ridgeway and Smith-Lovin 1999 and Turco 2010.

39. Similarly, women anthropologists have been allowed to enter and observe male-only spaces in communities when they were perceived as foreigners and therefore not expected to conform to local gender norms.

40. Thanks to Laura Frader for pointing out this possible interpretation.

41. See, for example, Gutiérrez y Muhs 2012; Massachusetts Institute of Technology 2010; and Ong 2005.

42. See Chapter 2.

43. Ridgeway 2011; see also Sandberg 2013, who calls women to "lean in" at the table.

44. Frehill, Vlaicu, and Zippel 2010.

45. There is, of course, also a selection bias; senior faculty who do not feel comfortable engaging in international collaborations are probably less likely to engage in them and thus would not have participated in our survey.

46. Singer 2003.

47. Czarniawska and Sevón 2008: 26; this interpretation, though, is controversial. Bailyn 2008 finds it most convincing, Calás 2008 asks for a different metaphor, and Acker 2008 is most critical and least persuaded that the notion of "stranger" applies to these women.

48. Of course, this marginalization experienced by academics could also be due to research fields that are less mainstream in the United States.

49. See of course also the experience of international women academics in the United States (Beoku-Betts 2004). Banerjee 2016 also shows how travel experiences by women faculty of color due to racial profiling at airports sheds light on barriers for women due to race and ethnicity compared to white women faculty.

Chapter 4

1. See also Leemann 2010 for her interpretation of the ideal internationally mobile academic.

2. This interpretation is based on Cole and Singer's 1991 key concept of cumulative disadvantages, that seemingly small gender differences as in negative setbacks and the like add up over time to create gender inequalities in academia. Cole and Singer reverse Merton's idea of the cumulative advantage of the Matthew's effect. According to Cole and Singer, gender inequities are based on the cumulative disadvantage in women's academic career paths. This theory is also central in Valian's 1998 explanation of the persistent underrepresentation of women in science, in her book *Why So Slow*.

3. I draw on Acker 1990, Bird 2011, Britton 2000, Fox 2010, Martin 2003, and Wharton 2015.

4. See also Leung 2014, who uses a very different theoretical framework of gender to study gendered inequalities in academic mobility with the case of Chinese academics in Germany.

5. See research on general obstacles to the involvement of faculty in international collaborations: Childress 2010; Dewey and Duff 2009; Finkelstein and Sethi 2014; and Green and Olsen 2003.

6. Mandelker 1994 coined the term *glass borders* for myths, assumptions, and stereotypes about women managers' availability, suitability, and preferences for assignments outside the United States; see also Adler 1994, showing the myth that women managers were not interested in expatriate assignments.

7. See Larivière et al. 2013.

8. Massachusetts Institute of Technology 1999; Shen recounts that the grant sizes of NIH to women are lower than to men (2013: 24).

9. Bailyn 2004; Jacobs and Winslow 2004; Misra et al. 2012; Misra et al. 2011; Sayer 2005; and Winslow 2010.

10. Fox 2009.

11. Jöns 2011; see Vabø 2012 for the argument about the gender-segregated academic system.

12. Bozeman and Corley 2004.

13. See also Freeman and Huang 2014, who show how coauthorship is also structured by ethnicity.

14. Only future large-scale studies can solve these questions comparing national and international collaborations in specific contexts.

15. I build here on Leemann's concept of the ideal type of academic entrepreneur developed in the context of transnational academic mobility. She argues that this ideal type creates inequalities in who can conform. Leemann argues that "complex formations related to parenting and partnering, gender and social class, as well as to embeddedness into the scientific community, result in inequalities in the accumulation of international cultural and social capital" (2010: 623).

16. Sassen 2001.

17. According to Merton 1979 (1942), 1996, claims to truth are evaluated in terms of universal and impersonal criteria, not only on the basis of race, gender, and the like.

18. In the American Institute of Physics Report 2005, Ivie and Ray state: "Women earn almost 40% of Turkey's bachelor's degrees in physics, 33% in France, and 30% in South Korea."

19. National Research Council 2010; see Chapter 1.

20. Connell and Wood 2005.

21. See literature overviews Salamin and Hanappi 2014 and Acker 2004.

22. See also Ecklund et al. 2012 and Jacobs 1999.

23. See National Research Council 2010; Institute of Medicine et al. 2007; Blackmore and Sachs 2001; and Hearn 2001.

24. Similarly, Fox and Xiao 2013 find that collaborations with businesses are perceived as risky activities that women faculty engage in less often than do men.

25. For example, in the historical list of the top twenty-nine famous explorers Sacagawea (c. 1788–1812) a Native American woman, is the only woman included (Famous Explorers 2016);. Modern women explorers also tend to be also less known (National Geographic 2016). .

26. Frehill et al. 2010.

27. Ibid.

28. Frehill et al. 2010 find that women traveled less internationally. See also Henderson 2015; and Settles and O'Connor 2014 analyze how incivility at conferences is a gendered phenomenon related to sexist contexts and women's perceptions of exclusion and sexism at conferences in particular. Blumen and Bar-Gal 2006 discuss how geography conferences are gendered spaces. Hesli and Lee 2013 find that, for women political scientists, conference attendance was associated with more reports of discrimination. And Brown and Watson 2010 find how work family conflicts keep already women PhD students from attending conferences.

29. See Lubitow and Zippel 2014 for gendered strategies that parents engage in to handle work–family conflicts when traveling abroad, and Tripp 2002.

30. See also Lubitow and Zippel 2014.

31. Etzkowitz et al. 2000; Larivière, et al. 2013; Siemieńska and Zimmer 2007; and Mellström 2009.

32. Arthur et al. 2007.

33. See Adler 1987. In general, the business literature has identified stereotypes about gender and leadership that can lead to cultural conflicts over gendered expectations when women are in leadership or managerial positions.

34. Survey data on the prevalence of such experiences do not exist. An exception is the study by Clancy et al. 2014, which focuses on trainees in fieldwork in physical anthropology, as I discuss further in the following pages. Also, (feminist) social scientists and anthropologists at times include encounters with sexism and unwanted sexual advances and behaviors in their methods sections. Mügge 2013 published a very frank account and analysis of how she experiences sexual harassment from gatekeepers when she conducted interviews in Surinam and Turkey as a Dutch researcher. For other scientists and engineers, however, there are still few "legitimate outlets" to challenge these experiences in public, so we know less about it.

35. Women professors report unwanted sexual advances and behaviors not only from superiors and colleagues but also from students (see Dziech and Weiner 1990; Jacobs 1996; McKinney 1990; Paludi 1990; Settles et al. 2006; and Zippel 2006).

36. I found that more men professors, the hosts and collaborators, and others were more concerned about the safety of women professors than they seemed to be for themselves, similarly to the business literature.

36. Similarly, research on construction work shows how doing gender for men often means that they endanger themselves, as taking reasonable precautions of wearing safety hats and the like would appear too "sissy," too feminine, and undermine hegemonic masculinities; Paap 2006.

37. Rubin 1976; Easterday et al. 1977; and Wong 2015.

38. West and Zimmermann 1987.

39. Clancy et al. 2014. In our interviews we did not ask women or men specifically about such incidents because the university would have demanded that I as an employee report such incidents.

40. Ibid.: 4.

Chapter 5

This chapter draws on material and interview quotes previously published in Uhly, Visser, and Zippel 2015; Lubitow and Zippel 2014; and Frehill and Zippel 2011. I thank Amy Lubitow, Emily Smykla, and Katrina Uhly for their work in coding and analyzing the interview and focus group data in this chapter.

1. A large and vocal strand in the gender and science and academia literature argues that children have a negative impact on women's academic careers and are the key explanation for the underrepresentation of women in the professoriate (see Ceci and Williams 2007, 2015 and Mason et al. 2013). In particular, studies show that that children impede women scientists' geographic job mobility (Kulis and Sicotte 2002 and Shauman and Xie 1996). Others also argue that gender and family issues need to be considered as interlinked but separate (Husu 2005 and Padavicet al. 2013). Research reveals gender gaps in work-related travel in general particularly for women with small children (Bergman and Gustafson 2008; Gustafson 2006; and Jeong et al. 2013). Interestingly, though, Leemann, Dubach, and Boes 2010 found that having a child reduces international mobility for both women and men postdoctoral researchers in Switzerland. And only a few studies discuss international collaborations of U.S. academics, for example, Agnete Vabø et al. include U.S. academic researchers in general and find that family status (marital status, spousal employment, and parental status) explains some but not all of the gender gap in international research collaborations (see Vabø et al. 2014 and Vabø 2012).

2. Steffen-Fluhr et al. 2012.

3. Bozeman and Gaughan 2011 found that family status (marital status and number of children) does not have a significant effect on gender differences regarding collaborations; they do not differentiate between national and international collaborations. Fox 2009 conducted a survey of participants in an international Women's International Research Engineering Summit (WIRES) and found that the women participants perceived family to be a lower barrier to international research collaborations than other issues such as obtaining funding, finding collaborators, or work commitments for themselves. However, they rated family issues as higher barriers for other women in their institutions. Of course, the fact that they themselves participated in an international workshop shows some selectivity.

4. See table 3, Frehill and Zippel 2011.

5. Ibid.

6. See, for more findings and discussions, Uhly et al. 2015. We analyzed the 2007 Changing Academic Profession, an international survey of faculty and academic researchers. The countries we analyzed are Argentina, Australia, Brazil, Canada, Finland, Germany, Italy, Malaysia, the UK, and the United States.

7. Ackers 2004.

8. See discussions in Uhly et al. 2015; Vabø 2012; and Ackers 2004. See also Leemann 2010, who finds for Swiss PhDs during the postdoc phase that the most likely person to go abroad "is a young scientist from abroad (i.e. who was already mobile

in former stages of his or her career), with an academic family background, without children and partner, who had career-oriented support during doctoral studies (i.e. is well integrated into the academic field) and got an approved fellowship from the SNSF or was funded by another research funding institution" (609).

9. Ibid.

10. Fox 2005 shows how marriage per se might not be an issue because women in second marriages often feel more supported than those in their first marriage. See also Kulis and Sicotte 2002; Moen 2003; Rusconi and Solga 2011; Schiebinger, Henderson, and Gilmartin 2008; and Wolf-Wendel, Twombly, and Rice 2004 for studies on the importance of dual career couples on gender inequalities.

11. Uhly, Visser, and Zippel 2015.

12. Etzkowitz et al. 2000.

13. Cech 2016.

14. Cech and Blair-Loy 2014; Fox, Fonesca, and Bao 2011; and Blair-Loy 2009.

15. Tripp 2002.

16. Ibid.

17. See Zippel 2011.

18. Starr and Curie 2009.

19. Aronson 1992; Bianchi 2011; Gerstel and Gallagher 2001; Kan, Sullivan and Gershuny 2011; and Walker, Pratt, and Eddy 1995.

20. Zippel 2011.

21. Ibid.

22. See also Tripp 2002. The following section draws heavily on my work with Amy Lubitow; see Lubitow and Zippel 2014.

23. Ibid.

24. Ibid.

25. Ibid.

26. Ibid.

27. See Smykla and Zippel 2010, citing Mason and Goulden 2004.

28. Lubitow and Zippel 2014.

29. Fox et al. 2011 and Gatta and Roos 2004.

30. Hays 1996.

31. MacDonald 2009.

32. Lareau and Weininger 2008.

33. Jeong et al. 2013.

34. Wall and Arnold 2007.

35. Schiebinger and Gilmartin 2010 and Wonch et al 2014.

36. Schiebinger and Gilmartin 2010; Mason and Goulden 2004; Misra et al. 2012; Misra et al. 2011; and Jacobs and Winslow 2004.

37. Bianchi 2011; Coltrane 1996; Craig 2006; Hochschild and Machung 1989; Suitor, Mecom, and Feld 2001; and Wall and Arnold 2007.

38. Hook 2006 and Sayer 2005.

39. Schiebinger and Gilmartin 2010 and Fox 2005: 137:

For women, the highest productivity is among those married to a scientist outside academia or to someone in one of the non-traditional professions (such as accountant, social worker, librarian, physical therapist, writer/artist). Among men, productivity varies less than women's by the occupation of their spouse.

40. I want to thank Kimberly Morgan, who first mentioned this term to me in 1999 when she asked me: "Do you have a portable partner?" Until then I had only considered the importance of a portable computer for my career.

41. Thanks to Amber Ault, who pointed out this connection.

42. Tripp 2002.

43. Soyer 2014 points out how the identity as a mother can serve women as a "nonsexual, gender-specific roles" enabling access to certain male-dominated communities.

44. Ibid.

45. Hardill 2002: 1; see also Chapter 2; Bourdieu 1984; and Bourdieu and Passeron 1977.

46. Khan 2011 and Weis and Cipollone 2013.

47. Tripp 2002.

48. Manrique and Manrique 1999: 121.

49. Brandth and Kvande 2002; Cole 2012; and Kvande 2002, 2009.

Chapter 6

This chapter is inspired by and uses some ideas developed at the NSF-funded 2010 workshop on international research collaborations, summarized in the final report to NSF (see Hogan et al. 2010).

1. Rilke 1996.

2. See also Ferree and Zippel 2015; Bilimoria and Liang 2012; Fox 2010; Risman and Adkins 2014; Skrentny 2013; and Williams et al. 2014 for discussions on how to promote gender equality and diversity efforts in male-dominated fields and universities.

3. Ferree and Zippel 2015 and Zippel et al.2016. See also the history of policies on equal opportunities in the United States in Dobbin 2009 and Skrentny 2013.

4. Larivière et al. 2013.

5. Childress 2010; Dewey and Duff 2009; and Finkelstein and Sethi 2014.

6. Childress 2010 and Trondal 2010.

7. Frehill et al. 2010; the WIRES survey results show for women that another obstacle is finding suitable collaborators; see Fox 2009.

8. Hogan et al. 2010.

9. Fox 2009.

10. Hogan et al. 2010: 1.

11. Hogan et al. 2010.

12. See also Uhly and Zippel 2014.

13. See also Fox 2009.

14. Nesmith 2009.

15. Of course, these expectations also depend on the field and the degree of internationalization. See also Arthur et al. 2007.

16. Cummings and Finkelstein 2012b: 107 argue that the U.S. tenure system is an institutional impediment against faculty's international research collaborations.

17. Adler 1984 and Salamin and Hanappi 2014.

18. See also Chapter 1; Cummings and Finkelstein 2012b: 101 find that the odds of U.S. faculty who spent one to two years abroad after their undergraduate degree were three times higher to engage in international research collaborations than were other faculty. See also Franzoni et al. 2012 and Freeman et al. 2015.

19. See Chapter 1; Institute of International Education 2014.

20. European Commission 2012; Marimon et al. 2009; and Morano-Foadi 2005.

21. Ackers 2008, 2010; similarly, Leemann 2010 and Leemann and Boes 2012 caution that mobility requirements both disregard and perpetuate complex inequalities among academics. For a similar argument, see also Costas et al. 2013.

22. Lincoln et al. 2012; see also Jöns 2011.

23. Hogan et al. 2010.

24. Rossiter 1982.

25. Zippel, Ferree, and Zimmermann 2016 and Ferree and Zippel 2015.

References

Abramo, Giovanni, Ciriaco Andrea D'Angelo, and Gianluca Murgia. 2013. "Gender Differences in Research Collaboration." *Journal of Informetrics* 7(4): 811–822.

Acker, Joan. 1990. "Hierarchies, Jobs, Bodies: A Theory of Gendered Organizations." *Gender & Society* 4(2): 139–158.

———. 2004. "Gender, Capitalism, and Globalization." *Critical Sociology* 30(17): 17–41.

———. 2006. "Inequality Regimes: Gender, Class, and Race in Organizations." *Gender & Society* 20(4): 441–464.

———. 2008. "Helpful Men and Feminist Support: More Than Double Strangeness." *Gender, Work & Organization* 15(3): 288–293.

Ackers, Louise. 2000. *The Participation of Women Researchers in the TMR Marie Curie Fellowships*. Brussels: The European Commission.

———. 2004. "Managing Relationships in Peripatetic Careers: Scientific Mobility in the European Union." *Women's Studies International Forum* 27(3): 189–201.

———. 2005. "Promoting Scientific Mobility and Balanced Growth in the European Research Area." *Innovation: The European Journal of Social Sciences* 18(3): 301–317.

———. 2008. "Internationalisation, Mobility and Metrics: A New Form of Indirect Discrimination?" *Minerva* 46(4): 411–435.

———. 2010. "Internationalisation and Equality: The Contribution of Short Stay Mobility to Progression in Science Careers." *Recherches Sociologiques et Anthropologiques* 41(1): 83–103.

Adams, Jonathan. 2012. "Collaborations: The Rise of Research Networks." *Nature* 490(7420): 335–336.

———. 2013. "Collaborations: The Fourth Age of Research." *Nature* 497(7451): 557–560.

Adler, Nancy J. 1984. "Women Do Not Want International Careers: And Other Myths about International Management." *Organizational Dynamics* 13(2): 66–79.

———. 1987. "Pacific Basin Managers: A Gaijin, Not a Woman." *Human Resource Management* 26(2): 169–191.

———. 1994. "Competitive Frontiers: Women Managing across Borders." *Journal of Management Development* 13(2): 24–41.

Adler, Nancy J., and Dafna N. Izraeli. 1994. *Competitive Frontiers: Women Managers in a Global Economy*. Cambridge, MA: Blackwell.

Altbach, Philip G. 2015. "Building an Academic Career: A Twenty-First-Century Challenge." In *Young Faculty in the Twenty-First Century: International Perspectives*, edited by Maria Yudkevich, Philip G. Altbach, and Laura E. Rumbley, 5–20. Albany: State University of New York Press.

Altbach, Philip G., and Jane Knight. 2007. "The Internationalization of Higher Education: Motivations and Realities." *Journal of Studies in International Education* 11(3/4): 290–305.

Altbach, Philip G., and Jamil Salmi. 2011. *The Road to Academic Excellence: The Making of World-Class Research Universities*. Washington, DC: World Bank.

American Association for the Advancement of Science (AAAS). 2015. A Primer on Recent Trends in Federal R&D Budgets. Retrieved on June 8, 2015, from www.aaas.org/news/primer-recent-trends-federal-rd-budgets.

———. 2016. 2016 AAAS Annual Meeting. Available at www.meetings.aaas.org.

American Council on Education. 2012. Mapping Internationalization on U.S. Campus: 2012 Edition. Available at www.acenet.edu/news-room/Documents/Mapping-Internationalizationon-US-Campuses-2012-full.pdf.

Anderson, Benedict. 1983. *Imagined Communities: Reflections on the Origin and Spread of Nationalism*. London: Verso.

Appelt, Silvia, Brigitte van Beuzekom, Fernando Galindo-Rueda, and Roberto de Pinho. 2015. *Which Factors Influence the International Mobility of Research Scientists?* Paris: OECD Publishing.

Aronson, Jane. 1992. "Women's Sense of Responsibility for the Care of Old People: 'But Who Is Going to Do It?'" *Gender & Society* 6: 8–29.

Arthur, Nancy, Wendy Patton, and Christine Giancarlo. 2007. "International Project Participation by Women Academics." *Canadian Journal of Education* 30(1): 323–348.

Bailyn, Lotte. 2003. "Academic Careers and Gender Equity: Lessons Learned from MIT." *Gender, Work & Organization* 10(2): 137–153.

———. 2004. "Time in Careers—Careers in Time." *Human Relations* 57(12): 1507–1521.

———. 2008. "Hierarchy of Strangeness: Negating Womanhood." *Gender, Work & Organization* 15(3): 294–297.

Banerjee, Pallavi. 2016. "Racial Profiling at Airports adds a Colour-coded Cost when I Fly on Business." *The Globe and Mail*. July 19. Available at www.theglobeandmail .com/life/facts-and-arguments/flying-while-brown/article30979345/

Baruch, Yehuda, and Cristina Reis. 2015. "Global Career Challenges for Women Crossing International Borders." In *Handbook of Gendered Careers in Management: Getting in, Getting on, Getting Out*, edited by Adelina M. Broadbridge and Sandra L. Fielden, 341–356. Cheltenham, UK: Edward Elgar Publishing.

Beall, Jeffrey. 2015. "Predatory Journals and the Breakdown of Research Cultures." *Information Development* 31(5): 473–476.

Beck, Ulrich, and Natan Sznaider. 2010. "Unpacking Cosmopolitanism for the Social Sciences: A Research Agenda." *British Journal of Sociology* 61: 381–403.

Belle, Deborah, Laurel Smith-Doerr, and Lauren M. O'Brien. 2014. "Gendered Networks: Professional Connections of Science and Engineering Faculty." In *Gender Transformation in the Academy*, 153–175. Bradford, UK: Emerald Group Publishing Limited.

Beoku-Betts, Josephine. 2004. "African Women Pursuing Graduate Studies in the Sciences: Racism, Gender Bias, and Third World Marginality." *NWSA Journal* 16(1): 116–135.

Berger, Joseph, M. Hamit Fisek, Robert Z. Norman, and Morris Zelditch Jr. 1977. *Status Characteristics and Social Interaction: An Expectation States Approach*. New York: Elsevier.

Bergman, Ann, and Per Gustafson. 2008. "Travel, Availability and Work–Life Balance." *Mobility and Technology in the Workplace* 9: 192.

Bianchi, Suzanne M. 2011. "Family Change and Time Allocation in American Families." *ANNALS of the American Academy of Political and Social Science* 638(1): 21–44.

Bilimoria, Diana, and Abigail J. Stewart. 2009. "'Don't Ask, Don't Tell': The Academic Climate for Lesbian, Gay, Bisexual, and Transgender Faculty in Science and Engineering." *National Women's Studies Journal* 21 (2): 85–103.

Bilimoria, Diana, and Xiangfen Liang. 2012. *Gender Equity in Science and Engineering: Advancing Change in Higher Education*. Routledge Studies in Management, Organizations, and Society 15. New York: Routledge.

Bird, Sharon R. 2011. "Unsettling Universities' Incongruous, Gendered Bureaucratic Structures: A Case Study Approach." *Gender, Work & Organization* 18(2): 202–230.

Blackmore, Jill, and Judyth Sachs. 2001. "Women Leaders in the Restructured University." In *Gender and the Restructured University: Changing Management and Culture in Higher Education*, edited by Ann Brooks and Alison Mackinnon, 45–66. Ballmoor, UK: SRHE and Open University Press.

Blair-Loy, Mary. 2009. *Competing Devotions: Career and Family among Women Executives*. Cambridge, MA: Harvard University Press.

Blumen, Orna, and Yoram Bar-Gal. 2006. "The Academic Conference and the Status of Women: The Annual Meetings of the Israeli Geographical Society." *Professional Geographer* 58(3): 341–355.

Børing, Pål, Kieron Flanagan, Dimitri Gagliardi, Aris Kaloudis, and Aikaterini Karakasidou. 2015. "International Mobility: Findings from a Survey of Researchers in the EU." *Science and Public Policy.* 10.1093/scipol/scv006.

Bourdieu, Pierre. 1984. *Distinction: A Social Critique of the Judgement of Taste.* Translated by Richard Nice. Cambridge, MA: Harvard University Press.

———. 1988. *Homo Academicus.* Cambridge, UK: Polity.

Bourdieu, Pierre, and Jean-Claude Passeron. 1977. *Reproduction in Education, Culture, and Society.* Beverly Hills, CA: Sage.

Bozeman, Barry, and Elizabeth Corley. 2004. "Scientists' Collaboration Strategies: Implications for Scientific and Technical Human Capital." *Research Policy* 33(4): 599–616.

Bozeman, Barry, Daniel Fay, and Catherine P. Slade. 2013. "Research Collaboration in Universities and Academic Entrepreneurship: The-State-of-the-Art." *Journal of Technology Transfer* 38(1): 1–67.

Bozeman, Barry, and Monica Gaughan. 2011. "How Do Men and Women Differ in Research Collaborations? An Analysis of the Collaborative Motives and Strategies of Academic Researchers." *Research Policy* 40(10): 1393–1402.

Brandth, Berit, and Elin Kvande. 2002. "Reflexive Fathers: Negotiating Parental Leave and Working Life." *Gender, Work & Organization* 9(2): 186–203.

Britton, Dana M. 2000. "The Epistemology of the Gendered Organization." *Gender & Society* 14(3): 418–434.

———. 2010. "Engendering the University through Policy and Practice: Barriers to Promotion to Full Professor for Women in the Science, Engineering, and Math Disciplines." In *Genderchange in Academia: Re-Mapping the Fields of Work, Knowledge, and Politics from a Gender Perspective*, edited by Birgit Riegraf, Brigitte Aulenbacher, Edit Kirsch-Auwärter, and Ursula Müller, 15–26. Wiesbaden: VS Verlag für Sozialwissenschaften, Springer.

Britton, Dana M., Chardie L. Baird, Ruth A. Dyer, B. Jan Middendorf, Christa Smith, and Beth A. Montelone. 2012. "Surveying the Campus Climate for Faculty: A Comparison of the Assessments of STEM and Non-STEM Faculty." *International Journal of Gender, Science and Technology* 4(1): 102–122.

Brown, Lorraine, and Pamela Watson. 2010. "Understanding the Experiences of Female Doctoral Students." *Journal of Further and Higher Education* 34(3): 385–404.

Browne, Irene, and Joya Misra. 2003. "The Intersection of Gender and Race in the Labor Market." *Annual Review of Sociology* 29: 487–513.

Calás, Marta B. 2008. "The Wedge or the Doorstop?" *Gender, Work & Organization* 15(3): 298–302.

Cañibano, Carolina. 2009. *Euro-Cv. Building New Indicators for Researchers' Careers and Mobility Based on Electronic Curriculum Vitae. Final Report.* Available at

www.enid-europe.org/PRIME/documents/EUROcvREPORT_FINAL_08_08_09
.pdf.

Cañibano, Carolina, Mary Frank Fox, and F. Javier Otamendi. 2015. "Gender and Patterns of Temporary Mobility among Researchers." *Science and Public Policy* 42.

Cañibano, Carolina, F. Javier Otamendi, and Francisco Solís. 2011. "International Temporary Mobility of Researchers: A Cross-Discipline Study." *Scientometrics* 89(2): 653–675.

Cantwell, Brendan, and Barrett J. Taylor. 2013. "Global Status, Intra-Institutional Stratification, and Organizational Segmentation: A Time-Dynamic Tobit Analysis of Arwu Position among U.S. Universities." *Minerva* 51: 195–223.

Carnegie Classification of Institutions of Higher Education. 2015. Center for Postsecondary Research, Indiana University School of Education. Retrieved on May 27, 2015, from www.carnegieclassifications.iu.edu/.

Castellani, Davide, Alfredo Jimenez, and Antonello Zanfei. 2013. "How Remote Are R&D Labs? Distance Factors and International Innovative Activities." *Journal of International Business Studies* 44: 649–675.

Castellani, Davide, and Fabio Pieri. 2013. "R&D Offshoring and the Productivity Growth of European Regions." *Research Policy* 42: 1581–1594.

Cech, Erin A. 2016. "Mechanism or Myth? Family Plans and the Reproduction of Occupational Gender Segregation." *Gender & Society* 30(2): 265–288.

Cech, Erin A., and Mary Blair-Loy. 2014. "Consequences of Flexibility Stigma among Academic Scientists and Engineers." *Work and Occupations* 41(1): 86–110.

Ceci, Stephen J., and Wendy M. Williams. 2007. *Why Aren't More Women in Science? Top Researchers Debate the Evidence*. Washington, DC: American Psychological Association.

———. 2015. "Why So Few Women in Mathematically Intensive Fields?" In *Emerging Trends in the Social and Behavioral Sciences*, edited by Stephen M. Kosslyn and Robert A. Scott. Hoboken, NJ: John Wiley & Sons.

Charles, Maria. 2011a. "What Gender Is Science?" *Contexts* 10(2): 22–28.

———. 2011b. "A World of Difference: International Trends in Women's Economic Status." *Annual Review of Sociology* 37(1): 355–371.

Charles, Maria, and Karen Bradley. 2009. "Indulging Our Gendered Selves? Sex Segregation by Field of Study in 44 Countries." *American Journal of Sociology* 114(4): 924–976.

Childress, Lisa K. 2010. *The Twenty-First Century University: Developing Faculty Engagement in Internationalization*. New York: Peter Lang.

Cho, Sumi, Kimberlé Williams Crenshaw, and Leslie McCall. 2013. "Toward a Field of Intersectionality Studies: Theory, Applications, and Praxis." *Signs: Journal of Women and Culture and Society* 38(4): 785–810.

Choo, Hae Yeon, and Myra Marx Ferree. 2010. "Practicing Intersectionality in Sociological Research: A Critical Analysis of Inclusions, Interactions, and Institutions in the Study of Inequalities." *Sociological Theory* 28(2): 129–149.

Clancy, Kathryn B. H., Robin G. Nelson, Julienne N. Rutherford, and Katie Hinde. 2014. "Survey of Academic Field Experiences (Safe): Trainees Report Harassment and Assault." *PLoS ONE* 9(7).

Clark, Burton L. 1987. *Academic Life: Small Worlds, Different Worlds.* Princeton, NJ: Carnegie Foundation.

Cole, Jonathan R., and Burton. Singer. 1991. "A Theory of Limited Difference: Explaining the Productivity Puzzle in Science." In *The Outer Circle: Women in the Scientific Community*, edited by Harriet Zuckerman, Jonathan R. Cole, and John T. Bruer, 277–310. New York: W. W. Norton and Company.

Cole, Nina D. 2012. "Expatriate Accompanying Partners: The Males Speak." *Asia Pacific Journal of Human Resources* 50(3): 308–326.

Collins, Jane. 2003. *Threads: Gender, Labor, and Power in the Global Apparel Industry.* Chicago: University of Chicago Press.

Collins, Patricia Hill. 1999. "Moving Beyond Gender: Intersectionality and Scientific Knowledge." In *Revisioning Gender*, edited by Myra Marx Ferree, Judith Lorber, and Beth B. Hess, 261–284. Thousand Oaks, CA: Sage Publications.

Coltrane, Scott. 1996. *Family Man: Fatherhood, Housework, and Gender Equity.* New York: Oxford University Press.

Connell, Raewyn W. 2011. *Confronting Equality: Gender, Knowledge and Global Change.* Sydney, Australia: Allen & Unwin.

Connell, R. W., and Julian Wood. 2005. "Globalization and Business Masculinities." *Men and Masculinities* 7(4): 347–364.

Corley, Elizabeth, and Meghna Sabharwal. 2007. "Foreign-Born Academic Scientists and Engineers: Producing More and Getting Less Than Their U.S.-Born Peers?" *Research in Higher Education* 48(8): 909–940.

Costas, Ilse, Céline Camus, and Stephanie Michalczyk. 2013. *Die Unternehmerische Hochschule Aus Der Perspektive Der Geschlechterforschung: Zwischen Aufbruch Und Beharrung*, edited by Kristina Binner, Bettina Kubicek, Anja Rozwandowicz and Lena Weber, 137–151. Münster: Westfälisches Dampfboot.

Cottom, Tressie McMillan, and Gaye Tuchman. 2015. "Rationalization of Higher Education." *Emerging Trends in the Social and Behavioral Sciences: An Interdisciplinary, Searchable, and Linkable Resource.* 1–17. May 15. Available at www.onlinelibrary.wiley.com/doi/10.1002/9781118900772.etrds0274/abstract.

Craig, Lyn. 2006. "Does Father Care Mean Fathers Share? A Comparison of How Mothers and Fathers in Intact Families Spend Time with Children." *Gender & Society* 20(2): 259–281.

Cresswell, Tim, and Tanu Priya Uteng, eds. 2008. *Gendered Mobilities.* Aldershot, UK: Ashgate.

Cummings, William K., and Martin J. Finkelstein. 2009. "Global Trends in Academic Governance." *Academe* 95(6): 31–34.

———. 2012a. "The Internationalization of the US Academy: A Disciplinary Perspective." In *Scholars in the Changing American Academy: New Contexts, New Rules and New Roles*, edited by William K. Cummings and Martin J. Finkelstein, 79–91. Dordrecht and New York: Springer.

———. 2012b. "Internationalization of Work Content and Professional Networks." In *Scholars in the Changing American Academy New Contexts, New Rules and New Roles*, edited by William K. Cummings and Martin J. Finkelstein, 93–109. Dordrecht and New York: Springer.

———. 2012c. "The 'Glass Ceiling' Effect: Does It Characterize the Contemporary US Academy?" In *Scholars in the Changing American Academy New Contexts, New Rules and New Roles*, edited by William K. Cummings and Martin J. Finkelstein, 63–78. Dordrecht and New York: Springer.

Czarniawska, Barbara, and Guje Sevón. 2008. "The Thin End of the Wedge: Foreign Women Professors as Double Strangers in Academia." *Gender, Work & Organization* 15(3): 235–287.

Davis, Angela. 1981. *Women, Race and Class*. London: Women's Press.

Dewey, Patricia, and Stephen Duff. 2009. "Reason before Passion: Faculty Views on Internationalization in Higher Education." *Higher Education* 58(4): 491–504.

De Wit, Hans. 2002. *Internationalization of Higher Education in the United States of America and Europe: A Historical, Comparative, and Conceptual Analysis*. Westport, CT: Greenwood Press.

Dietz, James L., and Barry Bozeman. 2005. "Academic Careers, Patents, and Productivity: Industry Experience as Scientific and Technical Human Capital." *Research Policy* 34(3): 349–367.

Dobbin, Frank. 2009. *Inventing Equal Opportunity*. Princeton, NJ: Princeton University Press.

Dziech, Billie Wright, and Linda Weiner. 1990. *The Lecherous Professor: Sexual Harassment on Campus*. Urbana, IL: University of Illinois Press.

Easterday, Lois, Diana Papademas, Laura Schorr, and Catherine Valentine. 1977. "The Making of a Female Researcher: Role Problems in Field Work." *Journal of Contemporary Ethnography* 6(3): 333–348.

Ecklund, Elaine Howard, Anne E. Lincoln, and Cassandra Tansey. 2012. "Gender Segregation in Elite Academic Science." *Gender & Society* 26(5): 693–717.

Ehrenreich, Barbara, and Arlie Russell Hochschild. 2003. *Global Woman: Nannies, Maids and Sex Workers in the New Economy*. New York: Metropolitan Books.

Elsevier. 2015. *Mapping Gender in the German Research Arena*. Available at www.elsevier.com/research-intelligence/research-initiatives/gender-2015.

Epstein, Cynthia Fuchs. 1973. "Positive Effects of the Multiple Negative: Explaining the Success of Black Professional Women." *American Journal of Sociology* 78(4): 912–935.

Espeland, Wendy, and Michael Sauder. 2007. "Rankings and Reactivity: How Public Measures Recreate Social Worlds." *American Journal of Sociology* 113(1): 1–40.

European Commission. 2012. "Structural Change in Research Institutions: Enhancing Excellence, Gender Equality and Efficiency in Research and Innovation." Luxembourg: Office for Official Publications of the European Communities.

———. 2016. *She Figures 2015: Gender in Research and Innovation. Statistics and Indicators.* Luxembourg: Publications Office of the European Union.

Etzkowitz, Henry, Carol Kemelgor, and Brian Uzzi. 2000. *Athena Unbound: The Advancement of Women in Science and Technology.* Cambridge, UK: Cambridge University Press.

Executive Office of the President. 2013. "Factsheet: Women and Girls in Science, Technology, Engineering, and Math (STEM)." Washington, DC: The White House. Available at www.whitehouse.gov/sites/default/files/microsites/ostp/stem_factsheet_2013_07232013.pdf.

Famous Explorers. 2016. "Famous Explorers." Retrieved on July 31, 2016, from www.famous-explorers.org.

Falkenheim, Jaquelina, and Nirmala Kannankutty. 2012. "International Collaborations of Scientists and Engineers in the United States." *InfoBrief:* National Science Foundation.

Ferree, Myra Marx, and Kathrin Zippel. 2015. "Gender Equality in the Age of Academic Capitalism: Cassandra and Pollyanna Interpret University Restructuring." *Social Politics: International Studies in Gender, State & Society.* November 7, doi: 10.1093/sp/jxv039.

Finkelstein, Martin. 2014. "How Does National Context Shape Academic Work and Careers? The Prospects for Some Empirical Answers." In *The Forefront of International Higher Education*, edited by Alma Maldonado-Maldonado and Roberta Malee Bassett, 49–60. Dordrecht, Netherlands: Springer.

Finkelstein, Martin, and Wendiann Sethi. 2014. "Patterns of Faculty Internationalization: A Predictive Model." In *The Internationalization of the Academy*, edited by Futao Huang, Martin J. Finkelstein, and Michele Rostan, 237–257. Dordrecht, Netherlands: Springer.

Fox, Mary Frank. 2001. "Women, Science, and Academia: Graduate Education and Careers." *Gender & Society* 15(5): 654–666.

———. 2005. "Gender, Family Characteristics, and Publication Productivity among Scientists." *Social Studies of Science* 35(1): 131–150.

———. 2009. *WIRES Survey: Research, International Research Collaboration, and Gender Equity.* Barcelona, Spain: Women's International Research Engineering Summit. Available at www.wires.gatech.edu/main.php.

———. 2010. "Women and Men Faculty in Academic Science and Engineering: Social-Organizational Indicators and Implications." *American Behavioral Scientist* 53(7): 997–1012.

Fox, Mary Frank, and Catherine A. Faver. 1984. "Independence and Cooperation in Research: The Motivations and Costs of Collaboration." *Journal of Higher Education* 55(3): 347–359.

Fox, Mary Frank, Carolyn Fonesca, and Jinghui Bao. 2011. "Work and Family Conflict in Academic Science: Patterns and Predictors among Women and Men in Research Universities." *Social Studies of Science* 41(5): 715–735.

Fox, Mary Frank, and Sushanta Mohapatra. 2007. "Social-Organizational Characteristics of Work and Publication Productivity among Academic Scientists in Doctoral-Granting Departments." *Journal of Higher Education* 78(5): 542–571.

Fox, Mary Frank, and Wenbin Xiao. 2013. "Perceived Chances for Promotion among Women Associate Professors in Computing: Individual, Departmental, and Entrepreneurial Factors." *Journal of Technology Transfer* 38(2): 135–152.

Franzoni, Chiara, Giuseppe Scellato, and Paula Stephan. 2012. "Foreign-Born Scientists: Mobility Patterns for 16 Countries." *Nature Biotechnology* 30(12): 1250–1253.

Freeman, Richard B. 2010. "Globalization of Scientific and Engineering Talent: International Mobility of Students, Workers, and Ideas and the World Economy." *Economics of Innovation and New Technology* 19(5): 393–406.

Freeman, Richard B., Ina Ganguli, and Raviv Murciano-Goroff. 2015. "Why and Wherefore of Increased Scientific Collaboration." In *The Changing Frontier: Rethinking Science and Innovation Policy*, edited by Adam B. Jaffe and Benjamin F. Jones. Chicago: University of Chicago Press for NBER.

Freeman, Richard B., and Wei Huang. 2014. "Collaborating with People Like Me: Ethnic Co-Authorship within the US." NBER Working Paper Series. Cambridge, MA: National Bureau of Economic Research.

Frehill, Lisa M., Alice Abreu, and Kathrin Zippel. 2015. "Gender, Science, and Occupational Sex Segregation." In *Advancing Women in Science: An International Perspective*, edited by Willie Pearson Jr., Lisa M. Frehill, and Connie L. McNeely, 51–92. New York: Springer.

Frehill, Lisa M., Sorina Vlaicu, and Kathrin Zippel. 2010. *International Scientific Collaboration: Findings from a Survey of NSF Principal Investigators*. Available at www. /nuweb.neu.edu/zippel/nsf-workshop/.

Frehill, Lisa M., and Kathrin S. Zippel. 2011. "Gender and International Collaborations of Academic Scientists and Engineers: Findings from the Survey of Doctorate Recipients, 2006." *Journal of the Washington Academy of Sciences* 97(1): 49–69.

Gaughan, Monica, and Barry Bozeman. 2016. "Using the Prisms of Gender and Rank to Interpret Research Collaboration Power Dynamics." *Social Studies of Science*. June 29, doi:10.1177/0306312716652249.

Gatta, Mary L., and Patricia A. Roos. 2004. "Balancing without a Net in Academia: Integrating Family and Work Lives." *Equal Opportunities International* 23(3/4/5): 124–142.

Gazni, Ali, Cassidy R. Sugimoto, and Fereshteh Didegah. 2012. "Mapping World Scientific Collaboration: Authors, Institutions, and Countries." *Journal of the American Society for Information Science and Technology* 63(2): 323–335.

Gerstel, Naomi, and Sally K. Gallagher. 2001. "Men's Caregiving: Gender and the Contingent Character of Care." *Gender & Society* 15(2): 197–217.

Gillett, Rachel Anne. 2013. "Jazz Women, Gender Politics, and the Francophone Atlantic." *Atlantic Studies* 10(1): 109–130.

Glänzel, Wolfgang. 2001. "National Characteristics in International Scientific Co-Authorship Relations." *Scientometrics* 51(1): 69–115.

Glänzel, Wolfgang, and András Schubert. 2005. "Analysing Scientific Networks through Co-Authorship." In *Handbook of Quantitative Science and Technology Research*, edited by Henk F. Moed, Wolfgang Glänzel, and Ulrich Schmoch, 257–276. Dordrecht, The Netherlands: Kluwer Academic Publishers.

Green, Madeleine F., and Christa L. Olsen. 2003. *Internationalizing the Campus: A User's Guide*. Washington, DC: American Council on Education.

Gustafson, Per. 2006. "Work-Related Travel, Gender and Family Obligations." *Work, Employment & Society* 20(3): 513–530.

Gutiérrez y Muhs, Gabriella. 2012. *Presumed Incompetent: The Intersections of Race and Class for Women in Academia*. Boulder: University Press of Colorado.

Hardill, Irene. 2002. *Gender, Migration and the Dual-Career Household*. London: Routledge.

Hays, Sharon. 1996. *The Cultural Contradictions of Motherhood*. New Haven, CT: Yale University Press.

Hazelkorn, Ellen. 2011. *Rankings and the Reshaping of Higher Education: The Battle for World-Class Excellence*. London: Palgrave Macmillan.

Hearn, Jeff. 2001. "Academia, Management, and Men: Making the Connections, Exploring the Implications." In *Gender and the Restructured University: Changing Management and Culture in Higher Education*, edited by Ann Brooks and Alison Mackinnon, 69–89. Buckingham, UK: SRHE and Open University Press.

Hearn, Jeff, and Liisa Husu. 2011. "Understanding Gender: Some Implications for Science and Technology." *Interdisciplinary Science Reviews* 36(2): 103–113.

Heilman, Madeline E. 2001. "Description and Prescription: How Gender Stereotypes Prevent Women's Ascent up the Organizational Ladder." *Journal of Social Issues* 57(4): 657–674.

Hemlin, Sven, and Soren Barlebo Rasmussen. 2006. "The Shift in Academic Quality Control." *Science, Technology & Human Values* 31(2): 173–198.

Henderson, Emily F. 2015. "Academic Conferences: Representative and Resistant Sites for Higher Education Research." *Higher Education Research & Development*: 1–12.

Hesli, Vicki L., and Jae Mook Lee. 2013. "Job Satisfaction in Academia: Why Are Some Faculty Members Happier Than Others?" *PS: Political Science & Politics* 46(02): 339–354.

Hochschild, Arlie Russell, and Anne Machung. 1989. *The Second Shift: Working Parents and the Revolution at Home*. New York: Viking Penguin.

Hogan, Alice, Kathrin Zippel, Lisa M. Frehill, and Laura Kramer. 2010. *Report of the International Workshop on International Research Collaboration*. Washington, DC: National Science Foundation. Available at: www.nuweb.neu.edu/zippel/nsf-workshop/docs/FinalReport_Oct22_2010.pdf.

Hook, Jennifer. 2006. "Care in Context: Men's Unpaid Work in 20 Countries, 1965–2003." *American Sociological Review* 71(4): 639–660.

Hsiehchen, David, Magdalena Espinoza, and Antony Hsieh. 2015. "Multinational Teams and Diseconomies of Scale in Collaborative Research." *Science Advances* 1(8).

Hunter, Laura, and Erin Leahey. 2008. "Collaborative Research in Sociology: Trends and Contributing Factors." *American Sociologist* 39(4): 290–306.

Husu, Liisa. 2005. "Women's Work-Related and Family-Related Discrimination and Support in Academia." In *Advances in Gender Research: Gender Realities: Local and Global*, 161–199. Bradford, UK: Emerald Group Publishing.

Husu, Liisa, and Suzanne Cheveigné. 2010. "Gender and Gatekeeping of Excellence in Research Funding: European Perspectives." In *Genderchange in Academia*, edited by Birgit Riegraf, Brigitte Aulenbacher, Edit Kirsch-Auwärter, and Ursula Müller, 43–59. Wiesbaden; VS Verlag für Sozialwissenschaften.

Husu, Liisa, and Paula Koskinen. 2010. "Gendering Excellence in Technological Research: A Comparative European Perspective." *Journal of Technology Management & Innovation* 5(1): 127–139.

Institute of International Education. 2014a. *Open Doors 2014: International Students in the United States and Study Abroad by American Students Are at All-Time High*. Washington, DC: US Department of State. Available at www.iie.org/en/Research-and-Publications/Open-Doors.

———.2014b. "International Students by Academic Level, 2012/13–2013/14." *Open Doors Report on International Educational Exchange*. Retrieved on October 25, 2015, from www.iie.org/opendoors.

Institute of Medicine, National Academy of Sciences, and National Academy of Engineering. 2007. *Beyond Bias and Barriers: Fulfilling the Potential of Women in Academic Science and Engineering*. Washington, DC: The National Academies Press.

Ivie, Rachel, and Kim Nies Ray. 2005. *AIP Report*. College Park, MD: American Institute of Physics.

Jacob, Merle, and V. Lynn Meek. 2013. "Scientific Mobility and International Research Networks: Trends and Policy Tools for Promoting Research Excellence and Capacity Building." *Studies in Higher Education* 38(3): 331–344.

Jacobs, Jerry A. 1996. "Gender Inequality and Higher Education." *Annual Review of Sociology* 22: 153–185.

———. 1999. "Gender and the Stratification of Colleges." *Journal of Higher Education* 70(2): 161–187.

Jacobs, Jerry A., and Sarah E. Winslow. 2004. "The Academic Life Course, Time Pressures and Gender Inequality." *Community, Work & Family* 7(2): 143–161.

———. 2004. "Overworked Faculty: Job Stresses and Family Demands." *Annals of the American Academy of Political and Social Science* 596(1): 104–129.

Jeong, Yu-Jin, Anisa M Zvonkovic, Yoshie Sano, and Alan C Acock. 2013. "The Occurrence and Frequency of Overnight Job Travel in the USA." *Work, Employment & Society* 27(1): 138–152.

Jones, Benjamin F., Stefan Wuchty, and Brian Uzzi. 2008. "Multi-University Research Teams: Shifting Impact, Geography, and Stratification in Science." *Science* 322(5905): 1259–1262.

Jöns, Heike. 2007. "Transnational Mobility and the Spaces of Knowledge Production: A Comparison of Global Patterns, Motivations and Collaborations in Different Academic Fields." *Social Geography* 2(2): 97–114.

———. 2011. "Transnational Academic Mobility and Gender." *Globalisation, Societies & Education* 9(2): 183–209.

Jöns, Heike, and Michael Hoyler. 2013. "Global Geographies of Higher Education: The Perspective of World University Rankings." *Geoforum* 46: 45–59.

Jules-Rosette, Bennetta. 2005. "Josephine Baker and Utopian Visions of Black Paris." *Journal of Romance Studies* 5(3): 33–50.

Kan, Man Yee, Oriel Sullivan, and Jonathan Gershuny. 2011. "Gender Convergence in Domestic Work: Discerning the Effects of Interactional and Institutional Barriers from Large-Scale-Data." *Sociology* 45(2): 234–251.

Kanter, Rosabeth Moss. 1977. *Men and Women of the Corporation*. New York: Basic Books.

Kapheim, Karen M., Hailin Pan, Cai Li, Steven L. Salzberg, Daniela Puiu, Tanja Magoc, Hugh M. Robertson, Matthew E. Hudson, Aarti Venkat, Brielle J. Fischman, Alvaro Hernandez, Mark Yandell, Daniel Ence, Carson Holt, George D. Yocum, William P. Kemp, Jordi Bosch, Robert M. Waterhouse, Evgeny M. Zdobnov, Eckart Stolle, F. Bernhard Kraus, Sophie Helbing, Robin F. A. Moritz, Karl M. Glastad, Brendan G. Hunt, Michael A. D. Goodisman, Frank Hauser, Cornelis J. P. Grimmelikhuijzen, Daniel Guariz Pinheiro, Francis Morais Franco Nunes, Michelle Prioli Miranda Soares, Érica Donato Tanaka, Zilá Luz Paulino Simões, Klaus Hartfelder, Jay D. Evans, Seth M. Barribeau, Reed M. Johnson, Jonathan H. Massey, Bruce R. Southey, Martin Hasselmann, Daniel Hamacher, Matthias Biewer, Clement F. Kent, Amro Zayed, Charles Blatti, Saurabh Sinha, J. Spencer Johnston, Shawn J. Hanrahan, Sarah D. Kocher, Jun Wang, Gene E. Robinson, and Guojie Zhang. 2015. "Genomic Signatures of Evolutionary Transitions from Solitary to Group Living." *Science* 348(6239): 1139–1143.

Kato, Maki, and Asao Ando. 2013. "The Relationship between Research Performance and International Collaboration in Chemistry." *Scientometrics* 97(3): 535–553.

Katz, Sandra, John Aronis, David Allbritton, Christine Wilson, and Mary Lou Soffa. 2003. "Gender and Race in Predicting Achievement in Computer Science." *IEEE Technology & Society Magazine* 22(3): 20–27.

Kauppi, Niilo, and Tero Erkkilä. 2011. "The Struggle over Global Higher Education: Actors, Institutions, and Practices." *International Political Sociology* 5(3): 314–326.

Kauppinen, Ilkka. 2013. "Academic Capitalism and the Informational Fraction of the Transnational Capitalist Class." *Globalisation, Societies and Education* 11(1): 1–22.

Kemelgor, Carol, and Henry Etzkowitz. 2001. "Overcoming Isolation: Women's Dilemmas in American Academic Science." *Minerva* 39(2): 239–257.

Khan, Shamus Rahman. 2011. *Privilege: The Making of an Adolescent Elite at St. Paul's School*. Princeton, NJ: Princeton University Press.

Kleinman, Daniel Lee, and Steven P. Vallas. 2001. "Science, Capitalism, and the Rise of the 'Knowledge Worker': The Changing Structure of Knowledge Production in the United States." *Theory and Society* 30(4): 451–492.

Knight, Jane. 1999. *A Time of Turbulence and Transformation for Internationalization.* Ottawa, Canada: Canadian Bureau for International Education.

Knobel, Marcelo, Tania Patricia Simões, and Carlos Henrique de Brito Cruz. 2013. "International Collaborations between Research Universities: Experiences and Best Practices." *Studies in Higher Education* 38(3): 405–424.

Krais, Beate. 2002. "Academia as a Profession and the Hierarchy of Sexes." *Higher Education Quarterly* 56(4): 407–418.

Kulis, Stephen, and Diane Sicotte. 2002. "Women Scientists in America: Geographically Constrained to Big Cities, College Clusters, or the Coasts?" *Research in Higher Education* 43(1): 1–30.

Kvande, Elin. 2002. "Doing Masculinities in Organizational Restructuring." *NORA: Nordic Journal of Women's Studies* 10(1): 16–25.

———. 2009. "Work–Life Balance for Fathers in Globalized Knowledge Work. Some Insights from the Norwegian Context." *Gender, Work & Organization* 16(1): 58–72.

Kyvik, Svein, and Mari Teigen. 1996. "Child Care, Research Collaboration, and Gender Differences in Scientific Productivity." *Science, Technology & Human Values* 21(1): 54–71.

Lamont, Michèle. 2009. *How Professors Think: Inside the Curious World of Academic Judgment.* Cambridge, MA: Harvard University Press.

Lareau, Annette, and Elliot B. Weininger. 2008. "Class and the Transition to Adulthood." In *Social Class: How Does It Work?*, edited by Annette Lareau and Dalton Conley, 118–151. New York: Russell Sage.

Larivière, Vincent, Chaoqun Ni, Yves Gingras, Blaise Cronin, and Cassidy R. Sugimoto. 2013. "Bibliometrics: Global Gender Disparities in Science." *Nature* 504(7479): 211–213.

Larivière, Vincent, Etienne Vignola-Gagné, Christian Villeneuve, Pascal Gélinas, and Yves Gingras. 2011. "Sex Differences in Research Funding, Productivity, and Impact: An Analysis of Quebec University Professors." *Scientometrics* 87(3): 483–498.

Latour, Bruno, and Steve Woolgar. 1986. *Laboratory Life: The Construction of Scientific Facts.* Princeton, NJ: Princeton University Press.

Ledford, Heidi. 2014. "Indirect Costs: Keeping the Lights On." *Nature* 515: 326–329.

Leemann, Regula Julia. 2010. "Gender Inequalities in Transnational Academic Mobility and the Ideal Type of Academic Entrepreneur." *Discourse: Studies in the Cultural Politics of Education* 31(5): 605–625.

Leemann, Regula Julia, and Stefan Boes. 2012. "Institutionalisierung von 'Mobilität' und 'Internationalität' in Wissenschaftlichen Laufbahnen: Neue Barrieren für Frauen auf dem Weg an die Spitze?" In *Einfach Spitze? Neue Geschlechterperspektiven auf Karrieren in der Wissenschaft*, edited by Sandra Beaufaÿs, Anita Engels. and Heike Kahlert, 174–203. Frankfurt am Main [u.a.]: Campus.

Leemann, Regula Julia, Philipp Dubach, and Stefan Boes. 2010. "The Leaky Pipeline in the Swiss University System. Identifying Gender Barriers in Postgraduate Education and Networks Using Longitudinal Data." *Swiss Journal of Sociology* 36(2): 299–323.

Leung, Maggi W. H. 2014. "'Academic Mobility for Development' as a Contested Notion: An Analysis of the Reach of the Chinese State in Regulating the Transnational Brains." *Tijdschrift voor economische en sociale geografie* 105(5): 558–572.

Levitt, Peggy. 2015. *Artifacts and Allegiances: How Museums Put the Nation and the World on Display.* Berkeley: University of California Press.

Lexington. 2009. "The Battle for Brains." *Lexington's Notebook American Politics* (blog). *The Economist.* Available at www.economist.com/blogs/lexington/2009/03/the_battle_for_brains.

Leydesdorff, Loet, Han Woo Park, and Caroline Wagner. 2014. "International Coauthorship Relations in the Social Sciences Citation Index: Is Internationalization Leading the Network?" *Journal of the Association for Information Science and Technology* 65(10): 2111–2126.

Leydesdorff, Loet, Caroline Wagner, Han Woo Park, and Jonathan Adams. 2013. "International Collaboration in Science: The Global Map and the Network." *El Profesional de la Información* 22(1): 87–96.

Leydesdorff, Loet, Caroline S. Wagner, and Lutz Bornmann. 2014. "The European Union, China, and the United States in the Top-1% and Top-10% Layers of Most-Frequently Cited Publications: Competition and Collaborations." *Journal of Informetrics* 8(3): 606–617.

Li, Eldon Y., Chien Hsiang Liao, and Hsiuju Rebecca Yen. 2013. "Co-Authorship Networks and Research Impact: A Social Capital Perspective." *Research Policy* 42(9): 1515–1530.

Liang, Xiang Fen, Simy Joy, Diana Bilimoria, and Susan Perry. 2008. "Establishing Advisor–Advisee Relationships: Impact of Decision Factors, Schemas and Time Periods." Paper read at the Academy of Management Annual Meeting, Anaheim, CA.

Liao, Chien Hsiang. 2011. "How to Improve Research Quality? Examining the Impacts of Collaboration Intensity and Member Diversity in Collaboration Networks." *Scientometrics* 86(3): 747–761.

Lincoln, Anne E., Stephanie Pincus, Janet Bandows Koster, and Phoebe S. Leboy. 2012. "The Matilda Effect in Science: Awards and Prizes in the US, 1990s and 2000s." *Social Studies of Science* 42(2): 307–320.

Lubitow, Amy, and Kathrin Zippel. 2014. "Strategies of Academic Parents to Manage Work–Life Conflict in Research Abroad." In *Advances in Gender Research*, edited by Marcia Segal, Catherine Berheide, and Vasilikie Demos, 63–84. Bradford, UK: Emerald Books.

Lucier, Paul. 2009. "The Professional and the Scientist in Nineteenth-Century America." *Isis* 100(4): 699–732.

Luke, Carmen. 2001. *Globalization and Women in Academia: North/West-South/East, Sociocultural, Political, and Historical Studies in Education*. Mahwah, NJ: L. Erlbaum Associates.

Luukkonen, Terttu, Olle Persson, and Gunnar Sivertsen. 1992. "Understanding Patterns of International Scientific Collaboration." *Science, Technology & Human Values* 17(1): 101–126.

Macdonald, Cameron. 2009. "What's Culture Got to Do with It? Mothering Ideologies as Barriers to Gender Equity." In *Gender Equality: Transforming Family Divisions of Labor*, edited by Janet C. Gornick, Marcia K. Meyers, and Erik Olin Wright, 411–434. New York: Verso Books.

Mandelker, Jane. 1994. "Breaking the Glass Border." *Working Woman* 19(1): 16.

Manrique, Cecilia G., and Gabriel G. Manrique. 1999. *The Multicultural or Immigrant Faculty in American Society*. Mellen Studies in Education volume 43. Lewiston, NY: E. Mellen Press.

Marimon, Ramon, Matthieu Lietaert, and Michele Grigolo. 2009. "Towards the 'Fifth Freedom': Increasing the Mobility of Researchers in the European Union." *Higher Education in Europe* 34(1): 25–37.

Martin, Patricia Yancey. 2003. "'Said and Done' Versus 'Saying and Doing': Gendering Practices, Practicing Gender at Work." *Gender & Society* 17(3): 342–366.

Mason, Mary Ann, and Marc Goulden. 2004. "Do Babies Matter (Part II)? Closing the Baby Gap." *Academe* 90(6): 10–15.

Mason, Mary Ann, Nicholas H. Wolfinger, and Marc Goulden. 2013. *Do Babies Matter? Gender and Family in the Ivory Tower*. Families in Focus. New Brunswick, NJ: Rutgers University Press.

Massachusetts Institute of Technology (MIT). 1999. *A Study on the Status of Women Faculty in Science*. Cambridge, MA: Massachusetts Institute of Technology.

———. 2010. *Report on the Initiative for Faculty Race and Diversity*. Cambridge, MA: Massachusetts Institute of Technology. Available at www.web.mit.edu/newsoffice/images/documents/women-report-2011.pdf.

McCall, Leslie. 2001. 2005. "The Complexity of Intersectionality." *Signs: Journal of Women in Culture and Society* 30(3): 1771–1800.

McKinney, Kathleen. 1990. "Sexual Harassment of University Faculty by Colleagues and Students." *Sex Roles* 23(7–8): 421–438.

McMillan Cottom, Tressie, and Gaye Tuchman. 2015. "Rationalization of Higher Education." In *Emerging Trends in the Social and Behavioral Sciences: An Interdisciplinary, Searchable, and Linkable Resource*, edited by Robert A. Scott, Stephen M. Kosslyn, and Nancy Pinkerton, 1–17. New York: John Wiley & Sons.

Melkers, Julia, and Agrita Kiopa. 2010. "The Social Capital of Global Ties in Science: The Added Value of International Collaboration." *Review of Policy Research* 27(4): 389–414.

Mellström, Ulf. 2009. "The Intersection of Gender, Race, and Cultural Boundaries, or Why Is Computer Science in Malaysia Dominated by Women?" *Social Studies of Science* 39(6): 885–907.

Merton, Robert K. 1968. "The Matthew Effect in Science." *Science* 159(3810): 56–63.

———. 1973. *The Sociology of Science: Theoretical and Empirical Investigations*. Chicago: University of Chicago Press.

———. 1979 (1942). "The Normative Structure of Science." In *The Sociology of Science: Theoretical and Empirical Investigations*, edited by Robert K. Merton, 267–278. Chicago: University of Chicago Press.

———. 1996. *On Social Structure and Science*. Edited by Piotr Sztompka. Chicago: University of Chicago Press.

Michaels, Ed, Helen Handfield-Jones, and Beth Axelrod. 2001. *The War on Talent*. Boston, MA: Harvard Business School Press.

Miller, David I., Alice H. Eagly, and Marcia C. Linn. 2015. "Women's Representation in Science Predicts National Gender-Science Stereotypes: Evidence from 66 Nations." *Journal of Educational Psychology* 107(3): 631–644.

Miller, James. 2008. "What Does It Mean to Be an American? The Dialectics of Self-Discovery in Baldwin's 'Paris Essays' (1950–1961)." *Journal of American Studies* 42(1): 51–66.

Misra, Joya, Jennifer Hickes Lundquist, Elissa Dahlberg Holmes, and Stephanie Agiomavritis. 2011. "The Ivory Ceiling of Service Work." *Academe* 97(1): 22–26.

Misra, Joya, Jennifer Hickes Lundquist, and Abby Templer. 2012. "Gender, Work Time, and Care Responsibilities among Faculty." *Sociological Forum* 27(2): 300–323.

Moen, Phyllis. 2003. *It's about Time: Couples and Careers*. Ithaca, NY: ILR Press.

Mohanty, Chandra Talpade. 2003. "'Under Western Eyes' Revisited: Feminist Solidarity through Anticapitalist Struggles." *Signs: Journal of Women and Culture and Society* 28(2): 499–535.

Moody, James. 2004. "The Structure of a Social Science Collaboration Network: Disciplinary Cohesion from 1963 to 1999." *American Sociological Review* 69(2): 213–238.

Morano-Foadi, Sonia. 2005. "Scientific Mobility, Career Progression, and Excellence in the European Research Area." *International Migration* 43(5): 133–162.

Mosbah-Natanson, Sébastien, and Yves Gingras. 2013. "The Globalization of Social Sciences? Evidence from a Quantitative Analysis of 30 Years of Production, Collaboration and Citations in the Social Sciences (1980–2009)." *Current Sociology*.

Mügge, Liza M. 2013. "Sexually Harassed by Gatekeepers: Reflections on Fieldwork in Surinam and Turkey." *International Journal of Social Research Methodology* 16(6): 541–546.

Musselin, Christine. 2004. "Towards a European Academic Labour Market? Some Lessons Drawn from Empirical Studies on Academic Mobility." *Higher Education* 48(1): 55–78.

National Academy of Sciences, National Academy of Engineering, and Institute of Medicine. 2007. *Rising above the Gathering Storm: Energizing and Employing America for a Brighter Economic Future*. Washington, DC: The National Academies Press.

———. 2010. *Rising above the Gathering Storm: Rapidly Approaching Category 5*. Washington, DC: National Academies Press.

National Center for Education Statistics. 2004. National Study of Postsecondary Faculty. 2004. Available at www.nces.ed.gov/surveys/nsopf/

———. 2015. "IPEDS data center." Available at www.nces.ed.gov/ipeds/datacenter/ Default.aspx

National Geographic. 2016. Women Explorers. Retrieved July 31, 2016, from www .nationalgeographic.com/explorers/women-of-national-geographic/.

National Research Council. 2010. *Gender Differences at Critical Transitions in the Careers of Science, Engineering, and Mathematics Faculty*. Washington, DC: National Academies Press.

———. 2014. *Culture Matters: International Research Collaboration in a Changing World (Summary of a Workshop)*. Washington, DC: National Academies Press.

National Science Board. 2008. International Science and Engineering Partnerships: A Priority for U.S. Foreign Policy and Our Nation's Innovation Enterprise. Arlington VA: National Science Foundation (NSB-08-4).

———. 2012. *Science and Engineering Indicators 2012*. Arlington VA: National Science Foundation (NSB 12-01).

———. 2014. *Science and Engineering Indicators 2014*. Arlington, VA: National Science Foundation (NSB 14-01).

———. 2016. *Science and Engineering Indicators 2016*. Arlington, VA: National Science Foundation (NSB-2016-1).

National Science Foundation. 2011. *Empowering the Nation Through Discovery and Innovation: NSF Strategic Plan for Fiscal Years 2011–2016*. Arlington, VA: National Science Foundation. Available at www.nsf.gov/news/strategicplan/ nsfstrategicplan_2011_2016.pdf.

———.2013a. *Graduate Students and Postdoctorates in Science and Engineering: Fall 2011*.

———. 2013b. NSF and USAID Jointly Announce Next Round of Global Research Collaboration Awardees. In *Press Release 13-110*. Arlington, VA: National Science Foundation. Available at www.nsf.gov/news/news_summ.jsp?cntn_id=128273.

———. 2014a. *Investing in Science, Engineering, and Education for the Nation's Future*. Arlington, VA: National Science Foundation.

———. 2014b. "International Science and Engineering (ISE) Section." Retrieved on November 22, 2014, from www.nsf.gov/od/iia/ise/index.jsp.

———. 2014c. "Office of International and Integrative Activities Welcome Page." Retrieved on February 24, 2014, from www.nsf.gov/dir/index.jsp?org=IIA.

———. 2015. "Partnerships for International Research and Education." Retrieved on March 25, 2015, from www.nsf.gov/funding/pgm_summ.jsp?pims_id=505038.

Nesmith, Robert. 2009. "WIRES Conference to Kick off International Networking and Research." *The Whistle*. Available at www.whistle.gatech.edu/archives/09/ may/18/wires.shtml.

Nielsen, Mathias Wullum. 2014. "Justifications of Gender Equality in Academia: Comparing Gender Equality Policies of Six Scandinavian Universities." *NORA-Nordic Journal of Feminist and Gender Research* 22(3): 187–203.

———. 2015. "Gender Inequality and Research Performance: Moving beyond Individual-Meritocratic Explanations of Academic Advancement." *Studies in Higher Education*: 1–17. 10.1080/03075079.2015.1007945.

Organisation of Economic Co-operation and Development (OECD). 1996. The Knowledge-based Economy. Available at www.oecd.org/sti/sci-tech/1913021.pdf.

Ong, Mia. 2005. "Body Projects of Young Women of Color in Physics: Intersections of Gender, Race, and Science." *Social Problems* 52(4): 593–617.

Paap, Kris. 2006. *Working Construction: Why White Working-Class Men Put Themselves—and the Labor Movement—in Harm's Way.* Ithaca, NY: Cornell University Press.

Padavic, Irene, Robin J. Ely, and Erin Reid. 2013. The Work–Family Narrative as a Social Defense. Presented at Research Symposium: Gender & Work, Challenging Conventional Wisdom. Harvard Business School.

Padilla-González, Laura, Amy Scott Metcalfe, Jesús F. Galaz-Fontes, Donald Fisher, and Iain Snee. 2011. "Gender Gaps in North American Research Productivity: Examining Faculty Publication Rates in Mexico, Canada, and the U.S." *Compare: A Journal of Comparative and International Education* 41(5): 649–668.

Paludi, Michele Antoinette. 1990. *Ivory Power: Sexual Harassment on Campus.* Albany: SUNY Press.

Park, Chan-ung. 2007. "Gender in Academic Career Tracks: The Case of Korean Biochemists." *Sociological Forum* 22(4): 452–473.

Pasupathy, Rubini, and Kamau Oginga Siwatu. 2013. "An Investigation of Research Self-Efficacy Beliefs and Research Productivity among Faculty Members at an Emerging Research University in the USA." *Higher Education Research & Development* 33(4): 728–741.

Patil, Vrushali. 2013. "From Patriarchy to Intersectionality: A Transnational Feminist Assessment of How Far We've Really Come." *Signs: Journal of Women and Culture and Society* 38(4): 847–867.

The Pew Charitable Trusts. 2015. Federal and State Funding of Higher Education: A changing landscape. Available at www.pewtrusts.org/en/research-and-analysis/issue-briefs/2015/06/federal-and-state-funding-of-higher-education.

Puuska, Hanna-Mari, Reetta Muhonen, and Yrjö Leino. 2014. "International and Domestic Co-Publishing and Their Citation Impact in Different Disciplines." *Scientometrics* 98(2): 823–839.

Pyenson, Lewis, and Douglas Skopp. 1977. "Educating Physicists in Germany circa 1900." *Social Studies of Science* 7(3): 329–366.

Qiu, Jane. 2014. "International Collaboration in Science: A Chinese Perspective." *National Science Review* 1(2): 318–321.

Radhakrishnan, Smitha. 2011. *Appropriately Indian: Gender and Culture in a New Transnational Class.* Durham, NC: Duke University Press.

Ramirez, Francisco O. 2006. "The Rationalization of Universities." In *Transnational Governance: Institutional Dynamics of Regulation*, edited by Marie-Laure Djelic and Kerstin Sahlin-Anderson, 225–244. Cambridge, UK: Cambridge University Press.

Ramirez, Francisco O., and Naejin Kwak. 2015. "Women's Enrollments in STEM in Higher Education: Cross-National Trends, 1970–2010." In *Advancing Women in Science: An International Perspective*, edited by Willie Pearson Jr., Lisa M. Frehill, and Connie L. McNeely, 9–25. Heidelberg, New York: Springer.

Ramirez, Francisco O., and Dijana Tiplic. 2014. "In Pursuit of Excellence? Discursive Patterns in European Higher Education Research." *Higher Education* 67: 439–455.

Ramos, Ana M. González, and Esther Torrado Martin-Palomino. 2015. "Addressing Women's Agency on International Mobility." *Women's Studies International Forum* 49: 1–11.

Rankin, Patricia, Joyce Nielsen, and Dawn M. Stanley. 2007. "Weak Links, Hot Networks, and Tacit Knowledge." In *Transforming Science and Engineering. Advancing Academic Women*, edited by Abigail J. Stewart, Janet E. Malley and Danielle LaVaque-Manty, 31–47. Ann Arbor: The University of Michigan Press.

Ridgeway, Cecilia. 2011. *Framed by Gender: How Gender Inequality Persists in the Modern World*. New York: Oxford University Press.

Ridgeway, Cecilia L., and Shelley J. Correll. 2004. "Unpacking the Gender System: A Theoretical Perspective on Gender Beliefs and Social Relations." *Gender & Society* 18(4): 510–531.

———. 2006. "Consensus and the Creation of Status Beliefs." *Social Forces* 85(1): 431–453.

Ridgeway, Cecilia L., and Lynn Smith-Lovin. 1999. "The Gender System and Interaction." *Annual Review of Sociology* 25(1): 191–216.

Rilke, Rainer Maria. 1996. *Rilke's Book of Hours: Love Poems to God*. New York: Riverhead Books.

Risman, Barbara J., and Timothy Adkins. 2014. "The Goal of Gender Transformation in American Universities: Toward Social Justice for Women in the Academy." In *Social Justice and the University: Globalization, Human Rights and the Future of Democracy*, edited by Jon Shefner, Harry F. Dahms, Robert Emmet Jones, and Asafa Jalata, 99–113. Houndsmills, UK: Palgrave Macmillan.

Robertson, Susan, and Ruth Keeling. 2008. "Stirring the Lions: Strategy and Tactics in Global Higher Education." *Globalisation, Societies and Education* 6(3): 221–240.

Roos, Patricia A., and Mary L. Gatta. 2009. "Gender (in)Equity in the Academy: Subtle Mechanisms and the Production of Inequality." *Research in Social Stratification and Mobility* 27(3): 177–200.

Rosenfeld, Rachel A. 1981. "Academic Men and Women's Career Mobility." *Social Science Research* 10(4): 337–363.

Rosser, Sue Vilhauer. 2004. *The Science Glass Ceiling: Academic Women Scientists and the Struggle to Succeed*. New York: Routledge.

Rossiter, Margaret W. 1982. *Women Scientists in America: Struggles and Strategies to 1940*. Baltimore, MD: Johns Hopkins University Press.

The Royal Society. 2011. *Knowledge, Networks and Nations: Global Scientific Collaboration in the 21st Century*. London: The Royal Society.

Rubin, Lillian B. 1976. *Worlds of Pain: Life in the Working-Class Family*. New York: Basic Books.

Rusconi, Alessandra, and Heike Solga. 2011. *Gemeinsam Karriere Machen: Die Verflechtung Von Berufskarrieren Und Familie in Akademiepartnerschaften*. Opladen, Germany: Verlag Barbara Budrich.

Salamin, Xavier, and Doris Hanappi. 2014. "Women and International Assignments." *Journal of Global Mobility: The Home of Expatriate Management Research* 2(3): 343–374.

Salmi, Jamil. 2009. *The Challenge of Establishing World-Class Universities*. Washington, DC: World Bank Publications.

Salzinger, Leslie. 2004. "From Gender as Object to Gender as Verb: Rethinking How Global Restructuring Happens." *Critical Sociology* 30(1): 43–62.

Sandberg, Sheryl. 2013. *Lean In: Women, Work, and the Will to Lead*. New York: Random House.

Sarsons, Heather. 2016. "Gender Differences in Recognition for Group Work." Working Paper. Cambridge, MA: Harvard University. Available at www.scholar.harvard.edu/sarsons/publications/note-gender-differences-recognition-group-work.

Sassen, Saskia. 1988. *The Mobility of Labor and Capital*. Cambridge, UK: Cambridge University Press.

———. 2001. *The Global City: New York, London, Tokyo*, 2nd ed. Princeton, NJ: Princeton University Press.

Sauder, Michael, and Wendy Nelson Espeland. 2009. "The Discipline of Rankings: Tight Coupling and Organizational Change." *American Sociological Review* 74(1): 63–82.

Sayer, Liana C. 2005. "Gender, Time, and Inequality: Trends in Women's and Men's Paid Work, Unpaid Work, and Free Time." *Social Forces* 84(1): 285–303.

Scellato, Giuseppe, Chiara Franzoni, and Paula Stephan. 2012. *Mobile Scientists and International Networks*. National Bureau of Economic Research Working Paper Series. Cambridge, MA: National Bureau of Economic Research.

Schiebinger, Londa, and Shannon K. Gilmartin. 2010. "Housework Is an Academic Issue: How to Keep Talented Women Scientists in the Lab, where They Belong." *Academe* 96(1): 39–44.

Schiebinger, Lorna, Andrea Davies Henderson, and Shannon K. Gilmartin. 2008. *Dual-Career Academic Couples: What Universities Need to Know*. Palo Alto, CA: Stanford University Michelle R. Clayman Institute for Gender Research. Available at www.stanford.edu/group/gender/Publications/index.html.

Schott, Thomas. 1993. "World Science: Globalization of Institutions and Participation." *Science, Technology, & Human Values* 18(2): 196–208.

Settles, Isis H., Lilia M. Cortina, Janet Malley, and Abigail J. Stewart. 2006. "The Climate for Women in Academic Science: The Good, the Bad, and the Changeable." *Psychology of Women Quarterly* 30(1): 47–58.

Settles, Isis H., and Rachel C. O'Connor. 2014. "Incivility at Academic Conferences: Gender Differences and the Mediating Role of Climate." *Sex Roles* 71(1–2): 71–82.

ShanghaiRanking Consultancy. 2016. "Academic Ranking of World Universities." Retrieved July 30, 2016, from www.shanghairanking.com/ARWU2015.html.

Shauman, Kimberlee A., and Yu Xie. 1996. "Geographic Mobility of Scientists: Sex Differences and Family Constraints." *Demography* 33(4): 455–468.

Shen, Helen. 2013. "Inequality Quantified: Mind the Gender Gap." *Nature* 495(7439): 22–24.

Sheridan, Jennifer, Christine Maidl Pribbenow, Eve Fine, Jo Handelsman, and Molly Carnes. 2007. "Climate Change at the University of Wisconsin-Madison: What Changed, and Did Advance Have an Impact?" Paper read at Women in Engineering ProActive Network (WEPAN) 2007 National Conference Proceedings: Imagining the Future of Engineering, June 10–13, at Disney's Coronado Springs Resort, Lake Buena Vista, FL.

Siemieńska, Renata, and Annette Zimmer. 2007. *Gendered Career Trajectories in Academia in Cross-National Perspective*. Warsaw, Poland: Wydawnictwo Naukowe SCHOLAR.

Singer, Sandra L. 2003. *Adventures Abroad: North American Women at German-Speaking Universities, 1868–1915*. Westport, CT: Praeger.

Skrentny, John D. 2013. *After Civil Rights: Racial Realism in the New American Workplace*. Princeton, NJ: Princeton University Press.

Slaughter, Sheila, and Larry L. Leslie. 1997. *Academic Capitalism: Politics, Policies, and the Entrepreneurial University*. Baltimore, MD: The Johns Hopkins University Press.

Slaughter, Sheila, and Gary Rhoades. 2004. *Academic Capitalism and the New Economy: Markets, State, and Higher Education*. Baltimore, MD: The Johns Hopkins University Press.

Smith, Janice W., and Toni Calasanti. 2005. "The Influence of Gender, Race, and Ethnicity on Workplace Experiences of Institutional and Social Isolation: An Exploratory Study of University Faculty." *Sociological Spectrum* 25(3): 307–334.

Smith-Doerr, Laurel. 2004. *Women's Work: Gender Equality vs. Hierarchy in the Life Sciences*. Boulder, CO: Lynne Rienner Publishers.

Smykla, Emily, and Kathrin Zippel. 2010. *Literature Review: Gender and International Research Collaboration*. Report for National Science Foundation Grant No. 0936970: "Incentives and Barriers to U.S. Academics' Participation in International Collaborations." Arlington, VA: National Science Foundation. Available at www.nuweb.neu.edu/zippel/nsf-workshop/docs/LitReviewOct22_2010.pdf.

Smyth, Frederick L., and Brian A. Nosek. 2015. "On the Gender-Science Stereotypes Held by Scientists: Explicit Accord with Gender-Ratios, Implicit Accord with Scientific Identity." *Frontiers in Psychology* 6: 1–19. 10.3389/fpsyg.2015.00415.

Sonnert, Gerhard, and Gerald James Holton. 1995. *Who Succeeds in Science? The Gen-der Dimension.* New Brunswick, NJ: Rutgers University Press.

Soyer, Michaela. 2014. "Off the Corner and into the Kitchen: Entering a Male-Dominated Research Setting as a Woman." *Qualitative Research* 14(4): 459–472.

Starr, Tina L., and Graeme Currie. 2009. "'Out of Sight but Still in the Picture': Short-Term International Assignments and the Influential Role of Family." *The International Journal of Human Resource Management* 20(6): 1421–1438.

Steffen-Fluhr, Nancy. 2006. "Advancing Women Faculty through Collaborative Re-search Networks." Paper read at WEPAN National Conference, June 11–14, at Pittsburgh, PA.

Steffen-Fluhr, Nancy, Regina Collins, Anatoliy Gruzd, Mingzhu Zhu, Brook Wu, and Katia Passerini. 2012. "Leveraging Social Network Data to Support Faculty Men-toring: Best Practices from NJIT Advance." Paper read at 2012 WEPAN Confer-ence, June 25–27, at Columbus, OH.

———. 2012. "More Than the Sum of Its Parts: Advancing Women at NJIT through Collaborative Research Networks." Paper read at WEPAN National Conference, June 25–27, at Columbus, OH.

Stephan, Paula E. 2012. *How Economics Shapes Science.* Cambridge, MA: Harvard University Press.

Stichweh, Rudolf. 2009. "Universitäten im Zeitalter der Globalisierung." In *Wissen und Geist. Universitätskulturen,* edited by Manfred Rudersdorf, Wolfgang Höpken and Martin Schlegel, 119–138. Leipzig, Germany: Leipziger Universitätsverlag

Suitor, J. Jill, Dorothy Mecom, and Ilana S. Feld. 2001. "Gender, Household Labor, and Scholarly Productivity among University Professors." *Gender Issues* 19(4): 50–67.

Teitelbaum, Michael S. 2014. *Falling Behind? Boom, Bust, and the Global Race for Sci-entific Talent.* Princeton NJ: Princeton University Press.

Traweek, Sharon. 1988. *Beamtimes and Lifetimes: The World of High Energy Physicists.* Cambridge, MA: Harvard University Press.

Tripp, Aili Mari. 2002. "Combining Intercontinental Parenting and Research: Dilem-mas and Strategies for Women." *Signs* 27(3): 793–811.

Trondal, Jarle. 2010. "Two Worlds of Change: On the Internationalisation of Universi-ties." *Globalisation, Societies and Education* 8(3): 351–368.

Tuchman, Gaye. 2009. *Wannabe U: Inside the Corporate University.* Chicago: Univer-sity of Chicago Press.

Turco, Catherine J. 2010. "Cultural Foundations of Tokenism: Evidence from the Lev-eraged Buyout Industry." *American Sociological Review* 75(6): 894–913.

Uhly, Katrina, Laura Visser, and Kathrin Zippel. 2015. "Gendered Patterns in Interna-tional Research Collaborations in Academia." *Studies in Higher Education*: 1–23.

Uhly, Katrina, and Kathrin Zippel. 2014. 'International Research Collaborations: Per-ceptions of Risk by Faculty." Paper at Annual Meeting of the American Sociologi-cal Association, San Francisco, CA.

UNESCO. 2005. *Towards Knowledge Societies: UNESCO World Report.* Paris: UNESCO. Available at www.unesdoc.unesco.org/images/0014/001418/141843e .pdf.

Vabø, Agnete. 2012. "Gender and International Research Cooperation." *International Higher Education* 69 (Fall): 19–20.

Vabø, Agnete, Laura Elena, Padilla-González, Erica Waagene, and Terje Næss. 2014. "Gender and Faculty Internationalization." In *The Internationalization of the Academy,* edited by Futao Huang, Martin Finkelstein, and Michele Rostan, 183–205. Dordrecht, Netherlands: Springer.

Valian, Virginia. 1998. *Why So Slow? The Advancement of Women.* Cambridge, MA: MIT Press.

van den Brink, Marieke. 2010. *Behind the Scenes of Science: A Gender Research on Professorial Recruitment and Selection Practices.* Amsterdam, Netherlands: Pallas Publications.

van den Brink, Marieke, and Yvonne Benschop. 2012. "Slaying the Seven-Headed Dragon: The Quest for Gender Change in Academia." *Gender, Work & Organization* 19(1): 71–92.

Vinkenburg, Claartje J., Channah Herschberg, Sara Connolly, and Stefan Fuchs. 2014. "Capturing Career Paths of ERC Grantees and Applicants: Promoting Sustainable Excellence in Research Careers." European Research Council. Available at www .erc.europa.eu/sites/default/files/document/file/ERCAREER_final_report.pdf.

Verloo, Mieke. 2013. "Intersectional and Cross-Movement Politics and Policies: Reflections on Current Practices and Debates." *Signs: Journal of Women and Culture and Society* 38(4): 893–915.

Wagner, Anne-Catherine. 2003. "La bourgeoisie Face à la mondialisation." *Mouvements* 26(2): 33.

———. 2007. "La place du voyage dans la formation des élites." *La Seuil/Actes de la Recherche en Sciences Sociales* 5(170): 58–65.

Wagner, Caroline S. 2009. *The New Invisible College: Science for Development.* Washington, DC: The Brookings Institution Press.

Wagner, David G., and Joseph Berger. 1993. "Status Characteristics Theory: The Growth of a Program." In *Theoretical Research Programs,* edited by Joseph Berger and Morris Zelditch Jr., 23–63. Stanford, CA: Stanford University Press.

Wagner, Caroline S., Han Woo Park, and Loet Leydesdorff. 2015. "The Continuing Growth of Global Cooperation Networks in Research: A Conundrum for National Governments." *PloS one* 10(7): p.e0131816, doi:10.1371/journal.pone.0131816

Wajcman, Judy. 2004. *Technofeminism.* Cambridge, UK: Polity Press.

Walby, Sylvia. 2007. "Complexity Theory, Systems Theory, and Multiple Intersecting Social Inequalities." *Philosophy of the Social Sciences* 37(4): 449–470.

Walker, Alexis J., Clara C. Pratt, and Linda Eddy. 1995. "Informal Caregiving to Aging Family Members: A Critical Review." *Family Relations* 44(4): 402–411.

Wall, Glenda, and Stephanie Arnold. 2007. "How Involved Is Involved Fathering? An Exploration of the Contemporary Culture of Fatherhood." *Gender & Society* 21(4): 508–527.

Weis, Lois, and Kristin Cipollone. 2013. "'Class Work': Producing Privilege and Social Mobility in Elite US Secondary Schools." *British Journal of Sociology of Education* 34(5–6): 701–722.

West, Candace, and Don H. Zimmermann. 1987. "Doing Gender." *Gender & Society* 1(2): 125–151.

West, Martha S., and John W. Curtis. 2006. *AAUP Faculty Gender Equity Indicators 2006*. Washington, DC: American Association of University Professors (AAUP).

Wharton, Amy S. 2015. "2014 PSA Presidential Address (Un)Changing Institutions: Work, Family, and Gender in the New Economy." *Sociological Perspectives* 58(1): 7–19.

White, Kate. 2014. *STEMing the Tide: Keeping Women in Science*. Melbourne: Melbourne University Press Academic.

White House Office of Science and Technology Policy. 2014. *Preparing Americans with 21st Century Skills: Science, Technology, Engineering, and Mathematics (STEM) Education in the 2015 Budget*. Washington, DC: The White House. Available at www.whitehouse.gov/sites/default/files/microsites/ostp/fy_2015_stem_ed.pdf.

Whittington, Kjersten Bunker, and Laurel Smith-Doerr. 2008. "Women Inventors in Context: Disparities in Patenting across Academia and Industry." *Gender & Society* 22(2): 194–218.

Wildavsky, Ben. 2010. *The Great Brain Race: How Global Universities Are Reshaping the World*. Princeton, NJ: Princeton University Press.

Williams, Christine L., Kristine Kilanski, and Chandra Muller. 2014. "Corporate Diversity Programs and Gender Inequality in the Oil and Gas Industry." *Work and Occupations* 41(4): 440–476.

Winslow, Sarah. 2010. "Gender Inequality and Time Allocations among Academic Faculty." *Gender & Society* 24(6): 769–793.

Wolf-Wendel, Lisa, Susan B. Twombly, and Suzanne Rice. 2004. *The Two-Body Problem: Dual-Career-Couple Hiring Policies in Higher Education*. Baltimore, MD: Johns Hopkins University Press.

Wonch, Patricia Hill, Mary Anne Holmes, and Julia McQuillan. 2014. "The New STEM Faculty Profile: Balancing Family and Dual Careers." In *Gender Transformation in the Academy*, 3–20. Bradford, UK: Emerald Group Publishing.

Wong, Rebecca W. Y. 2015. "A Note on Fieldwork in 'Dangerous' Circumstances: Interviewing Illegal Tiger Skin Suppliers and Traders in Lhasa." *International Journal of Social Research Methodology*: 1–8.

Wuchty, Stefan, Benjamin Jones, and Brian Uzzi. 2007. "The Increasing Dominance of Teams in Production of Knowledge." *Science* 316(5827): 1036–1039.

Xie, Yu. 2014. "Is U.S. Science in Decline?" *Issues in Science & Technology* 30(3).

Xie, Yu, and Alexandra A. Killewald. 2012. *Is American Science in Decline?* Cambridge, MA: Harvard University Press.

Yuval-Davis, Nira. 2006. "Intersectionality and Feminist Politics." *European Journal of Women's Studies* 13(3): 193–209.

Zippel, Kathrin. 2006. *The Politics of Sexual Harassment: A Comparative Study of the United States, the European Union, and Germany.* Cambridge, UK: Cambridge University Press.

———. 2011. "How Gender Neutral Are State Policies on Science and International Mobility of Academics?" *Sociologica* 5(1): 1–17.

Zippel, Kathrin, Myra Marx Ferree, and Karin Zimmermann. 2016. "Gender Equality in German Universities: Vernacularizing the Battle for the Best Brains." *Gender and Education.* January 29, doi: 10.1080/09540253.2015.1123229.

Zhang, Yingchan. 2016. "Tapping the Flow: The Global Circulation of Talent and Urban Development in China." Department of Sociology, Northeastern University. Unpublished dissertation manuscript.

Index

CPSIA information can be obtained
at www.ICGtesting.com
Printed in the USA
LVOW08*1434030317

526082LV00007B/106/P